**D**

Dervla Murphy was born in [...] Dublin parents. Since 1964 she has been regularly publishing descriptions of her journeys – by bicycle and on foot – in the remoter areas of four continents. She has also written about the problems of Northern Ireland, the hazards of nuclear power, and race relations in Britain. Her first book was the classic *Full Tilt*. More recent titles included *South from the Limpopo: Travels through South Africa*, *One Foot in Laos* and *Through the Embers of Chaos: Balkan Journeys*. She still lives in County Waterford and is accompanied by many animals.

*Other books by the author*

Full Tilt

Tibetan Foothold

The Waiting Land

In Ethiopia with a Mule

On a Shoestring to Coorg

Where the Indus is Young

Race to the Finish?

A Place Apart

Eight Feet in the Andes

Wheels Within Wheels

Muddling Through in Madagascar

Tales From Two Cities

Cameroon With Egbert

Transylvania and Beyond

The Ukimwi Road

South From the Limpopo

Visiting Rwanda

One Foot in Laos

Through the Embers of Chaos

# Through Siberia by Accident

A Small Slice of Autobiography

## DERVLA MURPHY

JOHN MURRAY

*For the Zvegintzov tribe – Caroline, Serge, Catherine, Anna, Ford, Nicholas. In their different ways, each contributed to the unlikely success of a stymied journey*

© Dervla Murphy 2005

First published in Great Britain in 2005 by John Murray (Publishers)
A division of Hodder Headline

Paperback edition 2006

The right of Dervla Murphy to be identified as the Author of the Work has been asserted by her in accordance with the Copyright, Designs and Patents Act 1988.

6

A CIP catalogue record for this title is available from the British Library

ISBN 978-0-7195-6664-6

Typeset in Monotype Bembo by Servis Filmsetting Ltd, Manchester

Printed and bound by
Clays Ltd, St Ives plc

Hodder Headline policy is to use papers that are natural, renewable and recyclable products and made from wood grown in sustainable forests. The logging and manufacturing processes are expected to conform to the environmental regulations of the country of origin.

John Murray (Publishers)
338 Euston Road
London NW1 3BH

# Contents

# Acknowledgements

Mrs Mary O'Sullivan of Townshend Street, Skibbereen, Co. Cork protected me from an eleventh-hour disaster.

Clem Cecil and Anna Zvegintzov made rough paths smooth in Moscow.

Rashit Yahin and his wife provided generous hospitality, sound advice and much practical assistance in Severobaikalsk – not least in giving my reluctantly abandoned bicycle a safe house in which to await my return.

My daughter Rachel provided editorial advice of such value that it transformed an unpublishable text into something (barely) publishable.

Diana Murray stood by me, as she has been doing for forty years, throughout the prolonged pangs of a literary delivery.

Anne Boston's eagle eye discerned and eliminated all inconsistencies and inaccuracies within her reach. Any that remain are the author's responsibility.

# Author's Note

I use 'Siberian' when referring to the European Russians who have been settled in Siberia for generations. The tiny indigenous population of that vast territory (hardly 3 per cent of the total) belong to many tribes: Tungus, Lamut, Negidais, Nanais, Manguny, Oroki, Oroch, Udehes, Buriat and Sakha. Apart from the last two, those native peoples are rarely encountered nowadays by the ordinary traveller.

The Baikal–Amur Mainline (BAM) was planned in the 1930s. At Taishet in Eastern Siberia it branches off from the Trans-Siberian Railway and runs north of Lake Baikal. Having climbed several mountain ranges, it descends to the Pacific harbour of Sovietskaya Gavan, 560 miles north of Vladivostok.

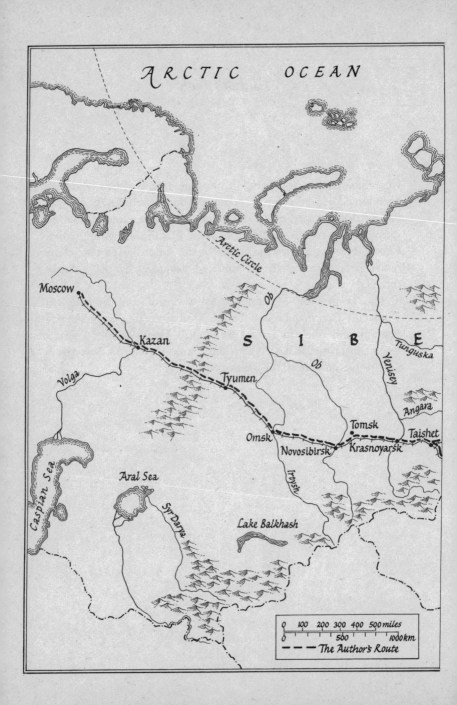

ARCTIC OCEAN

Arctic Circle

Moscow

Kazan

Volga

Tyumen

Ob

S I B E

Tunguska

Yenisey

Ob

Angara

Omsk

Novosibirsk

Tomsk

Krasnoyarsk

Taishet

Caspian Sea

Aral Sea

Syr Darya

Irtysh

Lake Balkhash

0   100  200  300  400  500 miles

0           500          1000 km

The Author's Route

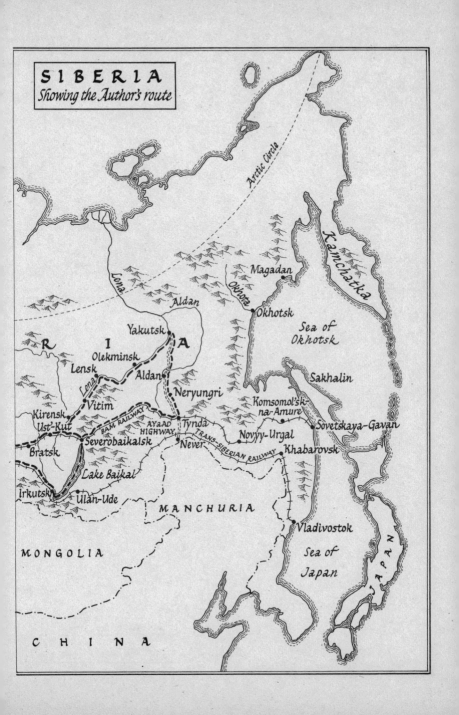

**SIBERIA**
*Showing the Author's route*

Arctic Circle

*Kamchatka*

Magadan

*Okhota*

Okhotsk

Aldan

Sea of
Okhotsk

Yakutsk

**R** **I** **A**

Olekminsk

Lensk

Sakhalin

Aldan

*Lena*

Neryungri

Komsomol'sk-
na-Amure

Kirensk

Vitim

Sovetskaya-Gavan

Ust'-Kut

BAM RAILWAY

AYaAD
HIGHWAY

Tynda

Novyyy-Urgal

Bratsk

Severobaikalsk

Never

TRANS-SIBERIAN RAILWAY

Khabarovsk

Lake Baikal

Irkutsk

Ulan-Ude

**MANCHURIA**

Vladivostok

**MONGOLIA**

Sea of
Japan

*JAPAN*

**C H I N A**

# Foreword

In retrospect the coincidence seemed uncanny: I decided to go to the Russian Far East at 9.05 a.m. (BST) on 11 September 2001. I was then working on a book about the Balkans and normally, when writing about the last journey, my mind is not allowed to hover over the next. But that morning I felt oddly restless; concentration was unaccountably difficult. I found myself recalling a recent World Service report from Vladivostok, mentioning that city's northern hinterland (Ussuriland) as a place 'at present without facilities for tourists'. By now accessible tourist-free zones are very scarce indeed...

At 8.55 I gave up trying to concentrate and opened my obsolete (1974) *Times Atlas*, feeling faintly guilty as one does when self-discipline breaks down. A minor coast road was shown, running north from Vladivostok between the low Sikhote-Alin mountains and the Pacific. Where it ended, an alluring network of tracks led inland, through the mountains, towards Khabarovsk and Komsomol'sk-na-Amure. 9.05 was decision time, marked by that joyous quickening of the pulse peculiar to the moment when the next journey begins to take shape.

Planning time came several months later and I acquired the *Siberian BAM Guide: Rail, Rivers and Road* by Athol Yates and Nicholas Zvegintzov (Trailblazer Publications). That invaluable little volume prompted me to become a travel snob, to ignore the Trans-Siberian railway and book a Baikal–Amur Mainline train ticket from Moscow to Komsomol'sk-na-Amure. The relevant Lonely Planet guide had little to say about Ussuriland, apart from recommending an excursion to a nature reserve where 'There is no guarantee ... you'll spot a tiger'. As solo cyclists don't yearn to meet tigers this didn't bother me. But when I confessed to total ignorance of the Russian Far East my more

twitchy friends registered slight unease. They seemed not to understand that after two and a half years' involvement in harrowing Balkan
problems I urgently needed a 'find out when you get there' holiday, a
light-hearted wander through a beautiful region where if people had
problems I couldn't identify them in advance – or discover them on
the spot, given an insurmountable language barrier.

By a happy chance two young friends of mine, Clem Cecil and
Anna Zvegintzov, had recently settled in Moscow. (It seems only yes-
terday I was changing their nappies.) Before I left home both rallied
round with sound telephonic advice and on my arrival in Moscow
they provided generous hospitality and much practical assistance,
including introductions to helpful Muscovites.

Clem explained that many Russians regard Siberia and the Russian
Far East as dangerous territories, mainly inhabited by criminals, bears,
wolves and mosquitoes carrying deadly diseases such as Kozhevnikov
epilepsy. However, a few of her friends are among the minority who
personally know the lands east of the Urals and on their advice I modified my original plan. As the new paved road from Komsomol'sk to
Khabarovsk is nastily trafficky, unlike the unpaved 1930s highway from
Tynda to Yakutsk, I would first pedal north to Yakutsk – then take the
paddle-steamer 1,300 miles up the Lena river to Ust'-Kut – then
rejoin the BAM, to Khabarovsk, and from there cycle south to
Vladivostok. At the end of October the Trans-Siberian would carry
me back to Moscow.

# I

## The Purchase of Pushkin

'Who', I asked myself on the way to the airport, 'flies Aeroflot from Shannon?' In the departure lounge, at 8 a.m., I saw the answer: a few West of Ireland natives employed in Holland and even fewer Russian entrepreneurs – serious-looking, expensively dressed young men, interacting with their lap-tops and not conversationally inclined. When we stopped for an hour in Amsterdam the Irish were replaced by a mix of Dutch entrepreneurs, Scandinavian tourists and (judging by their luggage) Muscovite traders in electronic goods.

At Sheremetyevo-2 airport, visually transformed by capitalism since last I saw it in 1983, the passport control queues were long yet all four 'Immigration' cubicles remained empty for twenty-five minutes. Most of the adult foreigners soon became agitated. The adult Russians queued calmly, many using mobile phones, and their children stood quietly beside them. A group of Swedish youths booed and gestured offensively when the passport officers eventually sauntered on to the scene, tired-looking young women with closed faces, replicating their Soviet predecessors. In a perverse way it cheered me that capitalism had not yet taught them to feign friendliness for the sake of the tourist industry.

Sluggishly the Shannon–Amsterdam–Moscow luggage was emerging – but not mine, or the luggage of fourteen other foreigners. For an hour confusion prevailed. A stout blonde Dutch matron, wearing tight pink slacks, a pea-green T-shirt and golden sandals, led the protesters, pacing to and fro near the roundabout, shouting at every official in sight whatever his/her function might be. Then she herded us to the Lost Luggage office, its long desk staffed by three surprisingly pleasant women – surprisingly because they were the innocent targets for every delayed passenger's rage. We each had to fill in three separate foolscap forms (in Russian only), identifying our lost property according to a code given on display boards. These illustrated almost every conceivable item of luggage, including a bicycle – but excluding two pannier-bags in a misshapen cardboard carton held together with masking tape. At last a Dutch businesswoman, long resident in Moscow, extracted an explanation from a passing air hostess. Our luggage had been transferred to a Helsinki flight and some official somewhere was trying to decide whether or not to delay that flight by retrieving it.

Meanwhile I was fizzing about Clem, waiting nearby but uncontactable; no public address system was operating and the surly exit guards, strolling around hugging rifles, forbade me to approach the barrier to send a signal. One woman offered me her mobile which for some arcane reason refused to link up with Clem's. And the missing luggage didn't appear until 9.30, almost three hours after our landing.

Outside, the taxi-drivers were tiresome until realizing that Clem speaks fluent Russian and knows exactly what fares should be. As we sped along the motorway the western sky looked strangely hectic, was an unbroken expanse of crimson, a sunset effect created by the smoke of nearby forest fires – prolonged, disastrous fires, said our driver.

Clem lived in a quiet, mellow corner near the city centre, her second-floor flat overlooking a grassy space shaded by tall trees that certainly witnessed the Revolution. Swings and a slide for small children stood in one corner and dogs relieved themselves all over the place. Such pleasant residential areas, close to the wide coiling river, are among Moscow's several saving graces.

Having dumped my luggage we walked through the warm dusk to Anna's flat, within sight of the Kremlin, drinking beer from bottles while dandering along the embankment. ('When in Moscow do as Moscow does.') Suddenly a piece of monumental kitsch smote my eye, a grotesque metal agglomeration of ships and sails and rigging seeming to rise out of the river, dwarfing every building in sight. Clem explained this towering example of old school tie activity in the new Russia: its designer, Zurab Tsereteli, once shared a classroom with Yuri Luzhkov, Moscow's first post-Soviet Mayor. The heroic figure standing astride the central ship, in triumphal pose, was conceived as Christopher Columbus when an American patron commissioned Tsereteli to commemorate the 'discovery' of America in 1492. On seeing the finished product this patron registered dismay and Tsereteli was left with surplus goods. Swiftly he renamed his hero 'Peter the Great' (founder of the Russian navy) and sold the whole bizarre ensemble to the City of Moscow. Its ugliness verges on the comic and makes many Muscovites giggle. Others, brooding on such a blatant and arrogant squandering of public money, are less amused – but resigned, though Tsereteli went on to secure several more major commissions from his classmate.

To me Moscow's central area felt quite safe after dark for two women – one young and beautiful, the other old and muggable. On our way home long after midnight (by which time I had received much valuable advice from Anna), Clem introduced me to Moscow's unofficial taxi service, a variant of hitch-hiking. One stands just off the pavement with the right hand slightly extended, palm downwards, and in most places a car stops within minutes, the driver usually a middle-aged man in a more than middle-aged vehicle. If going approximately in your direction he provides a lift for a negotiated fare much below the official rate. This sensible system, though only of use to Russian-speakers who know the city well, counters the new Moscow's crime-ridden image.

To the casual visitor, poverty is more evident than crime, the sort of poverty never visible in Soviet times. Next morning, as I approached a skip to dump the pannier-bags' carton, an old man, desperately seeking food amidst the household waste of this affluent district, seemed not to notice me. When he found a small plastic bag of stale crusts, discoloured lettuce leaves and chicken bones the relief on his face was harrowing to see. Later, near our Metro station, I passed an ancient, crumpled ragged man, wearing three incongruously splendid Great Patriotic War medals as he lay asleep on a bench in the sun. The soles of his feet showed through his shoes. I wondered where he slept in winter. He may have been among the foolish many who sold their flats when suddenly that was allowed, then a few years later found all those roubles virtually worthless.

That was a brutally hot day, the temperature over 32 °C, the heavy air made hazy by forest fire smoke. And for Clem and me it was an active day. We began by registering my visa with some quasi-official agency, another of those Soviet-era bureaucratic hurdles still put in the way of tourists. Then we visited *The Times* office where one of Clem's Russian colleagues kindly translated my publisher's letter of introduction 'To Whom It May Concern'. After that we unsuccessfully sought detailed maps of the Russian Far East. And finally we went shopping for a bicycle.

I lost pints of sweat as we walked the pavements of a city that has gained nothing in charm by the arrival of forty McDonald's, Lego-style financial blocks, advertisement hoardings on a US scale and speed-hogs who treat Stalin's absurdly wide boulevards like race-tracks. Happily the Metro has survived the rouble's vicissitudes and still makes London's tube feel like a pricey ordeal. Even for ill-paid Muscovites it remains inexpensive, perhaps because its splendour has been somewhat marred by advertisements and stall-holders. A train arrives at every stop every two minutes so there is no subterranean rush-hour to speak of in this city of nine million.

Moscow's cycle shops depressed me. I was seeking a normal bicycle but most of the machines on view looked abnormal. Many were of an ugly, bulky design no doubt aimed at young males who crave motor-bikes but are too young or too poor to acquire them. Some were hermaphroditic, distorted machines with crossbars at the wrong angles. Others had electronic attachments recording mileage, speed, temperature and wind-strength(!). And then the ultimate desecration – I saw my first power-assisted bicycle with promotional literature hanging from its handlebars boasting 'This motor is surprisingly quiet'. Despairingly I demanded, 'Is *nothing* sacred?' Clem made soothing noises but I could feel my blood pressure rising; I'm much too set in my pedalling ways easily to accept such a wimpish innovation. However, I later read, in a Sustrans newsletter, a plausible defence of power-assisted bicycles. If these induce some people to cycle to work, instead of motoring, they're environmentally sound and must be supported. Point taken...

In the biggest bicycle shop, a cavernous arcade, Ilya came to my rescue. Unlike those young salesmen-cum-mechanics I'd dealt with in Budapest and Zagreb, who saw bicycles as mere commodities, he himself was a serious cyclist and understood the importance of rider–machine harmony. Patiently he tolerated my spurning one

4

model after another – then had a sudden inspiration, retreated into some hidden space and returned with an old-fashioned roadster, sturdy and gimmick-free. 'Yes!' I exclaimed. 'That's it!'

From Ireland had come a saddle on which I have cycled so many thousands of miles that it now has a special relationship with my bottom. And also a top quality carrier, very light but very strong, well tested over some of Africa's roughest roads. The saddle is a bit battered around the edges yet when asked to do the exchange Ilya clearly appreciated its significance. After the purchase of a pump, spare tube, water-bottle and tin of oil, Pushkin and I were ready for action. But first came the five-and-a-half-day train ride to Tynda, and Pushkin was still wearing his protective suit of cardboard tubes as we walked to Kazansky Station where I was to board the BAM at 3.30 on the following afternoon. Clem had done some preliminary research and found that freight could be registered and loaded on the eve of departure.

This procedure involved penetrating several layers of bureaucracy and disentangling yards of red tape. Locating the bureaucrats' offices was difficult enough; the four were far apart, within the sprawling complexity of Kazansky. Yet it would have been unreasonable of me to grumble; much of the red tape had to do with BAM's security system. Reputedly, Russian freight wagons, particularly on BAM, often reach their destinations less full than when they started and alarmist friends had visualized my new bicycle vanishing at one of the innumerable stops between Moscow and Tynda. In fact Pushkin was locked in a Tynda-specific wagon, never opened en route, and his release would require the close scrutiny of a whole sheaf of triplicated documents.

Having secured most of those documents, and a $5.60 bicycle ticket, we walked at least a mile along various platforms in search of wagon No. 990290. Then, to my mortification, it emerged that Pushkin could not be accepted by Roman, the guard, because I had forgotten to bring my own ticket, essential for the completion of the final document. Therefore our 'freight' must be taken away and brought back on the morrow, not later than 8 a.m. But then Clem smiled at Roman. On previous occasions I had observed her uncon-sciously exercised charm bringing out the best in official Russia and now she won a considerable concession: Pushkin could after all be left overnight in the wagon (locked *to* the wagon) for retrieval next morning. Then he would have to be taken, with a chit from the guard, to one of those four offices because he was being registered on 31 July, not on the 30th, the date given on various other documents.

I confessed to Clem that too much heat always scrambles my brain, the most memorable example of this being a Galapagos Islands drama. When returning from Peru in February 1979 my daughter Rachel and I spent ten days on the islands and, on the ninth day, the equatorial heat caused me to break a lifelong rule by removing my money-belt from around my waist. Then I left it – containing all our cash, passports, return tickets to Quito and London – at one end of the shop's counter while I wandered off to the other end. Unsurprisingly, it disappeared. Communication between the Galapagos and the rest of the world was tenuous in those days and but for a freakish stroke of luck we might have spent weeks sitting on the equator, 600 miles from anyone who could help and dependent on local charity. Among our few fellow-tourists there chanced to be two young Norwegian women who, most improbably, had read some of my books and offered to lend us our fares back to Quito. There the British Embassy provided generous hospitality while in London my publisher was picking up the pieces. Where Ireland has no diplomatic representation it is customary for the British to look after the Irish, yet at that date most of the world saw Britain and Ireland as implacable enemies – an impression that persists, I was to discover, in Siberia.

Next morning I was escorted to Kazansky Station by Misha, a shy young freelance photographer, London bred but of Russian extraction and long resident in Moscow. For a reason best known to himself, he wished to photograph Pushkin and me beside the BAM. Confidently I led him through that bewilderment of platforms and barn-like sheds to No. 990290. Then a moment of panic: that wagon had vanished. But surely it couldn't have been moved far? Followed by Misha and clutching the scrap of paper on which Roman had scribbled 990290, I trotted anxiously from here to there and from there to yonder, peering at scores of identical freight wagons with metal numbers nailed to their sides – but not number 990290. At 8 a.m. the station seemed deserted but Misha suggested touring the relevant offices and at last we found a man who gestured towards a distant line, inaccessible to pedestrians, where stood all the loaded and locked Tynda wagons. He advised me to return at noon, when Clem and I found No. 990290 in its original position. Less than an hour later all Pushkin's documentation was in order.

# 2

## Riding a White Elephant

Kazansky Railway Station covers acres and as yet lacks multilingual signs; without my support group – Clem, Anna and their friend Jan – finding the Tynda platform would have been quite a challenge. At 3 p.m. the concourse was a scrambling mass of over-burdened passengers, each with their own support group. Most long-distance train travellers are seen off by numerous relatives and friends, some bravely smiling, others quietly weeping; few Russians can afford frequent three- or four- or five-thousand mile journeys so farewells tend to be emotional.

For those who can read them, BAM tickets are models of precision; without hesitation Clem led me to coupé No. 9, compartment 29–32, bunk 32. (For privacy's sake I had chosen an upper bunk.) On the platform, at the only entrance to each coupé, stands a gimlet-eyed *provodnitsa*, checking tickets and passports. As Anna explained me to our *provodnitsa* (who throughout this journey would be, I soon discovered, my Commanding Officer), she emphasized the babushka's communication problem.

My support group looked appalled when the Baranskayas joined me: a family of four, Aline the daughter aged twelve, Dima the son aged three, their destination the small town of Khani some 300 miles short of Tynda. How – wondered Anna – would a three-year-old react to five days' confinement? She needn't have worried; as a babushka of (then) almost seven years' experience I was deeply impressed by Dima. He never once woke anybody, always peed in his potty at convenient times, was carried out to the loo once a day for more substantial matters, ate everything put before him, contentedly gazed out of the window for hours on end, his lips moving, inventing a game in his mind. When it suited his parents and sister they played with him but he never demanded attention though lacking all those diversions we provide for long journeys. In nearby compartments four other toddlers and small children were equally well-behaved and happy. Do the Russians have something to teach us about child-rearing?

Russia's uniquely long train journeys have engendered their own conventions. At once you stow away your luggage, in a secure locker below your bunk if you're 'down', on a spacious shelf, extending under the corridor roof, if you're 'up'. This however is not a rigid rule; my pannier-bags left plenty of space on the shelf for some of the Baranskaya family's enormous cloth-wrapped bundles. Before settling down everyone changes into comfortable loose garments and hangs their smart street wear, often sheathed in plastic, on the hooks provided. Slippers replace shoes and are mandatory; going barefoot into the corridor, or even sitting barefoot in one's compartment, incurs the wrath of the *provodnitsa*.

After each meal the table by the window must be cleaned and left not too cluttered by anyone's food-related property – an admirable convention, allowing writing space. At bedtime men are expected to withdraw to the corridor while women don their nightwear. In our compartment this didn't arise as I had no nightwear, to my companions' evident puzzlement.

Food-sharing is immensely important, a way of rapidly establishing friendly relations between strangers who must live in close proximity for days on end. This put me at an embarrassing disadvantage; I had reckoned on needing no more than tea-bags, and a kilo of monkey-nuts and raisins, for five and half days without exercise. In contrast, the Baranskayas were supplied with two cold roast chickens, dried fish, salami, hard-boiled eggs, cheese, tomatoes, cucumbers, bananas, oranges, bread, butter, homemade jam, biscuits, thick slabs of chocolate and large bags of toffees, these last to be chewed with their tea. In addition, when we stopped for twenty minutes at Yekaterinburg, Mrs Baranskaya hurried out to buy from a platform trader plastic boxes of Chinese noodles, specially invented for train travellers. People take these to the communal samovar at the end of the corridor, add boiling water, replace the lid for ten minutes and hey presto! there's a hot meal. This was my introduction to the Siberians' capacity for consuming industrial quantities at a sitting.

The Baranskayas were an affectionate family, the parents in their mid to late forties. Unfortunately Mr Baranskaya – tall and burly with a bushy moustache and, as the days passed, an incipient beard – seemed to have a problem with the foreigner. He spoke a little English but was reluctant to use it and resolutely avoided all eye contact which I found rather disconcerting, given our sharing such a tiny space for five days. Yet he was consistently polite in his stiff way and helpful when misfortune left me in need of help. I did wonder about his occupational background, how he might have been conditioned as a young man. His wife and daughter were warmly friendly and eagerly curious about Ireland but he set the tone, subtly deterring the sort of diction-ary-cum-sign-language communication system we could have improvised.

Each long-distance train has its Captain (an august figure, rarely seen by passengers, enthroned in a mid-train office), its pair of highly skilled mechanics, its underworked restaurant staff, its smartly uni-formed security officer (apparently unarmed) and for each carriage a pair of conductors who work twelve-hour shifts. (Male *provodnik*, female *provodnitsa*, plural *provodniki*.) Our daytime *provodnitsa*, Olga Grekova – small and plump, with chestnut hair tightly drawn back from a high forehead – rarely smiled and obviously enjoyed her power. A *provodnitsa*'s authority may never be questioned and her vigilance is unceasing. As an institution, the *provodniki* guarantee orderliness, cleanliness, punctuality, sobriety. They discreetly but relentlessly observe alcohol intake and any veering towards over-indulgence is sharply corrected. Smoking is allowed only in the carriage vestibule, an uncomfortable, unventilated, cramped space to which none but the most nicotine-enslaved retreat. (Of course things may be different on the more cosmopolitan Trans-Siberian which allegedly transports 'criminal elements' – smugglers and wheeler-dealers of all sorts – from China and Mongolia, plus occasional groups of trouble-making young Western tourists whose unruliness can complicate life for the majority of well-behaved back-packers.)

As we trundled through Moscow's unexciting suburbs Olga Grekova toured her fiefdom, handing out to each passenger (for less than a dollar) a pair of sheets, a pillow-cover and a hand-towel, all cotton and well-worn but freshly laundered. The mattresses were stacked on the upper bunks and not really necessary, so comfortable are those bunks. Mrs Baranskaya volunteered to make up my bed, a touching gesture of welcome – characteristic, I was soon to realize, of the incomparably hospitable Siberians.

While exploring the rear half of the train (our carriage was about midway) I came upon the air-conditioned restaurant car, with dainty lace curtains, red plush chairs and slim vases of plastic flowers on each white-clothed table. This amenity is used almost exclusively by the train staff; BAM meals are notoriously bland, meagre and expensive and anyway the average Russian is not in the habit of eating out. The tiny bar sold soft drinks and cans and bottles of beer (*pivo* in Russian as in Serbo-Croat) but no vodka or other spirits. My ordering a *pivo* seemed to annoy the slim young waitress and pot-bellied mechanic who were drinking tea while collaborating on a crossword puzzle, one of the Siberians' favourite hobbies.

A long walk through several open *platskartny* carriages, each accommodating fifty-eight passengers, made me rather regret having taken Clem's advice to travel first class – as is not my wont. Here people were still settling in – arranging luggage, making beds, exchanging herbal teas, unpacking books, chess sets, photograph albums, Walkmans, laughing and arguing, quickly getting to know one another, creating an atmosphere of cheerful spontaneity not replicated in the staid coupés.

At the train's end I found myself in a cupboard-like space where, to my great joy, an unglazed window provided fresh air and a wide view of the landscape behind us. I looked forward to spending many happy hours here during the days ahead. But that was not to be...

Some forty-five miles from Moscow BAM's dawdle through a small deserted station (now again known as Sergiev Posad, formerly Zagorsk) allowed me to admire Trinity-St Serge's shimmering blue-green domes, gilded spires and crosses, tall brick belfries and towers – all tree-surrounded, on a slight rise above the railway. Here Russia's patron saint, Sergius of Radonezh, founded a monastery in the 1340s. Those were troubled times and it soon became the most important of many fort-monasteries dedicated to the defence of Moscow. Its founder earned his sainthood by uniting various Muscovite factions against the Tatars, after which the Mongol overlords experienced defeat for the first time, in 1380. Here was a certain irony. The Slav settlers in Russia, whose very gradual conversion to Greek Orthodox Christianity began towards the end of the tenth century, had never had a close or supportive relationship with Byzantium. Then came the Mongol conquest of 1237–41 which devastated the Muscovite territories, terrorized the population, disrupted trade – yet heralded the Orthodox Church's Golden Age. In his fascinating social history of Russia Richard Pipes explains:

> The Mongols exempted all the clergy living under their rule from the burdens which they imposed on the rest of the subjugated population. The Great Iasa, a charter issued by Genghis Khan, granted the Orthodox Church protection and exemption from tributes and taxes in return for a pledge to pray for the Khan and his family. The privilege was an immense boon to the Church at a time when the rest of Russia suffered from heavy exactions and violence … The main beneficiaries were the monasteries. In the fourteenth century, Russian monks undertook vigorous colonization and before it was over built as many new abbeys as had been established since the country's conversion 400 years earlier. [Those monks became] even more worldly than the monastic clergy of late medieval western Europe.

No notice was taken of the Orthodox ban on clerical trading. In 1558, Hakluyt records, one of the earliest English travellers in Russia described Trinity-St Serge as the wealthiest monastery, its monks 'as great merchants as any in the land … and have boats which passe too and fro in the rivers with merchandize from place to place where any of their countrey do traffike'. Around this date Trinity-St Serge had more than 100,000 peasant 'souls' (the Russian euphemism for serfs) working on its estates and at the beginning of the seventeenth century it complained to the government about the 'five year limit', which meant that runaway serfs who had lived elsewhere for five years could not be forced to return to base. In 1614, a year after the first Romanov ascended the throne, Czar Michael empowered Trinity-St Serge to reclaim all peasants who had fled since 1605.

Over the centuries, Trinity-St Serge continued to accumulate roubles beyond reckoning, its wealth being based not only on trading but on endowments and donations from czars, nobles and merchants anxious to secure extra-terrestrial backing. Millions were lavished on the construction and decoration of cathedrals, churches, bell-towers and a royal palace. From far and near, generation after generation, came fervent believers seeking spiritual sustenance from Russia's most beloved saint.

Remarkably, the Bolsheviks decided, when launching their anti-religion campaign, to spare this revered but indisputably capitalist place of pilgrimage. On 20 April 1920 Stalin himself, acting on behalf of the Council of People's Commissars, signed a special decree establishing Trinity-St Serge as the Museum of Historical and Art Relics of the Troitsko-Sergievskaya Lavra. When the Second World War initiated a State/Church truce of sorts the monastery was reopened as the Patriarch's residence and the Church's administrative centre. In 1988 the Patriarch and his bureaucracy moved to Danilovsky Monastery in Moscow, which apparently pleased the many thousands who annually make their way to this blessed place, their fervour not cooled (perhaps fuelled?) by decades of Soviet hostility. And the monks of Trinity-St Serge remain in money-making mode: US$10 per (foreign) person for a tour of the churches and grounds, $5 for the Old Russian Applied Art Museum, $4 for the Art Museum, $2 for a climb up the tower and $0.10 for a pee.

As the domes and crosses receded, I suddenly remembered my primary school classroom – the globe standing on a pedestal, the nun teacher's pointer sliding halfway across it as she said, 'All that's Russia, a bad place, the Soviet Union, the people are Communists who hate God and murder priests and nuns.' We eight-year-olds got the two messages. Russia is a big country, in fact the biggest by far covering one-sixth of the world's land-mass. And it was our Christian duty to hate Russians because they hated God.

Returning to my coupé, I noticed that most of the *platskartny* passengers were by now either eating or reading – usually hardbacks, their thickness proportionate to the journey's length. I wondered how the older generations felt and thought, deep in their hearts and minds, about the New Russia. It had all happened so suddenly: one day the Soviet Union was a superpower, the next day it didn't exist. Literally overnight – near Minsk, on 7/8 December 1991 – Boris Yeltsin had brought about its dissolution, acting in collusion with the Presidents of the Ukrainian Soviet Republic and the Belorussian Soviet

Republic. All three leaders were in theory accountable to their Supreme Soviets and according to the Law on Secession a Republic could not secede unless two-thirds of its electorate favoured independence. Yet only the Ukraine (on 1 December) had held the necessary referendum. Moreover, in a referendum held throughout the Soviet Union on 17 March 1991, 76.4 per cent of an 80 per cent turn-out had voted for the maintenance of a reformed USSR. Small wonder the Russians' abrupt exposure to capitalism rampant brought about the sort of economic chaos that punishes the majority while benefiting a fast-moving minority.

For the first 850 (or so) eastbound miles BAM is crossing Russia's Central Economic Region where thousands of factories employ millions of workers making everything from safety-pins to MIG fighters. However, the immensity of this region leaves plenty of rural space between the industrialized zones – relentlessly flat space, nowhere does European Russia rise above 1,400 feet. We have all read numerous descriptions of those conifer and birch woods, forming part of the world's largest forest. This extends for thousands of miles south of the treeless lichen-covered tundra and north of the equally treeless but comparatively fertile steppes. Known as the taiga, it occupies most of the northern half of Eurasia from the Arctic Circle to between 45° and 50° latitude north. But of course in European Russia it has long since been thinned out and my diary for Day One records:

> At irregular intervals gaps in the taiga: long arable fields or meadows.
> Elderly men cock hay with wide wooden rakes. Occasional small villages of one-storey dwellings, the traditional *izby*, solid log cabins set in picket-fenced vegetable gardens. Potatoes not planted in drills but look healthy. Odd to think the potato only arrived here in the 1830s, its introduction coinciding with a major cholera epidemic. Hence various taboos surrounded it and even forty years later only 1½ per cent of cultivable land under pot.s. Yet now among the most popular crops. Many old glass-houses converted to plastic. On rutted inter-village tracks horse-carts (convertible to sledges) being overtaken by antique tractors used as family cars. Small children herd goats with mega-udders. Huge flocks of geese but only a few bony solo cows –

black and white, always tethered. Livestock thrive on the steppes but have always done badly in taiga-land: short commons during the long winter, no spring grazing, even summer pasture not very nutritious – poor soil. 'Progressive' 19th-century nobles attempted to improve stock by importing Western European breeds; most immigrants soon died and the survivors rapidly degenerated – nothing achieved by cross-breeding. In contrast to the drab *izby*, village stations recently prettily repainted – to impress camera-wielding Trans-Siberian tourists? Along the embankments grow giant cow parsley and a tall elegant pink-flowered weed, very beautiful. (Memo: find out name.)

That weed brightened our route all the way to Tynda but botanical research is not my forte and I never did 'find out name'.

Towards sunset Aline became quite excited, sat close to the window, peered ahead, indicated that soon we would be crossing the Volga – to Russians 'the mother of all rivers', to the rest of us 'among those echoing river-names of Europe', if I may borrow a Lawrence Durrell phrase. He continued, in *The Spirit of Place*:

> Every great river gradually grows its own history, its own temperament, its own quite distinguishable personality … To the map-maker it suggests a living artery in the body of a country. But to historians it is always a road – a highway along which the peoples of the world have always undertaken their slow pilgrimages to distant shrines of worship; or more prosaically and more recently their business trips in search of customers for their wares.

Nowhere is a river's 'highway' function more important than in Russia. None of its great rivers runs east–west but many of their lateral branches do, providing a unique network of navigable waterways linked by not too demanding portages. These enabled the early Slav settlers to travel relatively safely and easily from the Baltic to the Caspian and back again; without them the Grand Duchy of Muscovy could never have expanded to imperial proportions. Given the distances involved and the limitations imposed by the climate on road-building, overland travel was practical only in winter when sledges ran (and still run) smoothly and swiftly on packed snow. In pre-railway days, most goods were transported by boat or barge, the latter towed by boatmen. As BAM speeded up on the slight descent to river level,

Mrs Baranskaya unsuccessfully sought Olga Grekova's permission to play me a tape of the Volga boatmen's melancholy songs. Those I would have enjoyed – but blessed is the carriage whose *provodnitsa* controls sound pollution.

On a long escarpment high above the river stood tyre and chipboard factories, oil refineries, chemical plants – their sinister plumes almost perpendicular in the still air, staining the pale blue evening sky, varying from pure white through yellowish-red to black and solid-seeming.

From the railway bridge I saluted the broad brown Volga, its 2,290 miles draining an area bigger than Britain, France, Germany and Italy combined. Too quickly it was lost to view and we paused briefly in Yaroslavl', one of Russia's oldest cities, founded in 1010 – it is said – by a Kievan Prince, Yaroslav the Wise, who reckoned that a lucrative trading post could be set up where the Kotorosol River joins the Volga. Eventually Yaroslavl' became the centre of an independent though Kievan-influenced principality. But then the Mongols invaded, sacked or burned every Russian town except Novgorod (there weren't many) and thus brought to an end the so-called Kievan period in Russian history which had started with the acceptance of Christianity by Vladimir I. (Russians, and others, still argue over the motive for this prince's conversion.) The Tatar Khans levied heavy taxes on all who used the Volga and the Don and not until 1552 did Ivan the Terrible capture Kazan, their capital on the Volga, hundreds of miles downstream from Yaroslavl' and now an industrial port.

Beyond the station a section of the old city appeared and the declining sun illuminated three McDonald's hoardings and the dazzling white towers of the twelfth-century Monastery of the Transfiguration of the Saviour.

I slept uneasily that night, wearing only a T-shirt yet dripping sweat.

As we crossed the Urals I failed to notice a conspicuous monument on the southern embankment at 1,777 kilometres from Moscow which supposedly marks the transition from Europe to Asia, an absurdly arbitrary border. Eurasia just goes on – and on, and on. When Asiatic tribes decided to incorporate the embryonic Russian state in their empire, and when the resurgent Russians chose to expand into Siberia and (much later) into Central Asia, the Urals hindered no one. Their role as an intercontinental barrier has been invented; here the merging of continents is amorphous, a phenomenon not celebrated by Nature.

To me 'the *conquest* of Siberia' rings false. The Russians' fur-inspired eastward move is not comparable to the Spanish Conquests of Mexico and Peru, the bloody English victories over North American tribes and Australian aborigines, or the prolonged czarist campaigns to seize the Caucasus from the Ottomans and then subdue Muslim tribes resentful of their new Christian overlords. (Unfinished business, as I write.) With a few exceptions, Siberia's numerous tribes were so small and scattered that a certain aura of inevitability surrounds the annexation by the more 'advanced' Russians of this vastness not separated from their homeland by anything more topographically decisive than the Urals.

Paradoxically, the Cold War with its emphasis on sophisticated weaponry engendered a widespread misapprehension of the USSR as simply a European superpower, its imperial status being blurred in many eyes by the geographical continuity of its possessions. Other European empires had been *overseas*, emphatically exotic, challengingly remote, the colonizers having confronted turbulent oceans on the way and unfamiliar cultures on arrival. Russia's colonizing, though no less physically perilous, was much less of a cultural adventure. None of western Europe's imperialists, except Spain, had experienced generations of subservience to a non-European power. In contrast, the Russians had long been intimately involved with and influenced by their Asiatic neighbours.

When the Mongols took over Muscovy it was, in their view, a primitive political entity, lacking an efficient tax-collecting system, dependable courier services, organized transport, trained diplomats and law-enforcers capable of cowing the public. We tend to think of the Mongols merely as bloodthirsty killers and the frenzied demolishers of civilized cities, which of course they were. Yet you don't establish an empire stretching from Manchuria to the Caucasus by bloodshed alone. As time passed the Golden Horde taught the Russian princes how to set up and run a centralized, predatory political authority – one without any sense of responsibility for the common good. Long after the Muscovites had liberated themselves, their own rulers adhered to this model of government. And when Peter the Great (1672–1725) set about the westernization/modernization of his country it was on a selective basis; he – and his successors, to their ultimate detriment – were resolved to compete with the European great powers on their own terms, without sacrificing one jot of what had become Russia's distinctive form of autocracy, blessed by the Orthodox Church. (Peter had brought the Church to heel, but that's another story.) In turn, the Soviet empire had much in common with the czarist empire: 'No democracy please – we're Russian!'

We were still chugging through the heavily industrialized Urals – their low sprawl extends for hundreds of miles – when misfortune struck. In the minuscule loo-cum-washroom passengers fixated on personal hygiene 'shower' themselves from the basin tap, leaving the metal floor soap-slippy. As I opened the door to leave, a young woman was approaching with babe in arms – a projectile-vomiting babe. Hastily I stepped backwards and simultaneously the train gave one of its not infrequent violent jerks. Losing my balance, I reached out to clutch the handbasin and didn't fall but twisted my right leg awk-wardly. At the time I felt only a slight momentary pain in my knee, seemingly of no consequence. But in fact a fall might have been less damaging; I woke next morning to find myself maimed, the pain intolerable when I put weight on my right leg. Because the knee was unblemished – no bruise, scratch, swelling or inflammation – the diag-nosis was easy: a damaged cartilage for which the only cure is rest.

Without visible evidence, explaining my plight to Mrs Baranskaya and Aline required much dictionary use, supplemented by a panto-mime which seemed to irritate Mr Baranskaya and sent Dima into convulsions of laughter. Mrs Baranskaya spent quarter of an hour excavating a tube of ointment from the depths of an enormous nylon sack, then expertly massaged the injury; she was a nurse by profession. Physically this treatment achieved nothing but emotionally it gave comfort.

Our compartment was mercifully close to the loo; I could hop there on one leg, hanging on to the corridor bar. Painlessness rewarded immobility and I thought positive: this misfortune having happened on Day Two left me three days of rest-time before our arrival in Tynda. What would happen there? I might still be incapable of getting myself and the panniers off the train, collecting Pushkin from No. 990290 and finding the hotel. But it's my habit to live one day at a time so I postponed worrying about that contingency. Then I registered a coincidence that made me chuckle: the vomit factor. In Rumania, in 1990, I broke three bones in my right foot when I slipped on a pile of vomit while carrying a heavy rucksack down an unlit stairway.

My secondary reaction to this setback was an odd sense of *relief*. While planning my Ussuriland journey I had had a strong premonition that something unpleasant would disrupt it – a premonition now explained, and the disruption could have been much worse. Strangely, my premonitory antennae gave me no warning of the far greater misfortune that lay ahead.

The building of the BAM railway and the BAM Zone towns (1933–1990) spanned most of the USSR's existence. According to the *BAM Guide*:

> This was the largest civil engineering project ever undertaken by the Soviet Union and probably by any country in the world. It devoured the same gigantic amount of resources as were used to conquer space in the 1950s and 1960s ... In the 1970s, probably 20,000 people lived in the BAM Zone ... Today over one million live in the Zone's three new cities and 100 settlements.

All very impressive, yet from its inception BAM provoked bitter dissension and was an outstanding example of Soviet muddling – in many ways a tragedy of errors.

When the Trans-Siberian railway was being planned in the 1880s two routes were considered, north and south of Lake Baikal. Geologists and engineers closely investigated both, then pronounced the northern route's terrain too daunting and its agricultural potential virtually non-existent. But Siberia's post-Revolution developers were either ignorant of this judgement or chose to ignore it. In 1924 a long-term USSR railway development plan included a map showing the northern BAM line and two years later, at the First Siberian Congress of Writers, one V. Zazubrin, a BAM enthusiast, sounded manic:

Let the crumbling green bosom of Siberia be clad in the cement armour of cities, armed with the stone muzzles of factory chimneys and fettered with the close-fitting hoops of railways. Let the taiga be burnt and chopped down, let the steppes be trampled underfoot. Let all this be, for it is inevitable. It is only on cement and iron that the fraternal union of all peoples, the iron fraternity of all mankind will be built.

By that date strategic considerations (forget fraternal union) were making BAM seem essential, at least in military eyes. The vulnerability of the Trans-Siberian, built between 1891 and 1916, had soon become apparent. Many stretches ran so close to the Chinese and Mongolian borders that the Russian Far East could again be easily isolated from the rest of the country, as happened in 1918 when British, American and Japanese troops took over. The Japanese had remained until 1922 and when they occupied Manchuria in 1931, and then extended their influence into Outer Mongolia, the case for a northern railway line was strengthened. In 1933 the second Five Year Plan proclaimed:

> The BAM will traverse little investigated regions of East Siberia and bring to life an enormous new territory and its colossal riches – amber, gold, coal – and also make possible the cultivation of great tracts of land suitable for agriculture.

That year the first tracks were laid, from Oldoi on the Trans-Siberian towards faraway Tynda, then an isolated village called Tyndinsky. Four years later, when this single track had been completed, a new organization, BAMProek, was established to coordinate the various government departments and other enterprises involved in different aspects of BAM construction. BAMProek found flaws in all the earlier surveys, apart from the Tynda–Urgal stretch, and a vicious purge followed. Among the many administrators, engineers and scientists then executed, on Stalin's orders, was the geologist wife of the renowned explorer V.K. Arsenev. Countless other victims were condemned to the railway workers' *gulag* camps, known as BAMLag.

Throughout the Cold War, Stalin's victims were generally believed to number more than thirty million. Then, in 1992, the opening of the state archives showed the true figure to be nearer five million, of whom 400,000 or so were BAM builders. Cold, hunger, disease and overwork allowed those exiles a short life span and no doubt many were glad to die. Several East Siberian *gulags* were pooled in 1937, to provide a steady flow of labour for taiga-clearing and track laying. The brave minority of engineers, geologists and senior managers who protested against being posted to Siberia were arrested, charged with some fictitious offence and sentenced to the required (by BAM) number of years in a corrective labour camp. However, their valuable skills ensured them tolerable living conditions unless they incurred Stalin's wrath by seeming unequal to the job.

No less important, from the beginning, were the railway troops (Railway Forces for the Construction and Maintenance of Railways), a unit first established in 1851 and part of the national army until 1992 but now controlled by the Ministry of Transport. These troops had a double appeal for governments: because their work was labelled 'training' they were paid only a pittance and as a military unit they could be ordered to work anywhere, under any conditions, at short notice.

Behind the scenes, throughout the 1930s, an anti-BAM lobby continued to mutter against the project and their mutterings seemed justified when the most immediate military threat was countered, in 1939, by Mongolia's defeat of Japan. But already work had begun on the Taishet–Bratsk–Ust'–Kut line, designated a State Priority Project because of the significance of the new and record-breaking Bratsk hydro-electric scheme. The BAM teams of explorers and surveyors were then using 26 aircraft, 28 motor boats, 28 tractors, 133 motor vehicles, 1,500 horses and reindeer sledges beyond counting.

Next came the Great Patriotic War. When Hitler attacked the Soviet Union in 1941 the railway's construction stopped, except in the Russian Far East, and soon those tracks laid at such an incalculable cost in human suffering were being torn up for use as part of a relief line to besieged Stalingrad. Only the stretch from Komsomolsk'-na-Amure to Sovietskaya Gavan on the Pacific coast was left intact; in 1945 it carried troops and equipment to defend Sakhalin Island and the Kuril Islands.

Soon the BAMLags were stuffed with German and Japanese PoWs. Only 10 per cent of the 100,000 Germans who worked on BAM's western end survived to be repatriated and most of the 46,082 Japanese prisoners who died in the Soviet Union were BAM builders.

Post-war, Stalin specified 1955 as the railway's completion date and in 1950 the Taishet–Ust'-Kut section was opened. But the *gulags'* closure, after Stalin's death in 1953, caused BAM building again to be suspended. European Russia's urgent post-war reconstruction needs meant that mineral- and timber-rich Siberia – at the top of the agenda for development in the early Five Year Plans – was now disregarded. However, huge quantities of copper had been revealed in 1949 at Udokan, halfway between Severobaikalsk and Tynda, and BAM came up for reconsideration in 1956, when Khrushchev doubled investment in Siberia's industrial development. The seventh Five Year Plan directed 10 per cent of the Soviet Union's capital investment to Siberia but dissension and debate continued for years. Did it make sense to spend billions in Siberia, given its climate, vastness and remoteness? Wouldn't European Russia yield better returns? It mattered that Brezhnev was then fantasizing about BAM's carrying Western Siberian gas and oil to the Japanese and US markets. (As those oil fields provided far less than expected his fantasy was short-lived.) The pro-BAM lobby monotonously quoted from the outdated second Five Year Plan (1933–7), adding that now the railway would also help development in the Russian Far East, relieve congestion on the Trans-Siberia line and speed up container traffic from the Pacific to Europe. BAM's route from the coast to Taishet, where it joins the Trans-Siberia, is 280 miles shorter than the Vladivostok route and – foretold the pro-BAMs – would attract much high-value container traffic.

Udokan's copper proved decisive, if that word may be used in a BAM context. In 1960 the USSR Council of Ministers decided to develop this deposit, which could not be done without the railway; but still nothing happened, apart from myriads of bureaucrats and experts designing many plans and having many arguments.

Meanwhile tension was rising between the Soviet Union and China. In 1969 there was fighting on the frontier, within a rifle-shot of the Trans-Siberia line, and the militarists again pushed forward, insisting that BAM had become vital to national security. The counter-argument was as strong as it was obvious: the northern route would be no less vulnerable than the Trans-Siberia to modern long-range bombers. But at last the pro-BAMs won and in 1972, two years before the Final Plan was officially approved, the relaying of the track to Tynda began.

Under Stalin the very word 'BAM' had made Russians sick with fear and, *pace* Soviet propaganda, few citizens then felt patriotic enough voluntarily to undertake pioneering construction work in Siberia. But by the 1970s all had changed, changed utterly. In March 1974 Brezhnev designated BAM a Komsomol Shock Project, to be completed by 1982, and six weeks later the first group of volunteers, none older than twenty-eight, arrived in Ust'-Kut. Two million students graduated annually and had to repay the State for their education; now many were given three-year BAM assignments by their regional Komsomols – in most cases manual jobs, a stupid waste of talent. When the Khabarovsk Komsomol sought fifty surveyors 200 applied, all recent graduates, and the surplus 150 had to make do with construction work.

Shock Project status brought access to scarce materials, the best available equipment and the most highly trained specialists. All BAM workers enjoyed a variety of privileges, queue-jumping being the major incentive. Back home, they would not have to wait the usual eight to ten years for a flat. Also, three years in Siberia entitled them to open a car account in the bank and, after saving for another three years, they could buy a special car voucher and jump the queue at the nearest official vehicle-supply depot. In addition, BAM workers got double holidays – 48 days annually – and those most at risk (the tunnelling and demolition heroes) were granted another six days. Rail travel was free and every third year workers were given air tickets to their home area, plus large discounts for themselves and their children at holiday resorts and Pioneer camps.

Predictably, these privileges aroused controversy and the *BAM Guide* quotes from the Spring 1983 issue of *Soviet Sociology*:

> Obviously, the primary emphasis on offering people the privilege of receiving scarce goods as a way of attracting a work force to the BAM region cannot be considered an adequate method ... It stimulates consumerist attitudes among young people, paving the way for various kinds of speculation and intrigue, and damage is done to the patriotic spirit which should prevail on an urgent construction project.

In two BAM towns I was to meet several older residents (themselves privileged in their youth and not *Soviet Sociology* readers) who expressed similar reservations about the 'incentive' sources of the current 'speculation and intrigue'.

When Brezhnev toured Eastern Siberia and the Russian Far East in 1978 his main purpose was to publicize 'the heroic achievements of the patriotic Komsomol volunteers'. This tour proved disconcertingly educational; soon after, the government admitted that their 1982 deadline had been over-optimistic. And so it proved. In 1982, according to the official Soviet news agency, BAM remained between 20 per cent and 30 per cent incomplete, though more than 200 stations and sidings had been constructed, plus 126 long, high bridges across rivers and gorges.

In September 1984 the eastern and western sections were solemnly connected by a golden spike in the new 'model town' of Kuanda; but no foreign journalists were invited to these rather misleading celebrations. In reality only a third of the track, and one of the six major bridges, were fully operational and the trickiest tasks still lay ahead. Now the track-layers were required to build more bridges, and a variety of complex railway infrastructures, and to become tunnellers – all skilled jobs for which the available workers were unqualified. Their retraining delayed progress for two years and by 1986 Gorbachev had come on the scene and vehemently declared himself to be anti-BAM. He pointed out that, for one thing, new speedy container ships were sailing from Japan to Amsterdam as quickly as goods can travel on trans-Russia railways – even using the Trans-Siberia, which is three times as fast as BAM. In 1988 the Academy of Sciences' Scientific Council on BAM Problems was disbanded, a signal decoupling the line from any new plans that might be made for Siberia's future prosperity. When Gorbachev described BAM as 'the greatest monument to the period of stagnation', and 'an example of Brezhnev's personal economic adventurism', Soviet journalists eagerly set about collecting facts and figures to prove the railway's futility. This was disheartening for the Komsomol teams and railway troops still slogging away on a dwindling budget – some of them, by that date, second-generation BAM workers. Not until March 1990 (fifty-seven years after the first tracks were laid!) did all of the line become fully operational, though the Severomuisk Tunnel remains unfinished. The

Ministry of Railways then suggested chopping the line up and presenting bits to other regional railways; but none was willing to give stable room to such a notorious White Elephant. Also, it has to be said, an endearing White Elephant. Despite much preferring trains to motor vehicles or planes, never could I have imagined myself falling in love with a railway. But the BAM *is* unique. A train that travels hundreds and hundreds of miles at an average speed of 20 m.p.h., often slowing to 15, surely represents the acme of civilized public transport.

On the afternoon of Day Three we pulled into Taishet, the BAM's starting point, once infamous as a *gulag* transit camp. This Trans-Siberian-created town (present population about 60,000) remains railway-centred; beyond colossal maintenance sheds, on a bewildering complexity of lines, much shunting of wagons and changing of engines takes place. From here the Trans-Siberian tracks can be seen curving away across flat land to the south-east while the BAM heads north-east, into the mountains.

Hitherto Olga Grekova had seemed indifferent to my misfortune but during this long stop she produced a woman doctor, one of BAM's own medical staff, complete with white coat and stethoscope. It then emerged that we had only one other English-speaker aboard, a young man named Maxim, found in some distant compartment and co-opted as interpreter. The doctor confirmed my diagnosis, apparently known in Russia as 'footballer's knee'. She applied a tight bandage and advised me to lie flat with my leg elevated rather than sitting all day by the window – which unwelcome advice made sense.

Maxim, aged thirty-one, spoke American rather than English. After a year in Ohio, being trained as a Pepsi Cola quality inspector, he was now based in Bratsk, his native place. That area was chosen, during the twilight of the czars, as a base for the tentative industrial development of Eastern Siberia. Under the Soviets Bratsk became one of the empire's Ten Most Polluted Cities and three of Maxim's American colleagues had recently returned home for health reasons. Ruefully he pointed to his 80 per cent bald pate and said that many of his contemporaries – and juniors – were similarly afflicted. He was now seeking an equally well paid job elsewhere but was hesitant about ever having children, so hesitant that after four years of marriage his wife had begun to utter divorce threats. The week before, at a godson's christening, he had defensively shown her the baby's webbed fingers. 'Very distressing for the parents,' she said, 'but a minor operation can sort it out.' What really unnerved Maxim were the several cases, within the previous few years, of monsters being born locally and at once 'put down', their parents misled to believe 'it was a stillbirth'. He added that the taiga, too, had been killed over a 100-mile radius from Bratsk – which I soon saw for myself as we ambled on through forests of naked black tree corpses. But by the time we reached Bratsk's lethal conglomeration of industries I was sound asleep.

BAM itself is responsible for other dead forests where its construction has created swamps by disturbing the permafrost. This permanently frozen soil may be hundreds of yards thick and is not, as many assume, a consequence of Siberia's low winter temperatures. Rather it is a leftover from the last Ice Age which hasn't thawed because of current low temperatures. When BAM building or similar upheavals promote a thaw, current temperatures cannot refreeze the ground to permafrost depths and swamps swiftly form and trees die.

Taishet is five hours ahead of Moscow (Tynda: six hours) and these time changes, so routine for air travellers, feel quite different – almost eerie – when happening slowly on a non-stop train journey. All Russia's railways keep Moscow time, showing it on station clocks, timetables and tickets, which sounds confusing until you're in the system when you realize how neat it is. I noticed some passengers adjusting their watches zone by zone; others, like myself, preferred to keep watch and body-clock synchronized – even if only an illusion of synchronicity can be attained, given the body's reaction to the sun.

Like most of her calling, Olga Grekova was scrupulously conscientious and scoured our carriage twice a day: every surface and the inside of every window polished – floors swept with a grass broom, then mopped with disinfectant – the litter-bin at the end of the corridor emptied regularly, the samovar kept full of boiling water, the loo promptly locked and unlocked before and after each stop, the passengers who got off at the few long stops closely watched and summoned back on board in good time. From all points of view, BAM is a shining (literally) example of how to run a long-distance train service. I have only two complaints: on this particular journey the windows were filthy *outside* and none could be opened more than twelve inches, which precluded leaning out to enjoy the view and take photographs of our sensationally long train as it rounded curves in the track overlooked by lordly mountains. Amiable discussions took place between the Baranskayas and myself about our window: how wide to leave it open during the night? The first two nights were so hot that we all opted for the full twelve inches but then the temperature dropped slightly and my companions suggested two inches. Politely I agreed, while still yearning for twelve.

At Ust'-Kut the railway runs parallel to the mighty Lena river (2,750 miles long) near its confluence with a minor tributary, the Kuta (a mere 255 miles long). Here I was planning to land (knee permitting) after my upstream voyage from Yakutsk and what is visible of this town from the station suggested that it would not tempt me to linger.

Beyond the low, pine-clad hills encircling Ust'-Kut we met the Kirenga, another Lena tributary, then for hours were crossing swampland and larch woods, occasionally interrupted by meadows where grey-brown haystacks stood awaiting the winter. New grass grew high around them and to me this looked like slovenly farming; later I learned that it is a Siberian labour-saving device. In November tractor-drivers put heavy chains around the bases of these stacks which then slide easily over the snow to their farmyard destinations.

That afternoon I wrote in my diary:

Rain is rare in Siberia; people exclaim in wonder when I describe our anxious rush to save hay before the next downpour. Here today a strong west wind is still blowing steadily, as it has been ever since we left Moscow. As a BAM passenger, gazing over these thousands of uninhabited and uninhabitable miles, one feels Siberia cannot be tamed or degraded, even by twenty-first-century Technological Man. Quite simply there's too much of it! Yes, the Russians (or their tribal surrogates) have slaughtered billions of furry animals, felled millions of trees, built intrusive railways and catastrophic dams, polluted hundreds of square miles, poisoned dozens of rivers, founded scores of little towns and a few cities. Yet between its scattering of railway-dependent settlements Eastern Siberia's immense silent isolation seems inviolable, aloof, able to ignore and survive the exploiters' wounds.

A comforting thought – of which I was soon to be deprived.

BAM allows only tantalizing glimpses of Lake Baikal as the line curves around the northern shore between Severobaikalsk and Nizhneangarsk, plunging frustratingly into four short tunnels where mountains rise sheer from the sapphire-blue waters of the world's deepest lake. Then we were gradually ascending, through the wide sloping valley of the Upper Angara river, and going even more slowly, for some 200 miles, around the steep flanks of sparsely forested mountains overlooking creeks, lakes, swamps, streams and young rivers. Only recently have all of Siberia's tens of thousands of rivers been named.

Suddenly, to everyone's astonishment, torrents of Siberia's rare rain swept across the landscape. This was cruelly bad luck; immediately ahead rose the Severomuisk Range, several of its now invisible peaks attaining 7,500 feet or more, and here BAM workers performed (and are still performing) their most spectacular feats. But as we climbed into dense cloud – at 10 m.p.h., so perilous is this stretch of track – I reminded myself that I would be here again, en route from Ust'-Kut to Khabarovsk.

The sky was clear when I woke next morning at first light – 4 a.m. local time. While hopping to the loo my knee felt much less painful and I reckoned on a short stay in Tynda, now only fourteen hours away. I perched then on one of the corridor's tiny fold-down seats where passengers needing a spell of solitude can quietly contemplate the landscape. Far below the track, a fat silver mist-snake showed the course of the winding river Khani. Shoals of crimson cloudlets swam in the blue-green eastern sky, then were lost in a surge of gold. Moments later the sun was up, giving to the sheer rock mountains on our left a rosy glow, perfectly mirrored in the still dark surface of a small lake. Hereabouts is BAM's most extreme permafrost area – the ground frozen to a depth of 1,800 feet. And soon we were crossing BAM's highest point, almost 4,000 feet above sea level and marked by a clumsy monument, a white rail six feet long and six feet high. Below this pass the deep Khani valley was now filled with lustrous morning cloud and ahead rose the Stanovoi Range, containing immeasurably rich coal-beds along all of its 440 miles. Very cautiously we descended, taking a roundabout route along the shores of gleaming creeks where a pair of duck – among the few birds seen on this journey – were diving for breakfast.

Meanwhile the Baranskayas, who usually slept until noon local time, were busily packing, washing, hair brushing, carefully donning their smart streetwear and, in Mrs Baranskaya's case, laboriously applying excessive quantities of make-up. They were the only passengers to disembark at Khani where the Uvarovs and their twenty-year-old daughter, Sveta, became my coupé companions.

Khani huddles at the base of steep rock-crested mountains and, like all these little BAM towns, has an air of despondency. At 8 a.m. the already hot sun shone brilliantly on half-a-dozen dingy five-storey apartment blocks with the usual fringe of rough-and-ready BAM builders' shacks, some still lived in, others used as stables or tool-sheds. Here we spent forty minutes, this being an engine-changing stop. Nothing else was happening around the station where lines of wagons, loaded with oil-tanks or timber, stood awaiting engines. Observing what I could of the town through binoculars, I saw no sign of life apart from a mongrel bitch being pursued by several would-be mates.

However, there may be more to Khani than meets the binoculars; the Uvarovs, who had never lived anywhere else, were as cheerful a trio as one could meet and instantly became my sign-language pupils. For them going to Tynda, to spend a week with Mr Uvarov's sister, was an annual adventure-holiday. They had never before actually met a foreigner, though they had seen a few visiting geologists, and their excited curiosity kept my Oxford mini-dictionary in constant use. For a time I assumed mother and daughter to be sisters; they looked very alike and only eighteen years separated them. This error naturally endeared me to Mrs Uvarov.

By now the traversing of such vast territories, only visible to train passengers and BAM workers, had left me feeling oddly but not unpleasantly disorientated. As the line remains close to Ireland's latitude, I had little sense of being in Asia – even on Day Five, when in fact I was further east than ever before in my life. Visually, in mid-summer, much of Siberia can seem quite home-like, the trees and vegetation generally familiar; to an Irish traveller southern Europe looks more 'foreign'. And Siberia's ferociously beautiful rock mountains, their peaks and precipices sometimes mirrored in jade-green lakes, resemble the Dinaric Alps rather than any of the great non-European ranges.

Remembering its history and observing its environmental consequences, one has to ride Siberia's White Elephant with mixed feelings. In the late 1940s, along the 230 mile stretch from Taishet to Bratsk, 300 BAMLags held more than 100,000 slave labourers. Of these camps few traces remain but each BAM settlement and the line itself – with its occasional adjacent dumps of discarded materiel – constitutes a profound insult to Siberia's unique environment. Yet it is easy enough to see BAM through Russian eyes, as a heroic achievement. Heroism hardly entered into the equation during the BAMLag era but the later Komsomol workers were indeed courageous, if not exactly 'heroic'. Any wimps tempted by the incentives on offer failed the test of their first winter on site. Also, despite the various vicissitudes and monumental misjudgements that bedevilled its construction, BAM is an awesome witness to Russian engineering ingenuity and sheer determination – this even the least technologically-minded passenger can appreciate.

We first saw Tynda from afar, a line of high white buildings gleaming on a long ridge embedded in taiga. Then it disappeared for twenty minutes as BAM descended to the left bank of the Tynda river, narrow by Siberian standards and now sparkling in the evening sun. When the little city reappeared, where the valley widened slightly, we passed hundreds of wooden shacks and converted railway freight wagons, the pioneer BAM builders' base. Then, at the end of this five-and-a-half day train ride, we arrived at 6 p.m. (local time) precisely: the arrival time given on my ticket. Later I was to acquire BAM-driver friends who explained that punctuality is a matter of honour; on some journeys, when conditions would allow an early arrival, BAM slows down over the last lap.

# 3

## The Children of BAM

The *BAM Guide* informs us:

> Tynda is a modern city in deep wilderness. It was the headquarters of
> the BAM Railroad until 1996 and it is still a major railroading town ...
> the third largest town on the BAM with a population of 70,000. The
> main street, Krasnaya Presnya, is lined with 16-storey buildings which
> is very unusual for Siberia ... The early years of Tynda were a litany of
> poor engineering with constant water and heating shortages, in-
> adequate housing, buildings subsiding into the permafrost and
> power interruptions. The situation now is vastly improved with the
> construction of a centralised heating system consolidating the town's
> 38 separate heating boilers in 1977. Air pollution was also a big problem
> due to the coal-fired power station but this closed when the supply of
> electricity arrived from Zeya, 225 km away ... Tynda has a sister-city
> relationship with Wenatchee, Washington, in the USA. In the early
> 1990s, an exchange programme for the children of these two cities
> started.

Major railroading towns have enormous stations and I quailed
when we stopped by a middle platform. Steep metal stairs gave access
to a long pedestrian bridge; hauling a loaded Pushkin up there would
have been difficult even with two sound legs and my dawn optimism
concerning The Knee had dwindled as a result of experimental walks
in the corridor. But at once the Uvarovs took charge: I didn't have to
ask for help. While Sveta took off for aunty's house, carrying their
meagre luggage, Mr Uvarov looked after the panniers and Mrs Uvarov
helped me on to the platform. There Mr Uvarov asked for Pushkin's
documentation and hastened away to No. 990290. The bustling
throngs around the freight wagons – waving sheafs of documents,
pushing handcarts – presaged a long wait so Mrs Uvarov and I sat on

the panniers, watching the freightless passengers rapidly dispersing. One woman, inexplicably, was carrying a sable in a mini-knapsack, its bright little eyes surveying the scene with apparent equanimity.

The air was pure and invigorating, the light clear, the sun still pleasantly hot, reminding me of an Indian Summer evening in Ireland. None of Siberia's infamous midges was in action, only an impressive display of giant flying cockroaches. Then Mr Uvarov came trotting back; without my passport he couldn't take delivery of Pushkin – a reassuring precaution but I was mortified by this added inconvenience for my Good Samaritan. Ten minutes later Pushkin appeared, unblemished, and the Uvarovs watched, fascinated, as I loaded him; in Siberia bicycles are uncommon and pannier-bags a novelty.

Mr Uvarov had already got permission for us to cross the numerous tracks at ground level. (Russia's current lawlessness does not extend into BAM-ruled territory.) Hobbling along behind him, leaning heavily on his wife, I allowed myself a brief wallow in self-pity. This was the moment I had been looking forward to for nearly eleven months – the moment when, all preparatory hassles overcome, I would mount my bicycle and ride away into an almost traffic-free unknown. Instead, I found myself incapable of even wheeling Pushkin and by the time we had covered the half-mile to the road I was almost fainting with pain.

Only one taxi remained, its driver a thin-lipped peroxide blonde. Mr Uvarov negotiated and settled on 100 roubles which seemed fair for the two-mile ride as Pushkin had to be roped to the boot. But then, outside the hotel, Ms. Peroxide pointed angrily to her number plate, allegedly damaged by Pushkin, and demanded an extra 300 roubles. When I laughed derisively and pointed to the wide variety of dents and scratches all over her vehicle she didn't pursue the matter.

Now I was stranded at the foot of six steep steps, utterly unable to get my possessions into the multi-storeyed Sovietesque Hotel Yunost. Three oafish-looking youths were sitting on a nearby bench, sharing a two-litre bottle of beer. Tentatively I appealed to them for help but they merely stared and sniggered though I was so obviously maimed. Moments later, two men emerged from the Yunost, talking animatedly. They looked startled when the foreigner sought assistance, then frowned and shrugged and swiftly walked away. I didn't blame them, given my inability to explain the problem in their language. Once a foreigner's reason for being in Siberia is understood, Siberian hospitality takes off and is limitless but the region presents some difficulties for solo non-Russian-speakers who may be viewed as inexplicable phenomena best avoided. Even in a city like Tynda, the majority have never met a western foreigner. Within recent decades many previously isolated parts of the world have been exposed to outside influences; wars, famines, diseases and oil or mineral interests have made them the focus for humanitarian aid, or military interventions, or corporate manipulations, or imported bureaucracies dedicated to 'guiding them towards democracy'. Most of Siberia has thus far been spared such exposures – though they loom.

The time had come to wield my publisher's introductory letter in its Russian translation. If all goes well these letters, tendentiously presenting me as a literary person of some consequence, are never used but in exceptional circumstances I deploy them shamelessly. When a tall, well-built, grey-haired man came down the steps I smiled at him ingratiatingly and firmly thrust the document into his hands. And that was the beginning of a brief but unforgettable relationship.

Perplexed, Igor unfolded the letter – then became very excited, shook my hand vigorously and said, 'I speak English *malinka* – small English but I help you, yes, all helps, every way helps!' I explained my disability and promptly he ordered the youths lounging on the bench to carry my possessions into the hotel's gloomy, high-ceilinged foyer where a stout, stern receptionist at first refused me admission, possibly because I didn't look respectable enough. Vigorously Igor fought my case and gradually she relented: I could have a room *if* I stayed for seven days and paid now in advance. This suited me; I had little hope of being able to walk normally in less than seven days.

Two swift lifts took Igor and me, and a young man and Pushkin, to the enormous, blue-carpeted second-floor lobby where tall potted plants flourished between fat shiny yellow armchairs and bamboo coffee tables; no one ever used this space, perhaps because of its conspicuous 'No Smoking' signs. Here Igor introduced me to Ira – matronly, efficient and affable, the descendant of those guardians who in Soviet times (when the Yunost was still state property) supervised all hotel guests on a given floor. She led us to my room – excellent value for $12 with a table and chair by the wide window, a bedside light, a shower that worked (apart from the water's tendency to flow out on to the bedroom floor), a sofa, easy chair and TV set. Little space remained for bicycle parking: Pushkin had to stand on his hind-wheel in a corner. Anxiously Igor inquired if I had all I needed and gratefully I replied, 'Yes, except for beer. May I order four bottles from the bar?' – a modest order, I thought, after five almost teetotal BAM days. But Igor smiled his gentle reproval and said, 'In Russia some people like beer and vodka, the people in this hotel – *no!*'

I stared at him in speechless horror. Could it be that immobilized me had paid for a week's accommodation in a 'dry' hotel? This, truly, was the stuff of nightmares.

Left alone, I hopped to the door, one hand on the wall, and called Ira; her room was conveniently near. '*Pivo?*' I queried hopefully, raising four fingers. She smiled and nodded and soon was back from the sixth-floor bar with four half-litre bottles – at twice the Moscow price for the same brand. (In Siberia vodka is much cheaper than beer.) I could then relax and settle down to diary-writing at the end, as I thought, of an interesting day.

Half an hour later a young woman doctor, tall and graceful, arrived with a nurse in tow; at Tynda hospital's A&E department Igor had swung into action. This fussy meddling irritated me but I tried to look pleasant and reached for the mini-dictionary. My own diagnosis was again confirmed by Dr Babenko who advised another week's rest. Then, as the nurse was rebandaging, Igor hurried in, sharply questioned the doctor, dismissed her diagnosis and declared that I must be taken at once to A&E for an X-ray. Dr Babenko snapped that this was unnecessary, then looked at her watch (it was 8.45 though the sun remained high) and said an X-ray now was *impossible*. There followed an astonishing ten-minute argument; from all three words poured forth like molten lava as I looked on, bemused. My BAM reading had been Dostoyevsky: lots of clashing personalities, dramatic declamations, flashing eyes – all a bit OTT, I had thought. Yet here was a *bona fide* Dostoyevsky scene complete with eloquent gestures, flashing eyes, defiant young women and a domineering, emotionally unstable male. At first the young women seemed to be holding their ground but Igor's tone became increasingly abusive. Finally Dr Babenko, looking demoralized, went out to make a telephone call and returned agreeing to the X-ray.

Now it was my turn to argue strenuously; I felt pain-exhausted and in no mood for further movement. The women, by now intimidated into silence, stood by giving me supportive glances. Igor assured me that I would be back in my room within twenty minutes, maximum. Having no reason to suppose that Tynda's A&E is exceptional I scoffed at this notion but at last gave in, for lack of energy to continue arguing. An ambulance was waiting outside the hotel; evidently Igor had presented me as an urgent emergency case which doubtless explained his insistence on the X-ray, to justify the ambulance. I felt an irrational twinge of guilt; possibly – even probably – there were other cases in Tynda at that moment in real need of an ambulance.

Igor disappeared (relief all round!) as Dr Babenko and her colleague helped me into a battered old vehicle with stale bloodstains on the floor and jolly graffiti on the ceiling where someone using black and red markers had drawn a skeleton dancing with a nurse.

Wryly I reflected that there must be something in my karma about Russia and ambulances. Only once before have I been thus transported to hospital: in 1975, in Moscow, when my daughter Rachel and I were on our way back from Baltistan and the Karachi-provided Aeroflot meal gave me (and scores of other passengers) acute food-poisoning. In those days long-distance passengers enjoyed a concessionary rate for a five-day stay at Aeroflot's hotel where I then experienced, to the extremes, both Russian individuals' kindness and Soviet officials' harshness. Luckily Rachel (aged six) had slept all the way from Karachi, stretched out on the floor at my feet, and had eaten nothing. But now she was abruptly abandoned in that vast hotel when her mother collapsed and had to be rushed off to hospital for tests. Vaguely yet vividly I remember struggling with my semi-delirium, begging people to allow her to come with me. But no, that would have broken some rule, so my suffering was exacerbated by worry verging on panic. Needless worry: back in the hotel I found my ewe lamb thoroughly enjoying the affectionate attention of three women who had deserted whatever their posts were to entertain her with jigsaw puzzles and picture books. Then came the next harshness. My condition had baffled the doctors, or so they claimed. Lest I might have some lethal Asian disease I was given a choice: three weeks' isolation in a fever hospital or immediate departure on the first Aeroflot flight to Western Europe – which happened to be going to Paris and never mind our onward tickets being for London. Then came more kindness. Somehow I had lost all our money and when this was explained the receptionist consulted the hotel manager who said, 'You have too much misfortunes, there is no bill to pay.' Several hours later we were sponging on a friend in Paris.

Tynda's huge hospital is now partially disused; BAM towns were built with industrial expansion in view, an expansion that never happened. The nurse helped me through two narrow doorways, stained at elbow-height with much fresh blood which she cautioned me to avoid. In a wide long corridor (standard hospital décor) the evening's genuine emergency cases were awaiting attention. A whey-faced mother stood over a small boy with a hideously smashed leg as he lay moaning on a bare wooden bench; on another bench a solitary unconscious young man was bleeding from one ear; nearby a woman sat with closed eyes and a blood-soaked towel around her head. Her husband (I assumed) knelt beside her holding her hand and muttering what sounded like prayers. Through an open doorway I could see the source of the blood trail on the floor: a large elderly very mangled man was being given a transfusion.

As I couldn't reasonably expect to be looked at before midnight I urged Dr Babenko to allow me back to the hotel; I could return next morning for an X-ray, which in any case she and I knew to be unnecessary. She nodded her agreement, but as the nurse was helping me to my feet Igor reappeared, took in the scene, then strode to the open door of the emergency treatment room, loudly demanding immediate attention for his important foreign friend. An angry Dr Babenko, her self-confidence quite restored, made it plain that even for Igor's protégée there could be no queue-jumping. He however persisted until two male nurse attendants, wearing long green gowns and surgical masks, briefly emerged and curtly said something that silenced him.

Hopefully I looked at my allies – but now, suddenly, they abandoned me without a backward glance. No doubt their shift ended at

10 p.m. Igor then adopted a sentry-like stance beside my bench and said something not polite to an exhausted-looking woman who had appeared with a bucket of disinfectant and a mop.

'Tynda is dirty place,' pronounced Igor. 'Why blood on a floor? Peoples here is not good to work.' Inconsequentially he added that he was a Lao.

I surveyed my companion's large frame, plump pink cheeks and pale blue eyes. 'From *Laos*?' I asked incredulously.

Igor frowned. 'What this Laos? I am laoer [lawyer], OK?'

'OK,' I assured him. 'I was being stupid and also I'm going a bit deaf in my old age.'

After a short pause Igor bent down, looked into my eyes and asked, 'Do you believe in God?' – which question then seemed but another manifestation of eccentricity. I was at the start of a steep learning curve; during the months ahead many uneccentric Siberians were to ask me the same question within half an hour or less of our first meeting.

'No,' I replied in a flat tone meant to convey that I was not just then disposed to debate the existence of God.

'So who created you?' demanded Igor.

'My parents,' said I, at which point a young woman wearing a radiographer's shield came hurrying down the corridor and took Igor's mind off soul-saving. He began to hassle her, repeatedly pointing at me, and when she laughed at him before vanishing he flushed crimson and angrily stamped his foot. 'More Dostoyevsky stuff,' said I to myself.

At 11.10 Dr Kutuzov beckoned me into the treatment room. A very young man with a thin pale face, he had dark rings under his eyes and a nervous tic; evidently Tynda, too, has its underslept interns. Igor had of course followed me, ostensibly to interpret though Dr Kutuzov spoke a little more English than he did. Dr Babenko's diagnosis was ignored and two flimsy grey forms had to be filled in: passport and visa details, next of kin address, medical history – drastically edited, or we would have been sitting there all night. When my trouser leg was rolled up Dr Kutuzov took off at a tangent, became extremely agitated about my varicose veins, seemed to regard them as my main problem. Summoning the dregs of my energy, I set about soothing him with the information that they were hereditary, that I had had them for fifty-four years, that apart from being an aesthetic handicap they caused me no trouble. All this took time, he and I poring together over the mini-dictionary.

Dr Babenko had examined my knee thoroughly but gently, Dr Kutuzov was much rougher and to my fury undid some of the healing already achieved. However, no one could accuse him of not devoting time to his patients. He drew several diagrams to illustrate what had certainly happened and what might have happened. Possibly fat had oozed in between cartilage and bone and was impeding healing in which case an operation would be inevitable. Hence the need for an X-ray next morning and now my leg must be put in gyps. That word made me flinch; in Rumania a ton-weight of nineteenth-century plaster of Paris, also described as 'gyps', had burdened my right leg for eight weeks. Nor was plaster the appropriate treatment: another waste of scarce resources. And anyway my knee had been healing slowly but surely until Dr Kutuzov jerked it. Forcefully I said 'No!' to the gyps – very likely with flashing eyes – but when the doctor showed signs of surrendering Igor threw a tantrum and attacked him for not being more resolute which provoked me to snap, 'I'm off to the Yunost!' (Momentarily I had forgotten that without assistance I couldn't go anywhere.)

Trapped between the hectoring Igor and a defiant patient, Dr Kutuzov's tic became more obvious. From the next room he fetched a packet of gyps with a diagram on the cover; this light twenty-first-century plaster was designed to go only on the back half of a leg. To deliver him from Igor's increasingly eloquent wrath, I consented then to the futile procedure. Looking triumphant, Igor withdrew to the corridor as I removed my trousers and Dr Kutuzov also withdrew – went off duty, leaving me at the mercy of a friendly adolescent tyro. She signed me to lie on that plastic couch recently occupied by the mangled man (most of his blood had been washed off) and moments later made me yelp by applying the gyps while it was still much too hot.

When we left the hospital, at half past midnight, the air was still warm and the western sky not quite dark. No ambulance was in sight, nor any other vehicle, and I realized that Igor expected me to walk back to the hotel, despite so much emphasis, by both doctors, on 'no walking'. This conclusively proved him to be more than slightly unhinged. Leaning heavily on his arm, I hobbled as far as the hospital entrance gates, then again felt literally faint with pain and sat on a step demanding a taxi. Igor looked surprised and made grumbling noises before disappearing for a quarter of an hour. Sitting alone under the stars, I registered for the first time that distinctive Siberian silence which reasserts itself when BAM towns go to bed.

In the taxi Igor announced that he was taking the early morning train to Khabarovsk – but I was not to worry, he had arranged everything for me. Dr Kutuzov would contact Reception about my X-ray appointment and have me collected by ambulance.

Back in my room, Igor glared at the *pivo* bottles but made no comment. We said our goodbyes, accompanied by ceremonial hugs and kisses, and as the door closed I felt liberated, opened another bottle and scribbled a few notes on the evening's surreal events. But alas! those goodbyes were not final. Igor had had after-thoughts and soon returned from a nearby all-night pharmacy to present me with 100 aspirins (to thin my blood because of those varicose veins), a roll of elastic bandage, a hot-water bottle and a large tube of ointment to be applied immediately to my knee to ensure a good night's sleep. The hot-water bottle's function was not specified. (Dr Babenko had advised 'Put an ice-pack on your knee', Dr Kutuzov had recommended 'Keep your knee very warm', and I had decided to ignore both.) My attempt to pay for these expensive items caused grievous offence and Igor departed in a huff – mouth compressed, shoulders hunched.

As I was undressing there came yet another knock on my door. Igor had awakened Ira's daughter Elena and instructed her to apply that ointment; he must have deduced from my expression that I had no intention of using it, for all my effusive thanks. And I was right – it caused a long-term stinging soreness where applied. That night my injury kept me awake for the first time, what with the ointment irritation, the damage done by Dr Kutuzov and the discomfort of the clumsily applied gyps which grated on my ankle and prevented me from lying in the position favoured by The Knee.

Next morning I sceptically awaited developments and to my great relief there were none; without Igor's prodding the hospital staff had sensibly forgotten about me and at noon I removed the gyps.

That first awakening in Tynda provoked another brief descent into self-pity. I opened my eyes to see a deep blue, cloudless sky; the sun shone warmly; a cool breeze touched my face – perfect cycling weather. And Pushkin stood in the corner, ready to go...

Soon Elena's arrival cheered me up. A biology student at Irkutsk university, she was tall, slim, raven-haired and shyly smiling. Her mother had delegated her to do my shopping because the Yunost's restaurant had recently been closed for lack of customers, a symptom of Tynda's decline since 1996 when it ceased to be BAM's headquarters. (Most of my fellow-guests ate in the market's excellent though quite expensive Chinese canteen.)

A one-minute walk from the hotel entrance took Elena to a new up-market bungalow-style shop from which she returned with a 250 gramme loaf of sourish, fawn-coloured bread, 350 grammes of delicious salami, 250 grammes of a well-matured local hard cheese, a one-and-a-half litre bottle of fizzy 'orange' juice and a half-litre bottle of vodka. All for the equivalent of $5.66.

My window, tall and wide, gave a fine view of the not hectic life of central Tynda. On the far side of Krasnaya Presnya – the four-lane main street, pleasingly lined with birch trees – sixteen-storey apartment blocks stretched in both directions, painted white with narrow vertical biscuit stripes between the windows. Soviet construction brigades used to boast that they could complete one such block, containing 360 flats, in six weeks – which must partly explain their many and various defects, like my shower's overflowing on to the bedroom floor. Gazing down that forenoon, I saw mothers or babushkas pushing babies in buggies, elderly couples taking dogs for walks, children eating ice-creams, youths drinking beers, women returning from the market with bulging plastic bags, teenage girls giggling over magazines, two men sitting on the bench near the hotel door sharing a crossword puzzle. I was coming to feel that Siberia is *somewhere else* – its own place, not belonging (except politically) to Russia or (except geographically) to what we think of as 'Asia'. Given the regional road shortage, the numbers of cars and jeeps puzzled me until I noticed that the same vehicles were being driven to and fro repeatedly. Those few Tynda residents who can afford a motoring holiday take their car beyond Siberia by rail.

Although Tynda is a mini-city, news spreads at village speed. Early that afternoon Viktor, the local daily's editor, arrived to interview the 'famous' Irish writer, with Tolya as his interpreter. Judging by that interview, Tynda now has a lively and thought-provoking newspaper, far removed from the dreary Party-controlled press of not so long ago. Viktor wasn't much interested in my sensational (by local standards) plan to cycle to Yakutsk. He wanted to discuss the conflict in Chechnya, the Northern Ireland Peace Process, the Israeli/Palestinian bloodiness, Nato's aggression in the Balkans, the enlargement of Nato and the EU (which he saw as two moves in the same game) and the UN's role in the world. At the end of our four-hour session I felt mentally exhausted and Viktor looked happy; he reckoned he had enough material for several articles. And of course I, too, had had a satisfactory time, riding a few of the numerous hobby-horses I keep in my ethical stable. Later, I realized that Viktor's interest in world affairs was unusual; most of my Siberian friends were indifferent to the politics of their own country, never mind the outside world.

As Viktor and Tolya were departing, Ira requisitioned Tolya: she needed an interpreter to explain to me why I must provide her with a bowl of my urine. In it she would boil cabbage leaves to be applied to The Knee at six-hourly intervals – not any old cabbage leaves but a particular sort, tried and tested over the centuries and guaranteed to speed the recovery of damaged cartilage. After a few *pivos* I made my contribution to this medication and an hour later Ira applied the poultice, Igor's bandage being used to hold it securely in place. Her treatment, continued for four days, certainly helped The Knee to heal.

Tolya had volunteered to return later with his friend Pavel, 'a historian of philosophy, our town's intellectual leader'. Tolya himself was rather remarkable, a polymath in the making who had already collected three university degrees and was about to start a post-graduate linguistics course at Irkutsk. As a seventeen-year-old he had spent a year in the US on a student exchange programme and been shocked by the low academic standards of a country believed by many Russians to be more advanced than their motherland. Especially shocking was his discovery that US teenagers knew nothing about nuclear physics. 'When I said I wanted to go on with that subject they said they don't do it and looked amazed because I'd been doing it for three years at our gymnasium here.'

According to Tolya, the exchange programme was not flourishing: too few Americans were keen to spend a year in Siberia. Also, some of Tynda's older generation had expressed reservations about the scheme, arguing that a year's exposure to the American way of life could have no obvious benefits for youngsters whose destiny it is to live in Russia.

Soon Tolya was introducing me to Pavel: fortyish, of medium build with thick, straight, auburn hair, a short neat beard, dark eyes, a soft voice, a gentle aura, a razor-sharp mind. In 1906 his army officer great-grandfather was posted to Irkutsk, fell in love with Siberia, sent for his wife and family and never returned to Europe. 'So here I am and happy to be here. Loving Siberia must be a hereditary peculiarity. But I sometimes wonder about my great-grandmother – how did she feel when she got her orders to say goodbye to Moscow and get on the Trans-Siberian with my four-year-old grandfather?'

Thus began what is likely to prove a lasting friendship.

On the following morning another healing aid was provided. Mikhail arrived with a little jar of ointment 'made from taiga mosses and lichens for your sort of injury. We have many twisted knees here when we slip on ice.'

Mikhail was aged thirty-one, tall and rather gangly in an adolescent way but going bald. He described himself as 'a BAM bureaucrat' and spoke fluent English. I was beginning to notice that Siberia's few English-speakers were either fluent or severely limited. There didn't seem to be that intermediate stage common in most countries where English is a school subject.

Soon Mikhail was showing me photographs of his three-year-old son – with trembling hands, which made me realize that something had gone wrong. 'He's in Moscow now,' said Mikhail and his voice, too, was trembling. After a moment's pause he continued, 'Last week his mother took him away and I don't know when I'll see him again.

I've no money to fight it legally and anyway mothers always win. My wife is divorcing me, she's gone to Moscow with her parents. They never wanted us to marry, they've always made difficulties between us. They're going into business in Moscow, they were big in the Party here and now Tynda is too small for them, for the sort of business they like. My wife is very clever, a lawyer, top of her class in Irkutsk. Her parents say she must have Moscow opportunities, that Tynda is going dead, that she'd be making no money here. But Tynda is my place. I'm a Siberian, I don't want Moscow. I was there once for our honeymoon, a week staying with my wife's uncle. It was horrible, in the streets everyone rushing and rude and rough. Her uncle and his friends were too rich and made me feel like a peasant. They joked about Siberians eating horses and not able to make love because they were too cold at night. My parents think I should go to Moscow to work so I can see my son even if we're divorced. But they're both BAM workers and I'm a child of BAM. What would I do in Moscow? My mother says I could earn good money teaching English. That's not enough. I earn all I want here. In Moscow my beautiful clever wife will soon give my son another father, someone rich like her uncle. How would that feel for me? What do you think?'

Disconcerted, I hesitated, then feebly said, 'I can't have an opinion, not knowing your wife and her parents and your parents.'

Mikhail frowned. 'But now you know me. Could I ever be a person happy in Moscow?'

Again I hesitated before asking, 'Can you be happy here, without your son? And there must be many different Moscows, it can't all be the way you saw it in uncle's milieu.'

'So you agree with my parents? I should think only of seeing my son?'

Hastily I backtracked and spoke honestly. 'I repeat, I can't have any opinion worth considering. But if you really want my gut-reaction, you should stay where you belong. I only say that because I know exactly how you feel about Moscow – I wouldn't want to live in Dublin.'

Mikhail picked up the photographs – from aged one day in the maternity ward to the third birthday party – and slowly looked through them and said, 'It's hard to forget you have a son. But

Moscow is very far away. Maybe I must try to forget. But always I'll hope when he's older he'll come looking for me.'

I was to meet many more BAM town residents who, like Mikhail, firmly identified themselves as 'Siberians'. When I expressed some surprise at this, Mikhail's parents having come from Smolensk and St Petersburg, he explained, 'Thousands of Komsomol workers stayed because so far from the central government they felt more free, in the past. I suppose I feel the same even now when everyone's politically free. It's another sort of freedom, about space and silence. In Moscow I felt trapped and sort of attacked by crowds and noise. I like to go into the taiga to hunt and fish and camp, I like the quietness we have. Tynda is a big town but only a small dot in Siberia – not important, not what's real for me. In the taiga I know that's my reality. And you can go there by foot, it's not a big excursion like Moscow people going to their dachas. In half an hour you can forget Tynda. My father grew up in our most famous and beautiful city but when they'd finished their three-year assignment he felt he didn't want to leave – and my mother the same, they didn't have a quarrel! Of course BAM had something to do with it, my parents got better pay here. And my age group, we do feel we're the children of BAM. We're proud of it and now able to take over our parents' jobs. BAM's like a big club, making work for so many. Like maintenance – see the size of our workshops for repairing and checking every little mechanical detail! BAM doesn't often have accidents, though our climate is so dangerous most of the year. And remember all those sheets and towels and pillow-covers to be laundered – *many* jobs! And the freight department where I work – very complicated, many more jobs.'

I asked, 'How did your English become so fluent?'

Mikhail smiled delightedly and said, 'Thank you! I liked English at school, most Siberians don't, they say it's a waste of time and don't *try*. I was lucky to have a very, *very* good English teacher, an elderly woman all enthusiastic about English literature, she got so angry if we used American slang! She liked me because I like English, lent me her own books to read, had me visiting her home to talk English. She was divorced and without children and we became friends. After I left school she still invited me to have discussions about Shakespeare, Shelley, Dickens, Hardy – her favourites. She wanted me to go to university and become an English teacher. That was in 1991 when every-thing was very uncertain, but even then my BAM job was secure, I was just starting my training. I gave that for my excuse. Inside myself – well, you know, I've explained already. I didn't want to be most of the year in some big university city. And teaching, it's so badly paid it's a woman's job. I prefer to have English as my hobby, dull bureau-cratic work makes me need an interesting hobby. But now I'm sad, my teacher died last Easter and I miss her the way I'll miss my mother.'

As he was leaving, Mikhail said, 'On Sunday, if you can walk a little way, I'd like you to visit my parents. Here we've not many foreigners, it would be exciting for them. They're only home on Sundays, they work very hard, my mother's an accountant, my father supervises maintenance.'

I felt that by Sunday I could certainly walk a short distance – and should do so, according to the Canadian doctor who advised me on a damaged foot in Vientiane. Some injuries, he had asserted, heal more quickly if not pandered to, despite the common belief that pain is a signal saying 'Stop!'

Eight sunny days passed, each bringing a few newcomers to my room – girls in pairs, shyly introducing themselves and asking if I needed any shopping, youths in pairs showing at least as much interest in Pushkin as in his owner. Those youngsters had spent six years or more learning English but for lack of speaking practice none could hold a conversation.

Sofya became a regular visitor. An electrical engineer in her mid-fifties, she was small, wiry and energetic with a mannish haircut, a strong triangular face and large bright brown eyes. In her spare time she wrote poetry; three not-so-slim volumes had been published and sold well. 'It was easy,' she said, 'to express things in verse that might have sounded subversive in prose.'

Sofya had come to Tynda as a twenty-four-year-old Komsomol volunteer, just graduated from Novosibirsk university and married to a twenty-seven-year-old Kiev-born seismologist whose skills were essential as the new railway line was being laid and the new town built. The young couple lived in a hastily constructed settlement of wooden shacks, augmented by worn-out railway carriages and freight wagons.

Both had grown up in urban flats but were undaunted by the lack of central heating, indoor sanitation, running water and electricity. 'Coming here was an adventure,' said Sofya. 'We also had material incentives, three times the average wage through hardship bonuses. We really believed in Siberia's future, saw the building of BAM as patriotic. Most of us felt good about being pioneers. The shared hardships made us a team though we came from all over the Soviet Union. My husband was Ukrainian, my grandparents were from a village in the Urals.'

Sofya's only child, a daughter, was born in 1974 'in a military sort of tent hospital'. Five years later the marriage ended; seismological duties had too often taken her husband to other sites while Sofya's work anchored her in Tynda. 'For my generation,' she explained, 'a woman's job came first. We were trained to think like that. Men and women were supposed to be equal, women not being distracted by family life, the State's needs coming first. Women workers were important, we'd lost so many men fighting Hitler, but as my daughter grew up official attitudes changed. There was pressure on her generation to marry young and be "womanly", not toughly equal to men but keen on cooking and sewing and knitting. Only that didn't mean women leaving the workforce, they were expected to keep their jobs *and* be model wives and mothers. Now my daughter is twenty-eight, a biologist with a four-year-old son and her husband has just divorced her. She married before she was ready for it. In the new Russia the pressure to marry early has become social, parents worry if daughters don't marry in their early twenties. A twenty-five-year-old having a first baby in our local hospital is called "an ageing first-time mother"!'

I asked 'How do you see the new Russia?' and laughingly Sofya replied, 'I don't try to see it! Here in Siberia we have our own concerns. In this town I helped to create I only look at how Tynda is faring. And we're lucky in one way. We've a good Mayor, as you'd call him – in past times an honest senior Party official, now an honest leader of his neglected community. I know how the outside world sees us, run by corrupt former Party bosses talking "democracy" while keeping control of their areas. That must be true in many places but it's not happening here.'

A few days later, as we were swapping rather intimate biographical details, Sofya described herself as 'socially engineered', one of the millions of children born out of wedlock during the decade following the Great Patriotic War. In 1944 Soviet women outnumbered men by some twenty-five million. Countless lives had been lost in the Civil War (1918–22) when many foreign troops – Japanese, British, Czechs and others – fought with the White Army against the Bolsheviks. Soon after, the forced collectivization of agriculture (another sort of civil war) and Stalin's purges eliminated further millions. Then at least twenty million, mostly young men, died fighting the Nazis. Confronting this demographic disaster, the Soviet government passed a law, in July 1944, making all children born out of wedlock wards of state, their fathers being explicitly relieved of any financial responsibility for them. Within a year 280,000 unmarried mothers had claimed state support; by 1950 the figure was 1,600,000 and seven years later more than three million 'wards' had been registered. The 'illegitimacy' label was eschewed, explained Sofya. Those mothers and their offspring (many women bore two or three children) were honoured for their contribution to the rebuilding of the Soviet Union. From the late Fifties, the numbers of wards rapidly decreased as parity between the sexes naturally happened among the younger generation. 'This was one of Stalin's few good ideas,' observed Sofya. 'It shocked a lot of people but what was the alternative? Young women don't like celibacy and were ignorant then about birth control. Most would have got pregnant anyway and aborted the babies we needed because they couldn't support them.'

As Sofya had pointed out, in the Soviet Union the family as an institution was badly damaged by state demands. (Although no more damaged, one of my Irkutsk academic friends was to argue, than the contemporary Western family, undermined by 'no respect for authority, promiscuity and women's greedy careerism'.) Most Soviet families suffered multiple handicaps: cramped accommodation, an inadequate diet, wives always overworked, husbands too often dedicated to vodka, children spending twelve hours a day in crèches. Yet I was to meet numerous young men and women who are now taking responsibility for parents rendered destitute by the new Russia, people whose vanished pensions have left them humiliatingly dependent on their children. And in various Siberian towns I was touched when those children confided in me, discussing family problems in often painful detail – perhaps because I was a transient person in their lives, from another world, and so they could unbutton without feeling disloyal to anyone.

Boris's dilemma was not unusual. His parents (father an agronomist, mother a factory manager) had looked forward to a modestly comfortable old age but were now so reliant on their only child that he couldn't afford to marry. His fiancée, Tanya, was in a similar but worse situation. Her long-since divorced and recently semi-invalided geologist mother (geologists are numerous and important in Siberia) lacked the state support available in Soviet times to disabled workers.

Being deliberately provocative, I asked, 'Does that make you wish the new Russia hadn't happened?'

Tanya threw back her head – long orange-tinted locks flying – and laughed almost jeeringly. 'How can you say this? Now everything is possible, in the past everything was stagnant! Maybe some nervous old people would like to go backwards but we want to go forwards. It's true, our new Russia is confused and difficult and insecure. We hear about mafia in Moscow and Khabarovsk and all over our big cities and we know there's no democracy – only our shops have all the things people can buy in democracies. But we're not *stagnant* any more, everything's *moving* and we're free to fight the mafia – or join them! I'm twenty-one, I don't remember Soviet times, I was four when *perestroika* was invented. But I know about Soviet times, I listen to my mother and her mother, I see in my mind how they lived and I'm happy I can live another way. It's bad for Boris and me not able to marry now because we've parents needing support. But if the State was still supporting *them* it would be controlling *us*. I don't want to be controlled. We're choosing to put our parents first, we have a choice. In Soviet times people had no choices.'

I looked at Boris who was exuding unease. Sharply he said, 'Tanya's talking like a woman, thinking on her personal level, being all sentimental about "choice". What choice does Russia have now? Gorbachev was a fool, pulling something down before he'd found something else to replace it.'

Tanya, flushed with anger, snapped something in Russian and left us, banging the door. Ignoring her departure, Boris continued: 'Gorbachev thought he could go back to the beginning, to real Communism, and make it work. But all the praise from the West, from people only wanting to kill the Soviet Union, made him dizzy. He couldn't see the result of restructuring with Western advice. Who gained first and most when our economic activity was no longer state controlled? The gang we call the "bureaucratic bourgeoisie"! They were ready to jump into the selling of shares in state enterprises. No one says we didn't need *perestroika*, done our way. Doing it the West's way was the mistake. The Americans don't have statesmen or even politicians, they're all businessmen wanting quick action for quick profits. In some ways, by Russian standards, the Soviet Union was OK. The masses were bullied but better off than they'd ever been before. No one can deny that. And now what? We've joined the Third World, with plenty of consumer goods there for the rich while our leaders take orders from the IMF and we wait for more American investors to exploit us – *hoping* they will!'

At that point Tanya returned, her eyes red and swollen. Looking directly at me she said, 'I go now to my mother. Tomorrow we can talk again – you and me.' But she didn't reappear on the morrow and next morning I left that city. Perhaps her being unable to many Boris at the age of twenty-one was no bad thing.

After a week in Tynda I could clearly see the wide silver lining around the cloud of my injury. So many congenial welcoming visitors, and the kindness of Ira and her cleaning-lady colleagues, had made me feel completely at home in my little room. Those cleaning-ladies were, I noticed, disproportionately numerous; the Yunost had not yet been transferred to private ownership and in a town seriously short of jobs the municipality was evidently putting people before profit.

Most of my fellow-guests were traders, former citizens of the Soviet Union, now foreigners from Azerbaijan and Armenia and the Central Asian republics, plus several Chinese and South Koreans – all staying long-term at the Yunost, paying $5 a night. Tynda's colony of North Korean loggers occupied one overcrowded apartment block and were strictly segregated from the town's other inhabitants, a restriction imposed from Pyongyang where the remittances they sent home were valued as much as they themselves valued jobs in comparatively prosperous Siberia.

After my third night the Yunost management began to fret because I hadn't yet registered with the police, a ritual still compulsory in Tynda though I came across it nowhere else. Elena and her friend Lynda (daughter of the relevant policewoman) offered to escort me to the correct police station – there are two, civilian and criminal – and arrived punctually at 11 a.m., the Siberians being admirably punctual. As we walked along Krasnya Presnya these children of BAM informed me that they had been 'born with the town' and proudly pointed out its various noteworthy (in their estimation) features – 'our school', 'our cinema', 'our new cathedral'. That last gleaming edifice had been, according to Tolya, a source of much dissension, the local clergy demanding that it should stand on the highest possible site, visible from afar, and the municipality insisting that it must go in the town centre, to enhance the six-lane Krasnya Presnya. Then there was another cacophonous row when the priests complained that the bells were insufficiently melodious because not enough had been spent on them. Neither Elena nor Lynda had ever been inside the recently opened church; women, they inaccurately warned me, were not admitted if bare-headed and wearing trousers.

This first venture outside the hotel disappointed me; The Knee was not as 'better' as it had felt when I was merely walking from my room to Ira's. I also realized that had I been awheel, en route to Yakutsk, the midday heat would have enforced a siesta.

All the BAM-Zone towns had 'sponsors': Tynda/Moscow, Severobaikalsk/St Petersburg, Kuanda/Uzbekistan and so on. Officially listed as 'urban settlements' (minimum population 3,000, of whom no more than 15 per cent work on the land), those towns' apartment blocks could be in Belgrade, Warsaw, Budapest – wherever Soviet urban planners cast their shadow. Yet Tynda does have a certain distinction: its planners made the most of the site's natural advantages and, as the *BAM Guide* puts it, 'The architecture is bold and self-confident'. From the railway station, at river level, wide streets slope gently up to the centre and one walks between double rows of birches, planted on grassy verges. The main street also has its shaded footpaths, much appreciated in the unexpected (by me) noon heat of Eastern Siberia's August. Above Krasnaya Presnya, immensely high archways and long flights of steps lead to the Moscow Boulevard – also wide: everything in Tynda is wide – a pedestrian zone overlooked by municipal buildings, schools, more apartment blocks and the Palace of Culture. To the visitor this uncrowded spaciousness is attractive, until one remembers that Tynda was not meant to be uncrowded. Had all gone according to plan (I forget which Five Year Plan) it would now be a bustling industrial hub from which spokes radiated towards the region's underground riches.

Elena and Lynda apologized for Tynda's carpet of litter which depressingly matched its many broken concrete steps with bits of metal sticking out at perilous angles. The police station, too, was in a poor state of repair, both externally and internally. In a small room on the ground floor three women clerks in civvies sat behind piles of fat files and overflowing cartons of documents. Lynda's mother – stout, young, fussily dressed – stood up to greet me warmly, as though I were making a social call, then directed her daughter to fill in my forms. These we took to a large adjacent room and sat at a long table to struggle with them under the not very friendly gaze of a young policeman. There was little space for whatever had to be inscribed and the questions baffled Lynda. After fifteen minutes she gave up and sought her mother's help. The fee was 112 roubles but when I took out my purse Elena shook her head; we must go to another office, half a mile away, and fill in more forms before paying.

My knee was throbbing painfully as we walked to the end of Moscow Boulevard and climbed two more flights of steps to an enormous ramshackle building, a hive of bureaucrats. Here Lynda had to queue for ten minutes to obtain a tiny but diabolically complex form, to be filled in according to specifications given on a bigger form requiring another ten minutes of queuing at a separate counter. Lynda spent almost an hour struggling with this task. Five times she took the tiny form to an L-shaped counter behind which four young women were doing nothing much yet looking harassed – and five times it was rejected, deemed 'not detailed enough'. As no seating was available, Elena and I sat outside on the balustrade of a long terrace looking down on another terrace where a dozen stallholders sold a limited range of goods and Marlborough umbrellas shaded little-used café tables. Our seat gave a fine view of the nearby cathedral, the distant triumphalist BAM station and the town's slender central heating chimneys, painted in bands of red and white, rising high above the vividly green taiga.

Elena asked if it were true that most Irish have red hair and are always fighting. Many Siberian women acquire red hair at a cost and she looked disappointed on hearing that I know only two redheads, a mother and son. As for fighting – TV images of the Omagh bombing, the Drumcree conflict and the Ardoyne school hostilities had convinced the average Siberian that Ireland is a country permanently engulfed in religious warfare. Even Pavel found it hard to believe that the Dublin government was not funding the IRA. Those letters, after all, stand for 'Irish Republican Army' and the country is known as the Republic of Ireland – so how can people in far-flung places be expected to sort it all out? Were less time spent showing pictures of violence more could be spent explaining its background: but TV has to prefer deeds to words. When Elena asked, 'You have how many TV channels?' I boasted of belonging to that élite 2 per cent of Ireland's population who enjoy TV-free homes. So how did I know what was happening, if I didn't watch the news? On being reminded of the existence of other media Elena remarked that her generation finds it easier to take things in visually.

Back at the Yunost, Tolya (by now established as my self-appointed interpreter) introduced me to Olga, a very beautiful young woman with waist-length golden hair (its gold genuine), grey-blue eyes and Greek goddess features. She wished to interview me for Tynda's 'official' newspaper, published by the municipality and admired for giving details of local government spending, down to the last kopek – one of the Mayor's anti-corruption measures. Although an apprentice, in the second week of her first job, Olga asked some excellent questions. For example, 'What's the difference in your reactions to new countries when you're aged thirty and seventy?' And, 'If you could make wishes for your granddaughters' futures, what would you want for them?' Olga's four grandparents lived in a town not far from Moscow and she could hardly remember them. 'We visited only once since I was born, the distance is so expensive.' Tolya commented, 'For many, living in Siberia is still permanent exile, like it often was in the old days, but now for economic reasons.'

Ivan joined us then, a hugely fat and effervescently cheerful elderly photographer, tenderly carrying his brand-new digital camera. He had been commissioned to provide pictures to go with Viktor's articles so I wasn't prepared for Tolya's turning to me, within moments of his arrival, and translating, 'He wants to know if you believe in an afterlife? Or are you an atheist?'

Olga made a few more notes as I replied that I don't believe in any of the afterlives currently on offer. However I don't care to describe myself as an atheist, a word with a bleak, negative, almost aggressive ring. 'Green Humanist' sounds better, though some humanists can be hostile enough in their attitude to 'believers'.

Ivan observed that many atheists pray unconsciously by putting their trust in Fate, which is really the God they say they don't believe in. He felt confident that even Russians who never go to church retain their faith deep within themselves because for so long 'believing' has been part of being Russian.

Having translated that much Tolya added, 'Among my friends, I can sense unbelievers being unhappy without knowing why. It's because they've lost something so important to all Russians but Stalin took it away. If priests tell me something I know they're right, not because they're forcing me to agree – we're left to make up our own minds, not like Roman Catholics – but because they're both trained and inspired to know best. My Orthodox faith and my Russian-ness are the same thing, those proselityzers being sent from the Vatican and the US are trying to weaken the Russian nation.'

Here was something too familiar to my generation in Ireland: religion as an expression of and confirmation of national identity. An exclusive religion, more political than spiritual: if you don't accept Russian Orthodoxy/Roman Catholicism you're not authentically Russian/Irish. Nasty stuff, imprisoning individuals' minds and threatening communal harmony. When I said as much to Pavel, later that day, he nodded, then did some explaining.

'Please try to understand why some need to regress, at this shift in our tectonic plate. We're confronting so much that's new, alluring, simultaneously very frightening. The West sees 1917 as Russia's dramatic break with the past: exit royalty, enter Communism. Yet really for most Russians it wasn't a *major* revolution. The Party went on from where the czars left off, only more so. It was another system of tyranny, of course a worse sort in Stalin's time. But it wasn't so different it confused people the way they're now confused. *Now* is our real revolution, when Russians must think completely differently to make a success of democracy, the rule of law, the free market. We must pretend to be like other Europeans though we're not – never were. We must retrain even our feelings so that we have emotional reactions comprehensible to outsiders. So if many are turning back to Orthodoxy it doesn't have to be as unhealthy as you imagine. They're needing comfort, reassurance about being Russian being OK. With the present making such unfamiliar demands, religion forms a link to the familiar past. I agree this is a dangerous stage, the Church showing so eager to regain power and property, some of its leaders cynics on the make. But others genuinely believe God has appointed them to control how people think and behave. Orthodoxy served the State for centuries, depended on that symbiotic relationship with the czars. In a would-be-democratic Russia, how can it re-establish its position? Only by waving the nationalist flag, taking advantage of the widespread insecurity, the fearful puzzlement as Russians experience their real revolution. Many are having a collective identity crisis, everything they were told was *good* about Soviet Russia is now *bad*! A lot's been made of Britain's loss of empire, so traumatic the British can't ever recover – and it's only a decade since we lost our empire! Sadly, the Church offers no sound guidance about coping with all this. It's allying itself again with the dominant trend – conspicuous spending, like giving Tynda a new church instead of a well-equipped hospital.'

The Knee had caused a printed matter famine; I wasn't equipped to deal with so many inactive hours. My hopes had been raised by Mikhail's enthusiasm for Eng.Lit. but an attempt to borrow from him uncovered a sad story. He knew his teacher friend had meant him to inherit her English volumes but there was nothing in writing. Then she died suddenly, of a heart attack, and a businessman nephew came from Vladivostok – not for her funeral, to pay his last respects, but a few days later, 'to loot'. Within hours all her possessions were in a BAM freight wagon and he was gone. 'She had nice old cut-glass, good china, beautiful Persian wall-hangings, three valuable nine-teenth-century landscapes from her family. All her friends here knew who she wanted to have those things, it was an understanding between friends. But even if that nephew wasn't so quick, how could we have persuaded a businessman like him to recognize our sort of arrangement? Businessmen don't believe that friends can trust each other.'

Tynda's public library (nowadays under-funded) contained nothing in English and only Tolya could provide emergency rations: James Michener's *The Bridge at Andau* and Hemingway's *To Have and Have Not*, both reprinted in Moscow with long Russian Introductions, and Notes in both Russian and English. I read the Michener with horrified fascination; an account of the 1956 Hungarian uprising, it reeks of McCarthy-era neuroticism. The author's appallingly ignorant condemnations of the Ottomans' behaviour in Europe foreshadowed the West's post-Cold War anti-Muslim paranoia. His descriptions of the tortures used by Soviet agents in Hungary might have been (and perhaps were) drawn from the textbooks used in the US School of the Americas for the instruction of Latin-American military allies of Washington. As for the Hemingway, one can see why that particular novel, emphasizing the misery endured by US workers in the 1930s, was translated – despite its incorrect English, carefully pinpointed in the Notes as 'illiterate usage'!

Tynda's large covered market is a five-minute walk from the Yunost, or a ten-minute hobble. On the way I passed a few pavement stalls selling everything a fisherman might need, from wide-brimmed canvas hats equipped with protective face-nets (antimidge) to waders, rods, reels and shoulder-bags whose many minuscule pockets were designed to hold the extraordinary variety of hooks and flies on display. A little further on, gaudy Chinese carpets were draped over poles on a patch of wasteland outside the market boundary; thus the traders avoided paying for space, a ploy that did not endear them to the locals. Several young Tajik women – copper-skinned, fine-featured, wearing the sort of costumes now rarely seen outside ethnographic museums – were also working the wasteland, holding armfuls of small carpet squares. Recognizing a foreigner, they crowded around me and became rather unattractively demanding.

Inside the high, wide food hall one-third of the stalls and long counters were bare. However, globalization has hit Tynda and there was no shortage of imported wines and spirits, together with the usual range of food industry items. All dairy products were local and limited: homemade butter, excellent hard cheeses and what the Siberians call sour cream and I call drinking yoghurt – one of my favourite foods. Prices (all clearly marked) were slightly lower than in the posh mini-supermarket near the hotel. The marble counters of the butchers' department, segregated at one end of the hall, were four-fifths bare, offering only expensive hunks of frozen beef and pork by courtesy BAM.

Outside, long rows of flimsy stalls under awnings sold fresh fruit and vegetables, household goods, cosmetics and toiletries, clothing, foot-wear, fabrics by the metre. Many of these traders were Chinese (men and women), though Azeris (men only) dominated the footwear section. (I was recognized and cheerfully greeted by a few of my Yunost fellow-guests.) Here one could also buy mushrooms – of all shapes, sizes, colours, textures – from weatherbeaten, unkempt pen-sioners who squatted on the ground beside their buckets. Some had also gathered buckets of blueberries, known in Ireland as whorts (pro-nounced 'hurts') and still with the power to carry me back to the 1940s, to long sunny July days in the woodlands around my home town. For a few weeks each summer our hands were permanently dyed purple.

Near the market, I came upon a large black and white cat lying on a bench beside a block entrance with one hind leg neatly bandaged. When I stopped to talk to him (I miss my cats) the young woman sitting on the other end of the bench asked, 'You are American?' Rejoicing to have met an English-speaker, I sat beside Katya and learned that the cat – Misha by name, belonging to her brother – had been attacked by a Doberman two days previously, then taken to the vet for an X-ray and injection. 'Tynda has only one vet but he's very, very good.' From my window I had observed two cats wrapped in towelling being carried by, respectively, an elderly woman and a teenage boy, presumably going to or from this vet. The Siberians, I was discovering, are devoted to their domestic animals; at weekends many families take a dog and/or cat to the dacha. Katya was pleased that the attack had not given Misha a phobia; he remained at ease with other dogs, including a neighbour's curly-haired golden cocker. On a nearby grassy path Katya's five-year-old daughter was playing with this long-suffering animal and with a pure white tomcat who enjoyed lying on his back trying to catch a blade of grass being dangled by the child.

Katya looked too thin and too pale, as did her daughter – an only child and no sibling was planned. 'Our housing crisis is getting worse, too many young couples must share with parents, so dangerous for relationships!' Since 1996 Katya had been teaching English in Novosibirsk and this was her first visit to her brother who had never before met his niece. Her husband worked as a laboratory technician at the once illustrious but now neglected Akademgorod, twenty miles from Novosibirsk; his pay had recently been halved without warning. Her own inadequate pay always came late and for a dire six months in 1998 it didn't come at all. 'So why are people surprised that school-leavers no longer want to become teachers? They only want to go into business, they are dreaming that everyone can be rich! What happens next as older teachers retire?' On average Katya taught classes of thirty. 'I divide them into three streams, according to ability and the will to learn. I tell them they must first speak good English if they want to get rich in the new Russia!'

Katya blamed that new Russia for pre-puberal children becoming addicted to drugs, mainly heroin. 'But in Tynda not yet heroin, I think there's not enough money here to make profit for dealers. I believe this craziness is because sports are not now possible unless parents can pay. Before, all were subsidized and organized, every child taking part and getting involved, not left with nothing to do.' She pointed straight ahead, to what had been tennis-courts on the long ledge above where we sat. 'There, that's what I'm talking about – all derelict now.' Only the iron posts for the nets remained, some leaning at an angle. 'For ten years we have democracy and all are free, no one telling children what to do and when, no one organizing anything for them. And what are they doing with their freedom? How can they be expected to organize themselves? The intelligentsia can use freedom but not the rest.'

Outside the Yunost a ten-year-old boy sold three-litre plastic bottles of beer from a small table on which he also displayed packets of disgusting crisps and bundles of tiny dried and salted fish – the local, more health-giving 'nibbles', particularly relished with beer. Nearby, lock-up kiosks sold cigarettes, pirated tapes and various types of bread. These all-weather kiosks have heat-conserving openings, only a foot square, through which purchases are made; in winter a shutter is drawn across between purchases. I often bought a cupful of blueberries, sold in a newspaper cone, from the wizened, arthritic babushka who sat all day on a wooden crate beside the steps leading down to the mini-supermarket. She did a slow but steady trade, her tall spotty grandson appearing occasionally to top up the bucket.

My being unable to explore Tynda's surroundings bothered Pavel and on the Saturday evening he organized a treat for me, a riverside picnic. Punctually at 6 p.m. we were joined outside the Yunost by Tolya and his musician friend Tikhon, both young men embracing large bottles and loaves of bread. From the short taxi rank Pavel chose a rickety minibus driven by a retired BAM mechanic whose small flaxen-haired granddaughter and mongrel terrier occupied the front passenger seat. Very soon we were jolting down a steep rough track, larch branches brushing the windows, and all those sixteen-storey blocks were invisible.

That morning I had written in my diary:

> Tynda feels like the oddest place I've ever stayed in. An urban community without a natural context, imposed on the taiga very far from any other town or city, an entirely European settlement east of Laos where the indigenous people register only as curiosities who might one day attract tourists. The *BAM Guide* mentions 'a nearby Evenki village' and Pavel suggested an excursion but understood at once when I said 'No thanks'. My memories of Canadian and American tourist-bait 'native reservations' are not pleasant.

Our track ended at the confluence of the Tynda river and an equally wide tributary that came racing and sparkling through the taiga. Half a mile downstream BAM's long white bridge spanned the Tynda and all around the dense green forest was unscarred, the flat stony shore unlittered, the silence broken only by the rivers' music – their waters at that hour shining sky-blue. We sat on warm round stones and opened our bottles: fruit juice for the teetotal Pavel, *pivo* for the rest of us. Then three pure white waterbirds, cormorant-sized, came flying upstream. A good omen, said Tolya, but no one knew their English name.

All evening nobody else appeared, apart from four children who suddenly swept around a bend in the tributary, travelling fast in mid-stream, using truck tyres as canoes and their arms as paddles. Through my binoculars I watched them landing below the bridge: two boys and two girls, aged about ten. Remembering Katya's outburst, I reckoned they must belong to the junior intelligentsia who know how to use freedom.

Tikhon – very tall, slim and olive-skinned, strikingly handsome – had never before met a Westerner. He spoke no English but his German was fluent because, explained Tolya, 'he wanted to read German musicologists'. Although his orchestral compositions had gained him quite a reputation in European Russia, parental needs bound him to Tynda where he taught at the College of Music. (This institution, Pavel informed me, is very proud of its alumni and alumnae, several of whom have distinguished themselves far beyond Siberia.)

Tynda didn't lag behind European Russia in the days when pop music fans risked nasty punishments. While the city was being built in the 1970s, the Soviet hippy decade, Tikhon's father always returned from his home leave in Novorossiysk, on the Black Sea coast, with a selection of illegal tapes known as *magizdat*. According to Pavel, the makers of these musical equivalents of *samizdat* literature began by merely echoing Western bands, then rapidly developed their own style with hard-hitting topical lyrics expressing the disaffected mood of the majority of youngsters. But now, ironically, the authoritarian pressure is coming from the West and Tikhon raged against the dumbing down and 'loss of identity' of Russia's pop music world in response to the demands of omnipotent record companies – demands including an insistence on lyrics being sung in English.

'But we don't *have to* obey those dictators,' said Tolya. 'Our bands are partly to blame. They won't give up the hope of getting rich quick though they've such a small chance of that. Except for a few rock groups like Kino and Splin, our style *isn't* "pop" in the West.'

On my sixth day in Tynda, Tikhon's first question to his first Western acquaintance – 'Do you believe in God?' – did not surprise me. He himself felt grateful to the village people who since the Revolution had kept Orthodoxy alive, cherishing in the privacy of their homes all its prayers, hymns, traditions and taboos.

Tolya said, 'In America I read about Stalin using religion during the Hitler war to stir up patriotism, making people ready to die for their country and go to Heaven. Then he couldn't go backwards to persecution, had to keep the truce going. When he died the Krushchev thaw made it easier for people to go to church though believing didn't do careers any good. And yet we know now some Party leaders were secret believers. Most Russians my age haven't heard this sort of thing and don't want to. Looking into our past can't make us feel good.'

'That's debatable,' Pavel said quietly. 'It depends on where you're looking from and what you're looking at.'

Then Tikhon infuriated Tolya by asserting that in some ways all the Christian Churches are less good at putting Christ's teachings into practice than the Soviets had been. He recalled participating as a schoolboy in May Day festivities when communities were united and felt happy celebrating together. Pavel translated: 'He says capitalism which Christian Churches support has broken this bond we had. Individuals are so busy competing they say "That's your problem" or "That's not my problem" when something goes wrong for you, instead of trying to help in the old way.'

An impassioned argument ensued, of necessity in Russian, and it promised to be lengthy. Pavel looked at me, his eyes twinkling, and murmured, 'Ivan and Alyosha!' This was serendipitous. Only the day before I had marked a passage in *The Brothers Karamazov* (published 1880) to illustrate Mother Russia's immutability. Ivan the would-be revolutionary is addressing his novice brother:

> For what have Russian boys been doing up to now? Some of them,
> I mean? Well, take this stinking pub, for instance. They meet here

and sit in a corner for hours. They haven't known each other all their lives and when they leave the pub they won't meet again for another forty years ... But, tell me, what are they going to talk about while snatching a free moment in a pub? Why, about eternal questions: is there a God, is there immortality? And those who do not believe in God? Well, those will talk about socialism and anarchism and the transformation of the whole of mankind in accordance with some new order. So, you see, they're the same damned old questions, except that they start from the other end. And thousands of the most original Russian boys do nothing nowadays but talk of eternal questions. Isn't that so?'

'Yes,' said Alyosha, 'to real Russians the questions whether there is a God and whether there is immortality, or, as you say, the questions that start from the other end, of course come first, and so they should.'

The sun still shone warmly, though the trees' shadows were lengthening on the stones behind us. We ate salami, cucumber and black bread and I remarked that this was the best sort of picnic spot, innocent of twee 'landscape furniture' and all those other 'amenities' that deface tourist routes.

'Every year we do have tourists here,' said Tolya, who seemed to be in rather a prickly mood.

'Not many,' said Pavel. 'Groups of railway buffs now and then. Foreign businessmen looking for opportunities who never come back. Specialists representing cultural organizations – we're a long way from having a tourist *industry*!'

Meanwhile, sitting beside the cool, clear water, and watching those children enjoying the rivers, had given me an exciting idea. As The Knee was being so slow to heal, why not go backwards to Severobaikalsk, on the northern shore of Lake Baikal, and enjoy a hydrotherapy course in the world's deepest and purest lake? (Normal people can swim in Baikal only during July and August, though some Siberians plunge into its shallower bays all the year round, having drilled through the ice to gain access.)

Pavel pronounced, 'That's a clever idea, but don't go until you're a bit more mobile and pain-free.'

Tolya volunteered to help me buy my ticket for the following

Thursday's BAM, and to negotiate Pushkin's ticket and documentation – a far more complicated transaction.

At 9.30, as the midges were beginning to swarm, our driver
returned and helpfully offered to dump our picnic litter under the
trees. This allowed me to glimpse the gentle Pavel in an eye-flashing
rage.

Mikhail's parents live uphill from the Yunost, on Tynda's highest residential ledge, approached by a steep path through a larch plantation
where broken bottles tinkle beneath one's feet. Then we skirted a
weedy, rubble-strewn space beside two long, six-storey, half-built
blocks, a rusted mega-crane looming over their floorless interiors and
empty window-spaces. This site was a commonplace symbol of the
sudden collapse of the Soviet Union. I asked, 'Why didn't they take
the crane away? Surely it was valuable, could be used somewhere else?'

Mikhail shrugged. 'In '92 Tynda's development was abandoned
overnight, without warning. There was no one in charge any more,
no one to make decisions, no one responsible for anything: I remember it being a strange time. Some people laughing and excited, some
shocked and frightened, others a bit of both. This area was probably
luckier than most, our BAM world kept going as usual – on time!'

The Stroganovs' block was outwardly slum-like: gross litter around
the entrance, crude graffiti on the lower walls, rows of vandalized
metal post-boxes never used, a filthy unpainted corridor leading to the
lift. And then – a roomy, clean, comfortable middle-class flat where a
French bulldog named Balzac gave me a wildly enthusiastic slobber-
ing welcome and thereafter sat on my lap though he was not of lapdog
dimensions. In the bright book-filled living-room Mrs Stroganov was
repainting a wall to conceal some construction defect. A mass of red
and yellow flowers bloomed gaily on the balcony and an indoor vine
had been trained around two walls. This was a typical BAM Zone flat
with a clothes cupboard in the hallway, the loo and bathroom small
but adequate, the dining-room/kitchen equipped with electric
cooker, fridge, washing machine. In the smaller living-room-cum-
bedroom where we sat, three TV sets were stacked in a corner (one
all the time in action with the sound off) and beside them stood an
elaborate Sony music system.

Mr Stroganov was tall, thin and sallow, his wife small, plump and fair. Neither spoke English but both had plenty to say. Mrs Stroganov smilingly recalled their arrival in Tynda as junior members of a specialist permafrost team. She described the engineering setbacks that plagued BAM building as unsurprising, given the 'specialists'' inexperience. Many, like the Stroganovs, were in their mid-twenties. Those 1970s Komsomol teams should have benefited from the lessons learned during the 1930s (BAM I) and the 1940s, when Yakutsk, Vorkuta and Norilsk were being developed on permafrost. But Soviet ineptitude led to all that construction experience being wasted. The Stroganovs were fascinated by page 313 of the *BAM Guide*: 'Track often had to be relaid after the ground beneath it subsided. Typical of this problem was one report that stated that ten million roubles a year was being spent in the early 1980s just relaying sagging rail foundations west of Tynda.' Mrs Stroganov chuckled and observed that she and her husband, as engineers involved with that stretch of track, would probably have been executed in Stalinist times. Mr Stroganov added that not only design faults were to blame; too often delays in the delivery of building materials upset careful permafrost-related calculations and not all those materials were of the specified top quality. He dismissed the boast that BAM had an almost accident-free record; within four months, in 1987, ballast disintegration and line subsidence caused three crashes.

We had been drinking cup after cup of black tea, deliciously sweetened with runny raspberry jam. It is deliberately made runny for this purpose, and served on individual saucers; some prefer to eat spoonfuls between sips of tea. Then suddenly it was lunchtime, an unexpected development as I hadn't been invited to a meal or yet learned that Siberians force-feed every guest. There was just enough room for the four of us to sit around a table laden with three different salads, red caviar on savoury biscuits, cheese, salami, hard-boiled eggs in sour cream garnished with lovage, smoked omul from Lake Baikal, cubes of bacon fat and grilled 'Bush's legs' – the notorious chicken legs imported by the ton from the US since the reign of Daddy Bush and the cheapest meat available to Siberians. The wine came from Moldova and was divine. The pudding was a chocolate cake (more chocolate than cake) and at that stage I desperately wondered if I could back off, claiming to be replete. But when Mikhail explained that this confection had been invented by his mother, and was locally famous, I accepted the inevitable.

Back in the living-room, fondling glasses of Georgian brandy, we talked of the future of the BAM Zone and of Siberia in general. This was an unusual family. Their decision to remain in Tynda went along with an awareness (on the parents' part: Mikhail thought otherwise) of Russians being Bad News in Siberia. Firmly they squashed my self-consoling thought about BAM's violation of the environment being tolerable, given Siberia's vastness. Not so, said Mr Stroganov, though he conceded that ecologists are right to praise the BAM-planners for having given detailed consideration to the environment and done the minimum damage. But still that damage was, inevitably, widespread and permanent. Siberia's vastness, emphasized Mr Stroganov, is no protection when science and technology move in. Because of its extreme ecological fragility all industrial developments – oil wells, dam-building, paper and pulp combines, logging, mining for coal, diamonds, gold, copper – can only be cataclysmic though the map may show them as mere flea-bites on a mammoth. Mrs Stroganov nodded, adding that flea-bites can become infected and infections can spread, and that's what's been happening, very quickly, in Siberia. Only its indigenous peoples, she asserted, could have preserved Siberia's uniqueness. Their numbers were so few and their technology so primitive, until 'civilized' outsiders armed them, that the environment was safe in their hands.

Here Mikhail broke off his interpreting to question that last statement. He reminded his parents of the plausible theory advanced by some experts to account for the mammoth's extinction: the tribes concerned fancied 'veal'. Archaeologists have found many more calves' bones than adult mammoths' bones on the relevant sites, though killing calves must have been by far the riskier operation.

Russia's colonizing of Siberia, continued Mrs Stroganov, was by global standards unusual. Most other colonial powers initially seized land for its own sake. Then settlers established cattle and sheep ranches, or plantations to produce rubber, cotton, tobacco, sisal, sugar, tea, coffee. ('And opium in India for the Chinese market,' I interjected.) As Siberia lacks much cultivable land, the Russians moved in as *industrial* developers with urban attitudes. Elsewhere, Europeans had to pay some attention to the locals' knowledge of environmental matters as they set up their enterprises. But the industrial-minded Russians could concentrate on doing their own thing, were made arrogant by having the necessary technological know-how, showed contempt for those who had another sort of know-how.

'And now?' I asked. 'Are there better or worse plans?'

Mr and Mrs Stroganov looked at one another and said something brief in unison. Mikhail translated, 'They don't have any answers. There's the same secrecy as before with a "free market" excuse – "commercial confidentiality". We only hear rumours and the names of the corporations who bought our national assets from the Party bosses. We don't know what they're doing but it won't be less than the Soviets did. Probably they do worse damage, they can afford more technology and there's the same lack of controls.'

Mrs Stroganov echoed Sonya on the Komsomol workers' *esprit de corps*. It wasn't, she insisted, a figment of the Party propagandists' imagination though naturally most wanted to leave Siberia at the end of their assignment, having qualified to jump the car purchase and housing queues. Mr Stroganov then recalled that a large minority, more than 25 per cent, also qualified for a medical certificate classifying them as 'disabled', either maimed for life or suffering from chronic respiratory problems.

Mikhail escorted me home – 'Balzac needs a walk' – and as we emerged from the block I wondered how Siberians can tolerate such external squalor when their domestic standards are so high. (They would be shocked to see the cobwebs that hang above me as I write.) For Balzac's sake we had to avoid the glass-strewn path through the spruces, the obvious place to exercise a dog. Other dogs were being walked on their leads on the streets: an obese dachshund, a muscular Alsatian, a magnificent golden collie with a long nose who wore his silken coat like a royal robe.

I asked, 'Why don't communities unite to improve their public spaces?'

Mikhail frowned and said, 'Most of us can't think that way yet – too used to depending on the State. And now local authorities can't afford to collect garbage and don't have the will or the means to enforce anti-litter laws. Our young people enjoy celebrating democracy by vandalizing. Some young men I know pay a little more for a *bottle* of beer – tins are cheaper. They want the satisfaction of smashing the glass on the ground wherever they happen to finish their drink. There must be specialists who can explain this – sociologists or psychologists.'

'Or criminologists?' I suggested.

BAM has a booking-office in the town centre, where Tolya and I queued next morning for forty minutes, not because of the queue's length but because of the procedure's complexity. Then we were informed that we must go, at once, to the freight office at the railway station to book Pushkin's place in a wagon though he would not be travelling for another three days.

At noon the town hall's 'temperature clock' registered 31°C. This long red-brick building looks attractive in Tynda, if only because it is not concrete and a mere three storeys high with eccentric arches decorating its façade. Nearby, on the grassy space bisecting Krasnaya Presnya, stands a stylized metal hammer and sickle, as tall as the birch trees. Tolya, sounding faintly apologetic, said, 'It's Communist but we like it so we keep it.' 'And so you should!' said I. 'Why distort history by demolishing what's suddenly become politically incorrect?'

The pedestrian bridge to the station is lined by colossal pipes – some twelve feet in circumference, two on each side –which carry boiling water to heat all of Tynda. In places the outer metal coating had fallen away to expose their soft golden 'thermal vest' and Tolya commented, 'That looks like vandalism – but why? Vandals need to be kept warm in winter! Unless maybe they come from the shacks that get no heating.'

Tynda's railway station contradicts the town's present reality. Marble stairways sweep up from the circular concourse to an open passengers' waiting gallery furnished with comfortable chairs. The restaurant (little used) is at a slightly higher level, several well-stocked shops are at a slightly lower level. The immensely high domed ceiling is supported by cleverly interwoven steel bars. The décor is black and white and gold. Nowhere is there a morsel of litter or a speck of dust. Smoking is of course forbidden. When I exclaimed at all this grandeur Tolya looked gratified and said, 'Yes, even Japanese visitors are amazed, they think we're savages in Siberia, they don't expect such a building in the middle of the taiga! It's like this because of the plan to have BAM's headquarters here, so Tynda's station was to celebrate the success of the whole project.' He paused before adding, 'Only now it's *not* a success...'

A quarter-mile walk through birch trees took us to the freight office. When at last our turn came the young clerk looked at me with interest. 'From *Ireland*? Where Protestants fight Catholics! Why do they fight so much?' He then broke the news that my Thursday train included no freight wagons – Pushkin must travel on the following Saturday. A fortnight previously I would have balked at entrusting a new bicycle to impoverished railway workers but since then my close-up view of the BAM system had fostered total trust.

As Tolya dealt with Pushkin's documentation (even more complicated now that he was to travel alone) I sat on a step studying the freight shed. Its high ceiling was elaborately insulated and the massive double doors, of wood and metal, had thick leather padding on their insides. The various offices were tiny with lowered ceilings and, like the street kiosks, only minuscule openings to the outside world. While sweating through August, it's hard to remember that for most of the year this is one of the coldest places on our planet.

As I was about to retire, on the eve of my departure, a soft knock heralded Pavel and Tolya. They had planned another treat for me, a short taxi-drive to see the sunset from a vantage-point amidst the taiga, high above Tynda. Unfortunately this beauty-spot's car-park ledge was now being used as an unofficial dump and I could sense poor Pavel's discomfiture as he repeatedly muttered, 'Don't look at the ground!' In fact one didn't have to look at the ground to be repelled: plastic bags and milk and juice cartons had been flung high into the surrounding trees. Happily the sunset didn't disappoint – a superb conflagration, its fierce redness dyeing Tynda's tall white blocks as the taiga turned from green to black.

Tolya then invited us to drink tea in his flat while awaiting the meteorite display due around midnight and guaranteed to be of unforgettable impressiveness. As our host did ritualistic things with a samovar, Pavel spoke of his beloved maternal grandfather, born in 1911 and a dedicated Communist all his long life. 'He was one of the kindest men I have ever known. I worshipped him and can see him still – rosy cheeks, white beard, deep blue eyes – so blue people used to say they were reflections of Lake Baikal!' Pavel himself only lost his faith in Communism when Gorbachev attempted to reform the Soviet system. 'Though of course he didn't realize what he was doing, he couldn't foresee the horrible monster that would be born after our leaders so passionately embraced the West.'

At midnight we were standing expectantly on the derelict tennis courts: but the meteorites were late. Tolya then revealed another of his many talents. Foreseeing this celestial unpunctuality he had brought his beloved flute and now I collected my most cherished Tynda memory, the poignant sweetness of J.S. Bach flute sonatas listened to under a golden glitter of stars.

The meteorites never happened. But that didn't matter.

# 4

## Backwards to Lake Baikal

At 6.06 p.m. (a minute late: my ticket said 6.05) BAM slid slowly away from Tynda where all my friends were grouped on the platform, vigorously waving. At 5.55 Pavel, a busy man, had arrived breathless to hug me tightly and provide lavish nourishment: bread, cheese, ham, tomatoes, grapes and a Siberian-sized slab of chocolate.

For this short journey (810 miles: twenty-six and a half hours) I had chosen a *platskartny* carriage accommodating fifty-eight passengers. On one side of the corridor two tiers of bunks form open, four-person compartments while on the other side, running lengthways, are another two tiers, each lower bunk easily convertible to two seats and a table. The *platskartny* provides more human interest than a coupé and seems almost as secure but does have certain snags; upper bunks lack reading lights and are so close to the ceiling that I felt encoffined. More important, none of the windows (cleaner than on my previous BAM) could be opened and night time did nothing to alleviate the stifling heat.

My companions were two young women and forty-four-year-old Yulia, widowed two months before and also going to Severobaikalsk. One of the young women, a slip of a lass, seemed upset as we left Tynda. Then for hours she sat upright in her corner, exhausted-looking, hands tightly clasped on her lap, staring fixedly through the window, not wanting to be sociable. Eventually it transpired that she was returning to her Bratsk job from a grandmother's funeral, the babushka who had brought her up when her mother was killed in a crane accident.

The two young Kirgiztan traders on the bunks at right angles to ours had round chubby faces and spent most of their time asleep but were cheerfully chatty when awake. One of them, noticing my efforts to open our window, led me to the small enclosure opposite the loo; its window was twelve inches open and I retreated there at intervals. (Incidentally, this loo had a raised iron grid on the floor which would probably have prevented my mishap.) Already, in mid-August, some leaves were burnished, the taiga glowing softly on wide slopes as the sun declined.

Nobody in our *platskartny* spoke English but everybody was friendly and as my photograph album travelled up and down the carriage Yulia proved unusually (for a Siberian) quick at sign language.

That was a memorably uncomfortable night; heat keeps sleep at bay as effectively as cold.

Not far beyond the marvellously named village of Shivery a new bridge, 560 yards long, took us over the Vitim river (low in August but still majestic) and into the Republic of Buryatia. As we approached Taksimo, a gold-mining and logging town, rain clouds gathered along the northern horizon and thunder mumbled distantly. Here the diesel engine is exchanged for an electric locomotive so we all went walkabout and Yulia asked someone to photograph herself and her foreign friend at the base of a Tupolev ANT-4 on a plinth. As the *BAM Guide* explains, 'This was one of the original planes that conducted the aerial surveys for the BAM in the 1930s. It crashed nearby into Lake Barencharoe. Its wreckage was discovered in the 1970s and restored voluntarily by the railway builders.'

No one had seemed worried about leaving their luggage and now I noticed that smartly uniformed Railway Policemen were vigilantly prowling. None of the few hawkers on Taksimo's long platform sold beer so my companions led me into the big unlovely station building where kiosks line one wall. As we ascended steep steps Yulia first noticed my limp – no longer very obvious – and showed great concern. Then I committed a solecism: babushkas of the better class do *not* sit around in public glugging *pivo* from two-litre bottles. Everyone looked so shocked – almost alarmed – that I hastily replaced the screw-top. We were then sitting on a low wall watching the engine change but we didn't sit for long. Here be midges!

Most of my fellow-passengers must have been familiar with this route yet a general excitement pervaded our carriage as we approached the Severomuisk Range with its famous bypass, a daring engineering feat achieved in desperation because another feat, the ten-mile-long Severomuisk Tunnel, remains incomplete. (One day it will rank as the sixth longest railway tunnel in the world.)

Travelling westwards, gazing up from the depths of the wooded Muya river valley, it seems impossible that any railway could find a way *over* the mountain barrier ahead. The BAM planners thought likewise and therefore designed a tunnel, begun in 1978, to be finished by 1984. In fact the service tunnels didn't meet until December 1997 and the train tunnels only met in April 2001. The *BAM Guide* explains:

> These mountains contain four major fault lines and are located in a highly seismic area which experiences 400 tremors a year on average. The entire tunnel is lined with seismic sensors. However, the biggest dangers faced by the tunnellers are the range's numerous underground lakes and rivers. After just a few metres of drilling, the tunnellers encountered streams of water and the epic of water drainage began. The further the tunnel went, the more water entered it. The subterranean water is at pressures up to 35 atmospheres, which means the water is always breaking through the tunnel walls. The huge granite fault lines, offering a conduit for underground rivers, must be approached very carefully ... In September 1979 a drilling team hit an unexpected fault line containing a 140-metre deep underground lake ... a massive 12,000 cubic metres of water, sand and rocks. The water surged into the gallery in just a matter of seconds, drowning several miners. Had most not escaped to the service tunnel, the death toll would have been significantly higher...

According to Vladimir Ignatovich, chief geologist for the Buryat Geological Production Association, the decision to build the tunnel was fundamentally wrong. 'Back when the route was being surveyed, we warned the designers about the highly complex conditions in the BAM's Buryatiya sector ... We felt it would be better to bypass it from the south with minimal excavation work. However, the shortest path was chosen...'

At one stage advice was sought from American, Japanese, French, German and Finnish tunnel experts. But the unique challenge of the Severomuisk Range made their combined knowledge almost worthless.

The BAM builders, left dependent on their own resources, had to devise novel technologies to meet this challenge – like injecting liquid nitrogen into the granite to freeze the water and temporarily stop seepage, allowing time to coat the tunnel with concrete, as a permanent seal. Channels on both sides of the rails will with luck (drainage by gravity) preclude any need for expensive pumping.

The first bypass (17½ miles) was completed in 1987 and not designed to last beyond 1992, the tunnel's new 'target date'. The *BAM Guide* quotes from a *Sotsialisticheskaya Industriya* report on this pioneering effort:

> Two or three electric locomotives pull the cars. The grades and the drops are so steep that, when the cars are heading downhill, the drivers literally ride on the locomotives' running boards so they'll be able to jump off in time if there's an accident.

Soon the 1992 target had been abandoned and the building of the present (34-mile) bypass begun. The *BAM Guide* assures us that 'it is safe for light-weight passenger trains though there are regular derailments of the heavily laden goods trains'.

We paused briefly at a jerry-built little station called Kazankan. Far below is the wretched settlement of Severomuisk, the tunnellers' eastern base, filling a bowl-shaped valley which must have been very beautiful, pre-BAM. Here a few passengers got off and even fewer got on.

Then began our two-hour crawl over the range. Looking up from Kazankan one can see four levels of track amidst the remains of the taiga and there are more around the mountain's shoulder. On this eastern side, extensive engineering yards – home to scores of gigantic machines, huge ugly sheds, stacks of materiel – do nothing for the bypass as 'a scenic experience'. Now I began to wonder about my fellow-passengers' silence; perhaps they were contemplating the remote chance that even a light-weight passenger train might fall over the edge. For quite a distance that edge not only seems but is a mere yard from the train's wheels. And the drop is a long one. However, all things considered – concrete coatings, drainage channels, seismic sensors – I'm thankful my BAM journeys pre-dated the tunnel's completion.

At 3,600 feet we crossed the pass and saw to the north a wild barren granite tumult, sharp 7,500 foot rock summits rearing above immense bleak expanses scattered with dwarf pines. During the gradual descent BAM curves slowly around the stony flanks of mountain after mountain, then jerks to a halt at the mini-station of Osypnoi, which serves Tonnelny. In theory this forlorn tunnellers' settlement will be demolished when the workers leave. Maybe – and maybe not. The Moscow authorities, Soviet or post-Soviet, seem able easily to live with blots on the landscape.

An almost vulgar crimson and purple sunset marked our arrival at Severobaikalsk's fanciful station – not immediately appealing, though it grows on one. Yulia had invited me to stay and delightedly I had accepted, not realizing that her eighteen-year-old son, Feodor, would have to move out to a neighbour's house. She ran a small drapery business and had been to Tynda to buy stock, imported from China, most of which would follow with Pushkin. A silent and unsmiling Feodor carried my pannier-bags to a taxi which sped up a wide road of broken tarmac past rows of five-storey blocks (the norm in the BAM Zone) to the Old Town. Yulia lived amidst a maze of dusty laneways, winding between high fences concealing small intensively cultivated gardens. Her wooden shack had been much extended, a porch, indoor loo and tiny bedroom added. It was semi-detached and the next-door home had been similarly enlarged.

Elvira, aged twenty, was busy in the cramped, hot kitchen, bottling tomatoes and pickling cucumbers. Later, I was shown the deep cellar below a trapdoor in the hall floor where many shelves were already laden with jams (blueberry, blackcurrant, raspberry, wild strawberry) and preserved mushrooms. Ungratefully Elvira reproached Yulia for having chosen a Nike T-shirt as her daughter's gift from Tynda. In Novosibirsk Elvira's student group – devotees of Naomi Klein – had vowed to boycott all Nike products, whether fake or real. (The T-shirt looked fake.)

Although understanding some English, Elvira couldn't or wouldn't speak it. I had just sat down in the kitchen when she showed me a photograph of her father, taken only a few months before he died, aged forty-six, of a fast-moving cancer. I intuited that she was still in shock, which might also explain her brother's surly tension. He wasn't seen again all evening so he missed a tasty casserole of liver, peppers, onions, tomatoes – of course eaten with bread, thick slices piled high in the centre of the table. The Siberians lean heavily on the staff of life.

For thirty-six sweaty hours I had been looking forward to a cold shower, or at least a cold wash. But this was not to be. As her home lacked a bathroom, Yulia had arranged for me to 'enjoy' a friend's *banya*, ten minutes' walk away. It was nearly midnight and very dark as we stumbled through a cabbage patch to a wooden hut on stilts, its stove pipe sticking through the shingle roof. Normally *banya*-dependent families light the furnace only on a Friday or Saturday, for their weekly cleansing of the pores, so Yulia's friends had gone to a lot of trouble on my behalf. Soon I wished they hadn't, as I stood naked enduring 36°C and not knowing what to do next. Jugs stood beside a big tin bath of hot water and a big enamel basin of cold water. The stove consisted of three tar-barrels welded together and half-full of red-hot stones. A slatted bench ran the length of one wall and above it hung big sheaves of leafy birch twigs. Sweat cascaded off me as I washed in the luke-warm 'cold' water. When Yulia came to collect me she was both amused and disgusted to find her guest throwing dirty water on to the cabbages. Had I used the *banya* correctly, the water poured over my body would have flowed away along the sloping floor to its appointed exit. Later I learned that one is meant to lie on the bench while an appropriate family member, or a friend of the same sex, beats one with the twigs, a process widely believed to cure most diseases.

Yulia and Elvira shared the annex off the kitchen where there was scarcely space to squeeze between their beds. In the living-room Yulia ignored my pleas to be allowed to use my flea-bag and firmly made up the double sofa-bed (Feodor's) with her best cotton sheets – meticulously ironed, which increased my guilt. In this doorless room, some fifteen feet by twenty, a gaudy Chinese carpet matched the upholstery and floor-length curtains. An enormous TV set (rarely used) stood in one corner and here again were packed bookshelves, part of that hybrid item of mass-produced chipboard furniture found throughout the former Communist world (it seems to go with blocks) and incorporating shelves, drawers, small cupboards, a mirror sometimes and what could be a dressing-table.

Elvira translated some of those volumes' titles: Russian classics, translations from the great European classics, a shelf of modern hard-back thrillers, romances and science fiction. The Soviets achieved 98 per cent literacy throughout the Soviet Union, a world record. And they not only made people functionally literate but encouraged reading as a recreation. I liked the flavour of this household with no bathroom but well-stocked bookshelves; to have both would be preferable but that's getting priorities right. I recalled then being made welcome in several South African homes complete with *en suite* bedrooms, swimming pools, two or three motor vehicles, perhaps a tennis court and/or a boat – and not one book in sight.

Lake Baikal can't be seen from Severobaikalsk's town centre which is overlooked, on three sides, by mountains of consequence – no mere hills, these. The New Town seems banal in contrast to Tynda, whose planners used topography and trees to counteract the worst effects of blockitis. Its total population is a matter of debate: the central government claims 35,000, the municipality suggests 30,000, local pessimists guess 'nearer 20,000'. Having been in decline since 1984, when Leningrad's Komsomol ceased to sponsor it, Severobaikalsk enjoyed no more than a decade of comparative prosperity. Without its acres of BAM repair workshops, joblessness would be at crisis point. Given its natural advantages, it of course longs to become a tourist centre, a reasonable (if environmentally questionable) ambition. The *BAM Guide* tells us 'Severobaikalsk is an unrivalled base for outdoor adventure ... It is probably the most popular destination on the BAM, yet fewer than 200 Western tourists a year visit.' This is unlikely to change unless air fares are considerably reduced: there is a small airport twenty miles away at Nizhneangarsk, linking Baikal's northern shore to Irkutsk. The BAM is not much help, tourist-wise; half the average person's holiday would be spent on train journeys.

Already I had a tenuous link with Severobaikalsk. Nicholas Zvegintzov, co-author of the *BAM Guide*, is a brother of one of my oldest friends and a colleague of Severobaikalsk's most eminent citizen, Rashit Yahin – editorial consultant to the *BAM Guide*, environmental activist and internationally acclaimed Master of Chess. Rashit advertises himself as 'Helping for Tourists on the Lake Baikal and Northern Baikal Area' and that word 'helping' is significant. Rashit could never make it as a cog in the tourist industry. For profit he organizes foreigners' holidays but the foreigners profit more than he does. Some years ago he was disabled by a stroke – physically, not mentally – and his courageous coping with this handicap is consistent with his heredity. In the mid-Thirties he was born in a prison camp, the son of a scholarly Tatar mullah exiled to Siberia as 'an enemy of the working class'. When his mother conceived him, during a fortnight's visit to her husband (who had by then been imprisoned for nine years) she, too, was imprisoned. Rashit faced discrimination as he grew up, being the son of a dissident, yet he gained an engineering degree, was employed by BAMProek and in 1974 arrived in Severobaikalsk to supervise the first contingent of BAM builders. His courageous protests against their hazardous working conditions soon came to the attention of the Minister of Railways and he was sacked – only to be conscripted, later, as a tunnel labourer. After all that, he might have been expected to move West ASAP. But he is another of those outsiders permanently in thrall to Siberia.

At 7 a.m. Yulia rang a friend of hers whose English-speaking son sometimes worked with Rashit. Then she beckoned me to the phone and Ivan offered to lead me to the Yahins' hard-to-find (and even harder to telephone) home in the Old Town. Yulia, on her way to work, would escort me to our meeting point.

Meanwhile there was work to be done, the blackcurrant bushes behind the house being so laden their branches were almost breaking. I was in practice, my daughter having recently had an identical crisis in Co. Clare. And those two households, so very far apart, were sharing another crisis: how to find a good home for a kitten in an over-kittened world.

Yulia's twelve-year-old Maria – long-haired, tortoiseshell-and-white – had had but one kitten, ginger-and-white and now seven weeks old. Watching him made me realize how deprived are only kittens. His elderly mother was not amused when he pounced on her tail and in general his activities were very subdued – just occasional attacks on the phone cord and curtains – compared with the antics of the seven I had left behind in Co. Clare. Mother and son monopolized the most comfortable chair and were fed with choice titbits as the family ate, an indulgence at which even I draw the line. A week before, Feodor had been given a large two-months-old mongrel pup – threatened by Maria if he even glanced at her offspring, therefore confined to an outhouse, allowed only half-an-hour of cuddling and frolicking each evening. At night his lonely whimpering distressed me. He and the kitten needed each other and had the situation been better managed would certainly have had a good relationship.

At 8.45 Yulia and I set off; every morning she walks to her drapery shop near the station, a leased premises in a grim grey disused warehouse divided into several such premises, mostly empty. When we came to the tallest construction in Severobaikalsk, the town hall's clock-tower, Ivan was awaiting me – another 'child of BAM', keen to promote the Northern Baikal 'holiday industry' and a naïve believer in the benefits of eco-tourism. He earned a meagre living by interpreting, translating and giving private English lessons to Severobaikalsk's more ambitious teenagers.

A wide belt of taiga, criss-crossed by pathlets, separates the attractive Old Town from the monotony of the New Town's blocks. Here, on a low, flat-topped hill, stands one of those colossal, brightly painted fun-fair wheels installed in every Siberian town and city I visited – and maybe to be found all over the former Soviet Union? Beyond the trees Ivan led me through a tangle of rough tracks and narrow paths where the ramshackle one-storey dwellings (no two alike) had been built of whatever materials came to hand as the Komsomol teams were being hurriedly housed. Some had ample gardens, others had none. Ivan pointed out the many fish-drying contraptions in sunny corners, a winter's supply of small fish hanging in rows behind cat-proof wire mesh. 'No one *planned* this district,' he observed superfluously. However, the State (never known for its class-unconsciousness) had provided a few comparatively spacious log houses for white-collar BAM workers and the Yahins now own one of these. In their half-acre garden behind a high picket fence we found Mrs Yahin, a small, wiry, energetic sexagenarian favoured by the sort of good looks dependent on bone structure and therefore unfading. She was picking blackcurrants with a swift skill that made my method seem cretinous. Unluckily Rashit was out, wouldn't be back before evening, would contact me then. Mrs Yahin speaks no English, and of necessity was blackcurrant-centred that morning, so we didn't linger.

'She works harder than ten men,' said Ivan. 'It's not easy for her since Rashit went sick. No one helps her in that big garden and big hot-house. All those potatoes you saw she planted and she'll dig them up.'

Soon I was to have my own reasons for singing Mrs Yahin's praises.

From Severobaikalsk's central square an almost traffic-free main thoroughfare, Leningradski Prospekt, slopes down to the BAM's high pedestrian bridge, spanning multiple railway tracks and platforms and the region's only tarred road. (This stretches for some forty-five miles from Baikalskoe, a fishing village, to Nizhneangarsk.) Beyond the bridge, a track took me through sadly littered taiga towards the still invisible lake.

Worldwide, people who know nothing else about Siberia can identify Baikal as our planet's deepest and purest lake. The oft-quoted statistics arouse awe:

- Maximum depth, 1,637 metres (more than a mile); average depth, 730 metres.
- Contains 20 per cent of the world's lake freshwater.
- Mineral content, 96.4mg per litre compared to at least 400mg for most lakes.
- In many cases Baikal water can be used instead of distilled water.
- Water transparency 40 metres, ten times the average.
- Age: at least 20 million and possibly 30 million years. This is the most vital statistic. The average lake's life-span is 10,000 to 15,000 years; then sediments take over and floating earth gradually forms a lid which eventually becomes a bog which may or may not dry out. What limnologists call 'its unique physico-geographic characteristics' explain Baikal's diverse and endemic organic life; 15 per cent of its plant species and 60 per cent of its animal species are found only here.

Finally, to quote Oleg Gusev, one of Lake Baikal's most eminent defenders in Soviet times:

The deepest point of the lake's rock basin is approximately 7,000 metres below sea level. Its stone bed is the deepest depression in the world whose 'roots' dissect the whole of the earth's crust, penetrating into the upper mantle to the depth of 50 or 60 kilometres. To put it figuratively, the Baikal depression is a window into the earth's depth making it possible to understand its inner processes.

Suddenly I was out of the taiga, approaching a steep cliff, overlooking a still expanse of blueness. On a calm day, under a clear sky, Baikal's blueness is intense, peculiar, indescribable, heart-stopping. I hastened down to the sandy shore and moments later Lake Baikal had received me. As one plunges into these blessed depths all the famous statistics seem irrelevant. Centuries before scientists had recorded its physical uniqueness, the few who lived around Baikal's shores – and many others who lived far away, in the mountains of Mongolia or on the northern tundra – recognized and revered this lake's magic, knew it as 'the Hallowed Sea'.

It boosted my morale to be able again to use my body vigorously without pain. The water's temperature was much the same as an Irish river's in early summer, exhilarating but not chilling. Sometimes I relaxed and floated and gazed at the surrounding mountains – ranges aloof and austere, known only to a few local hunters. (And allegedly, in their more formidable recesses, as yet known to nobody.) Half a dozen other swimmers were visible in the distance and smugly I pitied those millions who in August pullulate on the beaches of tourist destinations.

As I dressed, two fishermen were standing in the shallows, teaching small sons how to cast. And on my way back through the taiga mothers were teaching even smaller children how to identify edible mushrooms – picking inedibles, prodding and sniffing them, then decisively discarding them while grimacing. I would have liked to lie on the mossy cliff edge, in the shade of pines and larches, revelling in the Baikal blueness far below, but a coalition of vicious midges and tiny biting ants deterred me.

Thirstily I walked up Leningradski Prospekt with my mini-dictionary open at the Cyrillic alphabet. In these elaborately insulated towns a building's exterior, if one can't read Russian, rarely reveals what goes on inside. The search for a bar, restaurant, pharmacy, hairdresser or shoe shop involves traversing many long corridors and opening many doors. Then I rejoiced to see a rudimentary pavement bar, two trestle tables with wobbly benches, shaded by giant beach umbrellas. Nearby, under a mobile tin awning, Irina – chubby and cheerful – earned money for her university textbooks by selling homemade beer from kegs, served in disposable plastic half-litre 'glasses'. At intervals her father arrived with replacement kegs, in a rattling car which had lost its headlamps. Every day, I was to discover, Irina's adolescent silver tabby accompanied her to work and he needed little encouragement to sit purring on my knee. Some Siberians half-facetiously suggest that their dogs and cats are so important because, during long winters in cramped flats, animal family members serve as emotional buffer states. Not all BAM Zone residents take their winters for granted; photographs of Ireland in January – bare trees, vividly green fields – often aroused astonished envy.

Severobaikalsk is memorable for the spontaneity of its friendliness; the stranger immediately feels not merely welcome but *at home*. (There is a difference.) Irina's other customers were construction workers on a lunch break and teachers on holidays, residents of an adjacent block. Although no one spoke English everyone was interested in the foreigner. At once a stout jolly woman moved to sit beside me, offered me a half-pound smoked omul (peculiar to Lake Baikal, of the salmon family) and soon after poured half her glass of *pivo* into mine. The omul was a meal in itself, rather than a snack. Anywhere else, this most delicious fish – it makes salmon seem like whiting – would be an expensive delicacy. But here again distance handicaps Severobaikalsk; it is uneconomic to export omul, in any quantity, beyond the nearer BAM towns.

I was good for Irina's trade. Rapidly the group around me enlarged, all generations eager to see my photographs, and a two-hour party ensued as it would not have done were Severobaikalsk on the tourist trail. I'm sometimes accused of being perpetually in flight from tourists because I like to feel 'special' in a place, which to an extent is true. I do like being treated simply as a visitor, rather than as another unit in an economic asset.

Throughout Russia, according to official figures, beer has recently overtaken vodka as the most popular alcoholic drink. But this is not as healthy as it sounds. Because the multinational breweries' advertisements give the impression that beer is *almost* a soft drink, it is now openly imbibed in circumstances where vodka would not be tolerated. Frequently I saw small boys swilling from cans, sold by most pavement kiosks, while awaiting their school buses. As Russia has been notorious, over the past thousand years, for off-the-scale alcoholism, it is hard to forgive those corporations now enticing young Russians to develop a *pivo* addiction.

On my way back to Yulia's, I found myself walking behind a dangerously inebriated thirty-ish couple. She was wavering on her feet, he too was swaying and very angry indeed – repeatedly hitting her across the face, shouting abuse, pulling her hair as though to scalp her, putting his right hand to her neck in a strangling gesture which I felt could too easily prove fatal, by accident if not design. There was no one else in sight: this happened in the taiga, midway between the New and Old Towns. When the couple's path diverged from mine I stood uneasily watching them. Soon the man tripped, fell – and lay still. The woman stood gazing down at him, leaning against a birch. As I hurried towards her she vomited, then straightened up, yelled aggressively at me and ran away, now moving more steadily. Her partner was insensible but would certainly survive a warm night in the open air.

Yulia, having noted my own *pivo*-dependence, had laid in a supply and during the puppy's playtime we sat on the tiny verandah, our beers accompanied by salted omul. Then a car stopped by the garden gate, a most unusual event in this district. It was Rashit in his 1980 Zhiguli, being driven by a neighbour because he can no longer drive and Mrs Yahin never could. I went to the car to greet him and, as Nicholas Zvegintzov's brother's friend, was given a most touching welcome. He and Yulia then had a mild altercation about when I should become the Yahins' guest. Rashit said 'Saturday' (the next day), Yulia said 'Monday', I diplomatically decided 'Sunday'.

'Very well,' agreed Rashit, 'but you must be at our house by 7 a.m. on Sunday. You're going on a day-trip across the lake with two Americans. They've hired a boat to the hot springs and there's room for you.'

Rashit is like that, a kindly autocrat. Through him, I quickly acquired a network of English-speaking friends – real friends, not just people feeling obliged to be nice to me because Rashit had introduced us.

Severobaikalsk's enormous two-storey market, opposite the clock-tower and previously state-run, has by now acquired some of the worst characteristics of 'the shopping mall'. Surprisingly, it seems to cater for a more affluent community than Tynda's but its staff have not quite caught up with the free market. Sometimes they are AWOL, sometimes the girl behind the till is so immersed in her novel that she has difficulty returning to the real world and count-ing out the correct change. Occasionally the tills cease to function and long lines, reminiscent of Soviet times, patiently form while a Mr Fix-It is sought. Here, too, are many Chinese traders and a few Central Asians though the latter evidently feel more at home in the nearby open-air market. Dogs of all sizes wander to and fro, some with owners, others looking anxious because they have lost their person.

Having bought appropriate (I hoped) goodies for Yulia, I sat on the market terrace and, being hungry after my long swim, ate six bananas while observing the passing scene. Very tight micro-skirts, worn with very high heels and very little on top, were 'in' for girls; their male companions strutted or slouched in calf-length, multi-pocketed, baggy shorts and loose T-shirts, many imprinted with 'CCCP' and the hammer and sickle. I had been warned not to take this politically; it marked the younger generation's feeling so far from the Soviet era that they could use its logo as a fun decoration – one which might have the added advantage of irritating parents. On the pavement below hawkers hunkered beside their wares; our Kirgiz BAM friends were selling plastic and chrome handbags and glass ornaments. Seeing me they smiled and waved a handbag, their sign language suggesting I needed one. A doting granddad was also sitting on the wall; he had taken a toddler out of her buggy and happily he watched her exploring the world – until she made for the glittering ornaments.

Beside a hedge of listless-looking shrubs, recently planted along the pavement, a camera-wielding mother was positioning her small daughter against a background of foliage. This unfortunate child was on roller-blades and wearing fluorescent gear: special boots and gloves, helmet with chin-guard, knee and elbow pads, very short pants. Her mother spent fifteen minutes contriving poses to show every detail of the accoutrements to best advantage. Important photographs, these, perhaps to be sent to relatives thousands of miles away who had rarely or never seen the child. But why all this overprotection? Roller-skating used to be a simple, inexpensive activity, naturally involving some cuts and bruises. Now, like cycling and swimming, it has been hijacked to market superfluous accessories.

Strolling down to Irina's 'bar', I met an English-speaking couple, both studying at Irkutsk, aiming for degrees in 'Tourist Development'. (Are Russian universities, too, losing sight of the purpose of a university education?) Natasha was a raven-haired, large-eyed beauty, Lev had the rotting teeth and muddy complexion alarmingly common amongst his age group. They shared a lust for 'inward investment', preferably from the US. The whole Baikal area, they argued, needed a highly developed tourist industry.

Said Lev, 'OK, some people don't want high hotels and noisy discos and casinos and big marinas all around the lake. We believe there's no other future for the population and the same people admit the environment's already wrecked by BAM. What counts first, humans or beautiful landscapes? We know it's the same argument globally, you can't eat scenery. Anyway in big Siberia even mass tourism couldn't do much overall damage. And long ago the Soviets destroyed indigenous cultures, being anti-tourism can't protect them.'

I suspected that these arguments were not derived from any Irkutsk institute of learning but from outside sources. When I repeated what the Stroganovs had told me about Siberia's exceptional vulnerability Natasha and Lev didn't want to listen.

By then hydrotherapy had disappointed me; those walks to Lake Baikal, though short, were too long for The Knee and on our way to the railway station, to collect Yulia's merchandise and Pushkin, Yulia observed that my limp was worse. I had expected to be able to pedal when Pushkin arrived: instead, I had to walk him through the town. En route, I noticed some covetous stares; the few bicycles visible in Siberia were identical to the sturdy Russian model I bought in Nepal in 1965 – as basic as could be, no gears and pedal-braked. It felt surreal to have owned a bicycle for almost three weeks without riding it. Parking Pushkin in the narrow hall, I considered loading him then, in preparation for our early start; but that would have made him too bulky.

I urged Yulia not to forego her Sunday lie-in to see me off for my stay with the Yahins; I would be visiting her again. But at 5.15 next morning there she was in the hall – and in tears. Sobbing, she threw her arms around me. Pushkin was gone, stolen during the night. Soon after two o'clock odd noises had awakened her. Investigating, she saw no Pushkin, then rang a taxi-driver friend and spent more than two hours touring the town in the faint hope of catching the culprit awheel.

Pushkin being a mere acquaintance I had no emotional reaction, as I did when Lear was stolen in South Africa. My immediate concern was Yulia's distress; in lieu of comprehensible words I hugged her a lot before she rang the police. Moments later the plot thickened. A red-eyed, unslept Feodor, perceptibly beer-flavoured, was pushed through the front door by an angry Elvira. The precise details escaped me, but somehow Elvira had divined that Feodor's friend Drisha was the culprit. Yulia wept again, this time with relief, before ringing Drisha's mother to warn her that the police were on her son's trail but it was all a misunderstanding ... To me this warning seemed unnecessary; in our uncivilized era few police forces take bicycle thefts seriously.

At 6.10 we glimpsed Feodor leaving Pushkin by the garden gate, then fleeing. Yulia was now crimson with fury, the family atmosphere would be strained for a day or so. We've all been there, in various ways, with our adolescent young. Pushkin seemed none the worse for having been borrowed as a drunken prank, which suggests that his borrowers were not all that drunk but aching to ride this sophisticated machine, chosen by me as Moscow's least advanced model. When I left for the Yahins both boys were lurking around a corner, looking disarmingly guilty. Two days later I called on Yulia and immediately Feodor appeared. Staring at the ground and blushing, he said 'I'm sorry' in English. Yulia nodded approvingly, then beamed as I shook his hand and said 'Forget it!' It was the boys' bad luck that I happened to need Pushkin so early; by 7 a.m. he would have been back in the hall.

Mrs Yahin, in her role as the Americans' tour guide, accompanied me in the rattling Zhiguli to Severobaikalsk's port, some two miles from the town. There the Russian navy has a vestigial training base and behind it two mega-cranes dangle idly over an empty space where once BAM building materiels were unloaded. The long concrete pier creates a bay, bounded to the east by those steep mountains on which the railway runs close to the lake. Here too is the Severobaikalsk Yacht Club, founded by Rashit many years ago; three small yachts and four even smaller motor launches were moored by a short jetty. There is no club building but ten tiny wooden huts, standing near the water's edge, accommodate club members. I eyed them with interest; as an honorary member, my hydrotherapy problem would be solved.

At 7.40 the Americans arrived: Jane and Luke, a tall handsome couple in their forties, both fluent Russian-speakers who didn't have the aura of conventional tourists. In some quarters I am reputed to be virulently anti-American but this is a slander. My virulence is selective, some of my best friends are American and this couple would certainly be among them had the convergence of our destinies not been confined to Lake Baikal. Their home is TV-free, their library is extensive, their dogs are doted upon – how kindred can spirits get?

Siberian punctuality, when taken to extremes, can be tiresome; we couldn't leave before 8 a.m. though by 7.45 we were all ready to go and the captain/owner and his crew (his wife) stood nearby, chatting to a fisherman. As we scrambled aboard the motor launch (a locally made vessel, not designed for tourists) I swore at myself – the Pushkin drama had caused me to forget my bathing-togs. However, I'm not a hot springs aficionado and these springs are very hot – 86°C, only exciting in winter when one can come out and roll in deep dry snow.

We sat on deck, fore of the cabin, and beyond the bay's shelter donned our waterproofs. For hours the weather was unkind: an overcast sky, a strong cold wind – exceptional conditions said Mrs Yahin. Personally I enjoyed meeting Lake Baikal in this troubled mood, its leaping green waves irregularly splashing us because our little boat allowed intimacy with the water. Midway through this three-hour voyage the shores were invisible: Baikal is 400 miles long, an inland sea. Jane and Luke were entertained to hear that some years ago, at a London dinner party, a senior British politician with an unusual knowledge of Russian geography, and a not unusual impatience with 'the Irish problem', suggested dropping the Emerald Isle into the Pearl of Siberia.

Towards noon the sun suddenly shone, as we approached the massive blue-grey bulk of a mountainous shore. Here a long, narrow beach of soft pale gold sand was backed by dense forest, sloping up to the base of a fortress-like limestone peak. From the makeshift jetty a plank walkway took us over the sand, past a few log cabins, into woodland where the undergrowth was ledum, also known as Dahurian rhododendron – a spindly plant, not at all like our Himalayan variety, but in springtime a wonder to behold.

These hot springs, in a clearing surrounded by towering cedars, are beautifully undeveloped. Here every prospect pleases and man has not been vile. (Or not yet: wait for Natasha and Lev to have their way.) The *banya* is a low wooden structure, linked by stone paths to open-air shallow hot pools safe for small children. While the rest of the party were cooking themselves (they emerged looking pinkly overdone) I sat beside a deep well watching people drinking from an enormous, finely carved wooden ladle and filling plastic bottles, just as the devout do at places of pilgrimage. Siberia's indigenous tribes have always believed in the curative properties of various hot springs for every sort of illness, a belief shared by the Russian newcomers. Several Severobaikalsk day-trippers had already arrived by another launch and some were wallowing in warm black mud at the base of a slope, vigorously smearing themselves all over, their companions massaging the parts they couldn't reach. To rinse off they stood under steaming water gushing through a hollowed-out tree-trunk embedded in the slope at head-height. All the materials used to create this 'amenity' were native to the site and there were no refreshments or souvenirs on sale. Our mad world, where people are told it's patriotic to *spend*, whether or not they need what they're buying, seemed very far away. As so many economists, notably Richard Douthwaite, have forcefully pointed out, 'the growth society' contains the seeds of its own destruction. Mere self-preservation requires us to learn from those who have not forgotten that you can have fun for free by skilfully using what Nature has provided.

On board again, Mrs Yahin provided an excellent picnic lunch and the captain's wife brewed tea. As we sailed down the coast – steep taiga rising directly from a rocky shore – the shortage of birds was troubling: only a few small colonies of herring gulls appeared all day. Turning into a fjord-like inlet, the captain gently ran us aground on a pebble beach to pick up four fishermen; when these failed to arrive their absence alarmed no one. Such a futile ninety-minute détour seems very odd, Jane remarked, to those from 'mobile phone cultures' (her phrase).

Our next stop, after sailing far out to round a prominent headland, was more productive. Within a wide sheltered bay, on a sandy strip of beach below a grassy slope, three families had been camping for two nights and were busily packing up as we arrived. Such grassy slopes, though pleasing to look at, prove that where the gradient permits loggers have long been at work, with or without permission. These families were not serious campers and our steep narrow gangplank defeated four overweight ladies in long skirts who sportingly made a joke of their menfolk having to heave them up and haul them aboard. There were only eleven in the group, including three children, yet a ludicrous excess of gear had to be loaded, followed by many covered pails of mushrooms and taiga berries. But not fish, they had eaten all their catches. Meanwhile a fourteen-year-old girl was taking great care to extinguish with water every spark of the campfire, based on four giant logs.

Rashit told me that the Trans-Baikal taiga, an essential and irreplaceable contributor to Lake Baikal's uniqueness, is peculiarly flammable – the flammability of the deciduous forests' saplings comparable to gunpowder. A century ago the illustrious Russian biologist, Skalon, declared bluntly that since man is the main cause of forest fires, this region could only be protected by strictly limiting human access. When BAM workers arrived on the northern shore, hundreds of thousands of hectares were soon burnt out in the extraordinarily beautiful Frolikh area. And in the Barguzin district, because workers set fire to a hollow larch to drive a squirrel out for their supper, 7,000 hectares were lost. In one summer, in this Irkutsk Province, more forest was burnt than was planted in all the Russian Federation's ninety provinces.

As we left the bay, broken cloud cover created magical lighting effects; shafts of gold were striking expanses of red and yellow lichens on the bare rock cliffs of the headland, or picking out solitary gale-twisted pine trees growing amidst sharp crags. Then the shore receded and a rising wind sent many drenching waves over everybody – our little launch being now noticeably lower in the water. Beneath the restless clouds, Lake Baikal was fickle: at one moment its tints sombre and metallic, at the next gay and sparkling. All the way home we saw no other vessel. These mountainous, roadless hinterlands to the north-east and north-west are uninhabited, their only buildings a few log huts used by passing hunters. And the fishermen's summertime hamlets along the shore generate little traffic.

Three days later I rode Pushkin for the first time and found him very satisfactory. I then cycled to the Yacht Club with a note from Rashit to the Director, asking if I might rent one of the lakeshore huts for a week. My therapy plan was to swim four times a day, avoid unnecessary walking, cycle longer distances each day, then on 28 August take off on the BAM for Khabarovsk and Ussuriland.

Mr Krasotkin, the Director, lived with a grey and white kitten in a two-roomed hut perched on ten-foot-high stilts and approached by a shaky outside staircase. From his balcony he could observe all that was going on around the port (not that much ever went on) while drinking *chai* with his fishermen or yachting friends. He welcomed me warmly: certainly I could rent a hut ($6.50), Anna would show me which one and give me the key.

Anna was the 'cleaning lady', a round-eyed teenager who viewed me apprehensively as though I might at any moment turn into an Amur tiger and spring and snap. In my six-by-ten-foot hut three iron beds took up most of the floor space, leaving just enough room to park Pushkin. The only other furniture was a bedside locker – my writing-table, which I could carry out to the balcony, furnished with a short bench. The loo – 150 yards away, towards the red-brick naval base – was no more than a sentry-box of loose planks surrounding a squat-over long-drop. This orphan amenity, for which nobody took responsibility, was the local flies' favourite rendezvous.

As I pedalled back to the Old Town to collect my gear The Knee's response to cycling uphill delighted me. But then came an unexpected hitch; we notice exactly how we use our bodies only when some disability restricts use. Different movements are required for the mounting of an unloaded and a loaded bicycle. In the latter case, to clear bulky pannier-bags the right leg must be simultaneously bent and thrust outwards before the upward swing, an action of which The Knee was not yet capable. Again I had to wheel Pushkin, telling myself that a week's intensive hydrotherapy would certainly complete the cure.

Although Severobaikalsk's port looks shambolic – an unhealed developers' wound along the shore – Lake Baikal is what counts. My grass-surrounded hut was only thirty seconds' walk from the depths (I timed it) and on my balcony I could hear wavelets whispering over the sand. This didn't seem at all the sort of place where disaster would strike.

During the small hours on that first night I went out to pee by starlight. Had I been sensible and used a torch I would automatically have avoided those planks of rotten wood covering a four-foot-deep hole. (The hole's provenance is obscure and irrelevant; possibly someone at some stage had wanted to bury a body, it was of grave dimensions.) This, unlike the BAM accident, was serious; all my weight came down on my right leg and for long moments the pain was extreme. Having pulled myself out of the hole – I can't remember exactly how – I sordidly peed in my pants, crawled back to base on all fours and collapsed on the bed. I was too shaken to assess the damage but able luridly to curse my stupidity; this was a tormenting 'if only ...' situation. Then I slept: on such occasions the body's chemistry rapidly provides an analgesic.

At sunrise I woke, stood up, walked a few steps, rejoiced that no bones were broken. My diagnoses, based on previous experiences, were: a torn calf muscle, a twisted ankle (very swollen) and further damage to my knee, perhaps something displaced because when bent it made a funny-peculiar clicking noise and the pain was sharp. Oddly, the original problem hadn't been exacerbated; walking, though agonising, remained possible, as it had not been on the BAM. Initially the torn muscle caused the most pain, yet it was the first injury to heal completely.

Swimming, miraculously, was almost painfree and I took physical and emotional comfort from Baikal's magic while adjusting to the fact that I was not destined to visit Ussuriland in 2002. Then I counted my blessings: where better to be semi-invalided than Severobaikalsk, amidst a circle of congenial friends? Those friends of course viewed my simple accommodation as a hardship to which their town's foreign visitor should not be exposed. None looked convinced when I assured them that given a choice between this hut and a free week in Moscow's Hotel Ukraina I would choose the former. One or more of them came daily, usually on foot, bearing omul prepared in diverse ways, thermos flasks of soup, new potatoes cooked in butter and herbs, hard-boiled eggs in sour cream, cucumbers and tomatoes, litres of *pivo* and a selection of taiga-derived cures to be ingested, inhaled or rubbed on.

Soon I had a new plan. When fit to travel I would go to Irkutsk by hydrofoil, to Ust'-Kut by BAM, to Yakutsk by paddle-steamer, to Neryungri by bus and from there back to Severobaikalsk, via Tynda, by BAM.

How to explain the premonition phenomenon? Normally, when planning a journey, I expect everything to go well and never even consider what *might* go wrong. Yet this time a vague unease about *something* going wrong had overshadowed the days before my departure. And, as I later discovered, three of my close friends, not usually given to being jittery on my behalf, had experienced similar unease though not knowing about mine.

In retrospect I could discern a pattern of bad omens, a series of minor misfortunes, since my choice of the Russian Far East on 11 September 2001. (Resolutely I dismissed that date as itself a bad omen: one mustn't get too fanciful.) In March I had had to postpone my departure for three months because of a slight family complication. Then a plan to spend those months cycling around Ireland came unstuck when my animal-minder's husband had a serious accident. Exceptional rainfall from April to July kept the river Blackwater too high for regular swimming so my fitness level was reduced. In June my thirty-year-old pannier-bags – veterans of many campaigns, with mascot status – fell apart. Soon after, Dublin vandals attacked Ruairi, my trusty Zagreb-bought bicycle, leaving him too badly damaged to undertake a long journey. Shortly before departure date an old enemy, bronchitis, struck me down, just as a prolonged visa saga was overtaxing my patience.

A curious miasma envelopes this whole Russian visa scene. To obtain a three-months' business visa (tourist visas are valid for only thirty days) one must provide the relevant Consulate with a phony letter of invitation from some fictitious Russian-registered company which guarantees accommodation throughout one's stay. A covering letter from the traveller's company, stating 'purpose of visit', is also required; if one doesn't work for a company, this too may be faked. Scores of 'visa-support services' compete to send invitations for a fee, on receipt by fax or e-mail of passport details, entry and exit dates and the Consulate's address. It seems bizarre that this overt, officially required deception, universally recognized as such, has been able to survive the demolition of the Soviet bureaucracy.

In February it transpired that my 'invitation' could be expeditiously arranged through the kindness of a Moscow friend of a friend. Alas! too expeditiously. When I had to postpone my journey Russian officialdom proved unsympathetic and neither my visa fee ($175) nor my BAM fare to Tynda ($90) was refundable.

In June I reapplied for a visa and the Dublin Consulate admitted to having the first invitation still filed away – but no, it was definitely not re-usable. As that kind friend was no longer in Moscow, I used a London travel agency specializing in Russia, sending them the necessary details and cheque by recorded delivery. On the appointed date I rang the Consulate, who had received no invitation. Angrily I rang the travel agency whose spokesman, sounding defensive, denied having received my package. Within half an hour, Lismore's astoundingly efficient post office had produced a fax recording its delivery in London at 15.03 on 27 June, two days after it was posted. The agency brazenly persisted in their denial yet I had no alternative but to send them a replica package and then pay for an expensive 'quickie' visa, to be collected on 26 July with only two days to spare. By 25 July I was staying with my daughter in Co. Clare. At noon the telephone rang and a Kerrywoman's voice asked, 'Have I got Rachel Murphy?' Mrs O'Sullivan's son and three of his friends were soon going to Moscow for a holiday, their passports had just arrived in Skibbereen from the Consulate – and so had a passport belonging to someone called Dervla Murphy. It included next-of-kin details so Mrs O'Sullivan, having noticed my visa date of entry (28 July) was volunteering to Swift Mail the straying passport to Co. Clare instead of to Dublin. She was the one good omen, without whom I might well have missed my flight and lost several hundred pounds.

That night my throbbing calf muscle kept me awake and as I lay listening to Baikal, and gazing out at a sparkle of golden stars, I remembered an e-mail from Nicholas Zvegintzov in which he wondered if my travel karma was bad ... Indignantly I had retorted that it was excellent, the proof being my return from each journey outside a coffin. But now I counted my injuries and diseases, as some sleepless people count sheep, and the list seemed to justify Nicholas's speculation.

1963 A cycle ride to India coincided with the northern hemisphere's coldest twentieth-century winter. In Afghanistan a few broken ribs and a disabling scorpion bite. In Pakistan my first and last attack of amoebic dysentery. In New Delhi heat-stroke. In Dharamsala mumps at the age of thirty-one.

1967 In Ethiopia a dislocated right knee 300 miles from the nearest motor road after being robbed of almost everything in the Simien Mountains by *shifta* who threatened to kill me.

1973 In South India brucellosis, a prolonged and extremely nasty illness.

1976 In Belfast a deep dog bite above my right ankle; at intervals that indelible scar is still sore for weeks on end – perhaps the bone was affected.

1978 In Peru a pack-mule with a dangerously infected hoof which when you are high in the Andes, totally dependent on your pack-animal (and when you love her dearly) is a major crisis on a par with personal illness.

1983   In Madagascar acute gout in left wrist caused by a forest hooch famous for killing French colonists. Several broken ribs. Hepatitis A which meant enduring a teetotal year – part of the cure and perhaps quite beneficial (this has just occurred to me) for a hooch-hammered liver.

1987   In Cameroon a lost pack-horse because a leopard panicked him near our campsite. A triple tooth abcess beyond reach of dental care.

1990   On the Hungarian–Rumanian border robbed of all possessions by Rumanian police: nothing recovered. Concussion and a fractured coccyx after a car crash on an icy mountain road. Two months later three broken bones in right foot.

1992   In Zimbabwe malaria for the first and (so far) last time.

1993   In South Africa tick-bite fever, a debilitating disease with alarming early symptoms. Then the writing of that book was delayed by a shattered left arm, now containing seven metal pins. But perhaps that doesn't count; it was 'domestic', falling over a cat outside my kitchen door.

1996   Returning from what was then Zaire, a life-threatening clot in my right leg (it's always the right leg!) after an outrageously overcrowded (with other people's luggage) Nairobi–London flight.

1998   In Laos a torn tendon in my right foot.

2000   In Albania three attempted robberies within a day.

2002   In Siberia multiple injuries.

Strangely, in sixty years of pedalling I've never had a cycling accident. Nor, until 2002, did misfortune ever compel me to abandon a jouney totally, though my Rumanian, Laotian and Albanian plans had to be drastically modified. In the present case Fate had changed not only my method of transport but my destination and, despite the frustration involved, this seismic shift was engendering some excitement. Having left home regarding Siberia as a mildly interesting obstacle en route to fascinating Ussuriland, I was about to embark on an involuntary 'mystery tour' of a territory which by now seemed much more than 'mildly' interesting.

From the lakeside huts' grassy ledge a short iron step-ladder, directly outside my hut, led to a narrow strip of sand and a communal 'kitchen' for the use of all boat-owners, fishermen and visitors. This consisted of a log fire, lit every morning by whomever first needed it and kept going all day. Over it, suspended from a horizontal pole, hung two big black saucepans – one for tea, the water fetched from the lake three steps away, the other for food: soup, potatoes, cabbage, occasionally a hunk of gristly meat. Fish (usually omul) was fried on skillets. Two long benches were dual purpose: seats and dining tables. From my balcony I had a grandstand view of the enclave's culinary activities.

Throughout most of the day, few people were visible. As I drank my morning tea, a platoon of crew-cut conscripts from the naval base, wearing loose scruffy uniforms, ill-fitting caps and heavy down-at-heel boots came half-heartedly jogging along the track beyond the wire-mesh periphery fence. At noon they reappeared, sweating hard in the midday heat but now jogging faster, being chivvied by a sergeant-major type. Sometimes pairs or trios of these youths, palpably underfed, drifted listlessly past the huts, the bolder ones begging cigarettes and looking sulky when told they could not try my mini-cigars (unobtainable in Siberia). Twice a week they 'went to sea', rather briefly, in a smallish battered training vessel thirsty for paint. Despite my anti-militarism, I felt there was a certain poignancy about this isolated, impoverished outpost of a once-mighty navy.

I could see a few fishermen far away on the long pier – and a group of Irkutsk holidaymakers had rented two small yachts – and a man and his two young sons were building themselves a motor-launch. Sometimes Mr Krasotkin sauntered past with his brindled sheepdog, tethered at night near the main gate though he never barked and was admitted to lack guard dog qualities.

At intervals the outside world agreeably intruded when prodigiously extended trains, needing two engines, chugged sedately along the shore. Once I counted ninety-five freight wagons, each thirty yards long. How many motor engines would be required to transport those goods?

Every afternoon a stern-faced man led sixteen boys and girls, aged ten to twelve, towards the lake – the lucky participants in one of

Severobaikalsk's children's sailing camps. Their instructor stood watching as they carried six-foot dinghies from the ledge to the slipway, then fetched from a padlocked boathouse masts, sails, rudders, seats and paddles. Eagerly each child assembled his/her craft – unaided, their competence impressive – and donned a life-jacket before launching the dinghy with a push of a paddle. Those striped sails – orange, red, yellow, blue – made a pretty picture as the children wove to and fro across the bay, not always avoiding collisions. Then their instructor, standing on the slipway with a megaphone, would yell reprimands and instructions in an abusive tone which seemed not to faze his pupils in the slightest. Their guardians were a man and woman in a little rowing-boat with an outboard engine, both champion swimmers. One windy afternoon several dinghies capsized and the guardian boat hovered nearby but left the children to cope alone – right their craft, clamber aboard and sail on though soaked to the skin. A pigtailed ten-year-old girl had to struggle long in the water but when the guardians offered help she waved them away. Those children were cool and tough, in the best sense of both adjectives. In our wimpish world they would be seen as promising material for the SAS.

My therapy régime was rigorous: half-hour swims every four hours, starting and ending at 6.30. This soon brought about a physiological paradox; though stiff and sore on land, I otherwise felt much fitter than I had on leaving home. While swimming, I avoided looking west, where the two red and silver chimneys of Severobaikalsk's central heating plant soared eighty metres above the taiga. On clear days, the 6,000-foot mountains of the eastern shore were visible, their bases seeming to touch the water, and this range extends south for hundreds of miles in an unbroken barrier. Here be bears – lots of them. Rina, a new friend from Nizhneangarsk, had a bear story. In September 1986 a family friend, a famous (throughout the Soviet Union) photographer, foolishly sought bear portraits carrying a gun loaded only with bird-shot. This he fired into his attacker's stomach and the bear bled to death nearby, but not before he had killed the photographer. By the time the poor man's body was found, another bear had left little flesh on the skeleton.

What geographers call the Baikal Basin enjoys weather more varied and more windy than elsewhere in inland Siberia and the cloudscapes rival Ireland's for unpredictability. I enjoyed my dawn swims most: no one around, the light grey-blue as I left the hut, the silence Siberian (*different*). Then perhaps a low red ribbon lying along the eastern crests and moments later a luminous golden path crossing the iron-grey lake. Or a jagged pattern of dark scattered clouds towards the zenith, and soon a crimson globe sliding up from behind a slim, sharp peak, turning those clouds to copper before they coalesced and filled the sky, extinguishing the sun. On that particular morning a pale mist settled along the far shore, veiling the mountains, and a few hours of heavy rain followed. Yet the air was warm when I went for my 10.30 swim and the ground soon dried under a hot sun.

Next morning the sky was clear but for one long cloud, scimitar-shaped and blood-red, floating in isolation above that slim peak. Plunging in, I was gripped by an icy vice and momentarily lost my breath. Within eleven and a half hours, Lake Baikal's temperature had gone from summer to (by my standards) winter. In April the Blackwater river is quite cold yet one's body quickly adjusts if one remains immersed. Not so in Lake Baikal in late August and here it would have been foolhardy to play endurance games. Lighting the communal fire to brew warming *chai*, I noticed a light covering of new snow on the mountains.

End of therapy, I assumed, and decided to take the next hydrofoil, three days hence, to Irkutsk. But on the following morning, paddling in to fetch drinking water, I rejoiced to find Lake Baikal again in the mood to receive swimmers though colder than before.

However, autumn was nigh. On 28–29 August a gale blew all night, coming from the east, the wind not cold but powerful. Often I woke to hear it whistling, whining and rattling through the rigging of three small sailing boats moored by the slipway; all were overturned by morning. Waves were coming noisily and hastily ashore, drenching the pile of 'kitchen' firewood. Yet my frail-looking hut stood steady and admitted no draughts; the Russians know all about building with wood.

Surprisingly, the turbulent water remained swimmable and Lake Baikal's turbulence was relative, no deterrent to anyone bred on an Atlantic island and accustomed to six-foot breakers during what passes for summer in Ireland. But to my surprise the locals, many of whom enjoy rolling naked in the snow in January, registered alarm on seeing me splashing happily through those minor waves. They like to swim only in calm water. As one of my friends sagely observed, 'It all depends on where you're coming from.' The same friend warned me that that noon swim was my last. Within hours, the night's gale would have brought Lake Baikal's permanently cold waters to the surface and the thin, summer-warmed layer would be no more. She was right; by 4 p.m. even a two-minute immersion was intolerable. Those who live by its shores know their lake.

That afternoon the sailing class arrived looking even more eager than usual, excited by the waves and the wind – still blowing strongly enough to make it difficult for such small people to carry their sails from the boathouse and to hoist them. They had to help each other, the instructor barking orders, the guardians giving advice in gentler tones. It all took much longer than usual – and then, as everyone was about to push off, came the decision to cancel the class. A wise decision, I felt, but it should have been made much sooner. Two of the youngest, the intrepid pigtailed lass and her Buryat friend, were quietly weeping as they passed me, carrying gear back to the boathouse.

It was time to test my damaged parts so I limped quarter of a mile uphill to a little eating-house. From the port this looked like a yellow railway coach parked alone against a dark green taiga background. In fact it was a wooden dwelling with a deep verandah giving a panoramic view of lake and mountains. Here customers had no choice: pork *shashlik* (kebab) was served with rings of raw onion and thick slices of dry grey-brown bread. This meat was exceptionally flavoursome and, for a generous helping, surprisingly cheap at 40 roubles; the family bred their own free-range pigs. As customers were few, apart from the weekend trade, one had to wait while Father sharpened a two-foot knife, took a slice off the current carcass – sprawled on a table under a bloodstained anti-fly cloth – and then adjusted the logs in a huge mud-stove before grilling. An EU Hygiene Inspector would not have been impressed. In one corner Mother sold drinks both soft and hard, chocolate, toffees, cigarettes and an alternative to potato crisps. These packets of tiny cubes of fried bread, flavoured with something synthetic and horrible, are probably a greater health-hazard than the flies on the carcass.

The damaged parts passed that test and next day I ventured further – to the Yahins, about three miles, which was two and a half miles too far. On arrival my injuries were throbbing, especially The Knee. I then did my stiff upper lip bit and chatted cheerfully about the sailing class but Rashit, watching my movements, was not deceived. I needed medical attention, he decided, since hydrotherapy and folk medicines seemed inadequate. Meekly I agreed and duplicitously I promised to consult a doctor in Irkutsk. At that Rashit – Severobaikalsk's most doughty champion – took umbrage. Why Irkutsk? I must go, now, to the local hospital, he would give me a letter to an English-speaking doctor who was his friend and Mrs Yahin would accompany me.

The hospital – big and gaunt, dilapidated but clean – seemed disconcertingly unbusy. Rashit's friend wasn't on duty, was attending to his private practice – understandably, given a state salary of 500 roubles (less than $100) per month. Mrs Yahin and I wandered along endless silent corridors, climbed endless stairs (more s.u.l. required), saw a few injured out-patients slumped on benches wearing clumsy slings or blood-soaked gyps, knocked on several doors, were impatiently brushed aside by two doctors and four nurses all looking at the end of their professional tether. Mrs Yahin wanted to stick it out: eventually someone would pause to consider my case. But very obviously a foreigner with some minor injury was superfluous to requirements. Reluctantly Mrs Yahin conceded this point and we left, she to walk home, I to hobble to the taxi rank in the town centre.

The Yahins kindly volunteered to shelter Pushkin and most of my gear while I was being a tourist. As I now needed a rucksack, the only car-owner among my young friends drove me to a market near the station, a long row of kiosks capable of being securely insulated in winter but in summer open at the rear, as stalls. None of the Chinese-made rucksacks, poor quality though expensive, would have served a trekker's purpose. I paid 600 roubles for a jungle camouflage model, without a frame or waistband, and embarked on the hydrofoil (*raketa*) at 8 a.m. on 31 August as a superannuated backpacker.

Shortly before leaving home I had contributed to an anthology on old age and ended my essay thus:

Now, though the spirit is willing, the flesh is weakening. Recently, sciatica afflicted me and I fancy creaks are audible when I move. So perhaps, in Vladivostok, I'll be buying a zimmer-frame instead of a bicycle.

How prescient of me!

# 5

## Commerce at a Crossroads

Seen in the distance, skimming the lake's surface, our grey-blue *raketa* looked like some monstrous insect, a long fat grub with legs, left over from twenty million years ago when Baikal was young. One wouldn't choose to travel down the lake by this noisy, speedy, smelly contraption, its black diesel fumes desecrating the Hallowed Sea. However, the steamer service (a quiet five-day meander) has long since been scrapped so Port Baikal must be reached in ten hours at 40 m.p.h.

By the time the insect had drawn up its legs and moored beside Severobaikalsk's pier I was a culture shock case. Since leaving Moscow I had met only two foreigners, Jane and Luke. Now suddenly Westerners surrounded me, all intent on having their 'Baikal experience' by *raketa* to Irkutsk. They were globalization incarnate: a Polish couple who had been collecting material for a Kamchatka guidebook, an English couple who had been on a TEFL assignment in Vladivostok, an American couple on their way home via China after a year translating for a Moscow bank, a Danish couple on their way home after a year of voluntary medical work in Ulan Bator. Envy swamped me when it became apparent that the majority spoke Russian more or less fluently. I brooded then on genetic unfairness. My father knew seven languages (if you count the dead ones), and my mother four, yet I could never get a syllable beyond English. Then I cheered myself with the thought that this limitation has not been passed on to my daughter, who benefits from grandparental genes.

The *raketa* was only half full though three days previously it had been packed with students returning to Irkutsk's numerous seats of learning. I took a seat towards the stern where four women were anxiously debating what to do about two minute tabby kittens, en route to a good home in Irkutsk and mewing piteously in their cardboard carton. Should they be released or would they panic and try to throw themselves overboard? When set free they seemed unfazed by the *raketa*'s vibration and engine noise which made conversation quite difficult, at least for a babushka no longer in full possession of her senses. Having frolicked briefly and endeared themselves to everyone, they slept happily on the English couple's laps.

I soon moved outside and settled down on a small platform, close to the water, where huge coils of steel rope, empty beer crates, milk churns full of salted omul and buckets of red forest berries or dried mushrooms left little space for passengers. Here I spent most of the day, basking in warm sun, sheltered from the wind, occasionally joined by smokers and at each stop having a ringside seat. Officially the *raketa* stops once, halfway down the lake at Cape Bazarnaya; unofficially it stops on request, being an essential summer link with Outside for the few hamlets along the north-western shore. These are inaccessible by land; the craggy mountains behind them could be crossed only by well-equipped rock-climbers.

We kept within binocular range of the western shore, the far shore often invisible. At intervals one or two little boats with outboard engines sped towards us and we drew closer to the land before subsiding to meet them. Barter was commoner than cash transactions, tea, sugar, cigarettes and vodka being exchanged for forest berries, mushrooms and fresh, salted or smoked fish. Those taiga dwellers were mahogany-skinned, sinewy, raggedly-dressed and hard-bargaining. If they didn't get what they considered a fair exchange, they weren't dealing. Yet they and the crew obviously enjoyed good relations; much teasing and laughter accompanied their haggling. Then cash transactions took place between crew members and passengers, many of whom had brought plastic bags known to contain a given weight of berries. As a foreign babushka, I was presented with more omul than I could eat in a week and any attempt to pay caused offence.

Only a few fishing boats appeared in the distance – the majority, and the bigger ones, south of Cape Bazarnaya. In winter Lake Baikal would be less peaceful though it has no official *zimnik* (winter road). From February to April motor traffic traverses the ice on which, people assured me, vehicles cannot overturn. This I found hard to believe, but perhaps it's another of Lake Baikal's many idiosyncrasies. Infrequently, vehicles hit a weak spot and are never heard of again. No dead body, human or animal, has ever been recovered from Baikal. Among its unique species are crabs (epishura) which eat all foreign organic matter, including bones and non-synthetic garments, keeping the water so pure that you can drink it as you swim. I had marvelled at this while staying in my hut. Normally the water of even such a tiny port would show some discoloration and other signs of use. But not Baikal's water – and as I swam I searched for traces of mankind. There is something almost eerie about so immaculate a lake; no wonder Baikal's accretion of legends, in half a dozen languages, fills volumes.

Lowering my eyes from the shore – clouds were shifting slowly among fang-like crags, new snow-fields gleamed near the highest summits – I leaned over the low platform rail, gazed into the depths and thought about epishura. A minority of my readers may know as little about them as I did before Rashit informed me: so I'll explain. The epishura is a minute crustacean and it works in teams of millions rapidly to eliminate dead bodies – & etc. On this first link in the food chain depend all the lake's fauna, up to the unique Baikal varieties of whitefish, cod, grayling and seal. In the northern waters epishura make up 98 per cent of all the mass of zooplankton, to the south a little less. Epishura can live only in this lake; even when kept in Baikal water in a laboratory they die. Apart from being an irreplaceable food, they are a peculiarly powerful biological filter. Collaborating with diatomic algae (no, I don't know what those are), epishura annually extract approximately quarter of a million tons of calcium from the river waters flowing into Baikal. The lake's purity, and its saturation with oxygen even in winter, is entirely owing to these minuscule crabs which over the past four decades have been gradually but inexorably dwindling in the southern waters. They are being killed by extremely toxic effluents from the Baikal Paper and Pulp Combine (BPPC), with predictable consequences for all the lake's fauna.

As yet the casual traveller wouldn't notice that Lake Baikal is doomed – despite the part it played, forty years ago, in the arousal of environmental concern throughout the Soviet Union. The first warning came from V.A. Chivilikhin who, in April 1963, publicized the construction on Lake Baikal's southern shore of two gigantic paper and pulp combines certain to poison the lake while transforming the surrounding taiga into cellulose. He wrote, 'What will this mean – goodbye Baikal? No one wants to believe it! The disease can still be cured, and Baikal, that radiant orb of Siberia, will be healthy again.' But the disease was not cured, though agitated articles in *Pravda*, and many other newspapers and magazines, echoed Chivilikhin's alarm call. These writers proposed various rescue plans for Baikal and revealed that most of the scientists consulted, an impressive array of names from nine of the Soviet Union's most esteemed academies, had been steadfastly opposing the BPPC development since 1958. No one then knew of the hidden military agenda. The Committee on the Forestry Industry was taking its orders from the Ministry of Defence, which urgently needed new durable cord, hitherto bought from Sweden and Canada, for heavy bomber tyres. The manufacture of this cord required vast quantities of exceptionally clean water. Even the Soviet Council of Ministers never discussed such matters; bomber tyres were among the 'strategic interests of the country', tightly wrapped in a paranoid silence. Therefore no one could see the tragic irony when, in 1961, while BPPC was still being constructed, some scientist discovered how to make that durable cord from petroleum. By then so many tens of millions of roubles had been invested in BPPC that there could be no second thoughts, not even to protect Siberia's 'radiant orb'.

Meanwhile the State Planning Committee was producing documents by the ton: surveys, estimates, evaluations and so on. But these 'scientific' papers were held close to the Committee's collective chest; only a very few scientists were allowed to see a very few documents. Amongst them were judgements of this quality:

> The [BPPC] sewage water will create conditions for the propagation of life within the radius they cover, and this will mean an increase, rather than a decrease, in fish reserves.

A Commission chaired by the Director of the Institute of Geography thought otherwise:

> . . . even after treatment, effluents containing dissolved matter each year would dump more than 30,000 tons of sodium sulfides and chlorides,

toxic lignin, foul-smelling mercaptan compounds into Baikal. The concentration of mineral compounds in the waters after purification would be thirty to forty times higher than the normal Baikal levels. How could this not have an effect on the sensitive flora and fauna when many of them cannot even live in the Angara [river], where the water is only slightly worse than in Baikal?

From all over the Soviet Union angry protests continued. A collective farm chairman, Ivan Sysosev, wrote, 'To allow these factories will be a gross, irrevocable historical mistake.' A Moscow engineer, A. Provorovskii, wrote, 'We must take into account the moral damage done by such projects in developing industry.' Eleven distinguished Academicians signed a joint letter: 'Baikal has been turned into an experimental reservoir for testing sewage treatment systems, systems not tested in production, to say nothing of the severe climatic conditions of the Trans-Baikal Region.'

By 1966 world opinion (or the fragment of it then environmentally aware) had rallied to Baikal's defence and embarrassed Moscow. At the Twenty-third Congress of the Communist Parry, Mikhail Sholokhov suggested, 'Perhaps we will find the strength to renounce felling the forests around Baikal ... Later generations will not forgive us if we do not conserve this glorious sea, our blessed Lake Baikal.' Soviet public opinion became increasingly inflamed, though my Cold War generation was then being conditioned to believe it didn't/couldn't exist. Eventually the authorities took evasive action to quench this bonfire of anger, contempt and *grief*. (Leonid Leonov represented millions when he declaimed: 'Baikal is not only a priceless basin of living water but also a part of our soul.') Late in 1966 the government announced its intention to protect Baikal by installing the most up-to-date treatment facilities for BPPC's waste, no expense to be spared. A flood of films and articles gave people to understand that because of these 'facilities' Baikal would be only slightly polluted. Catastrophe had, it seemed, been averted.

Fast forward to 1975 when a 'Special Commission on Baikal' report revealed that the 'facilities' had in fact exacerbated the damage being done and taken the entire lake to the brink of irreversible degradation. But this report was confidential – *very*. By then the authorities had learned the wrong sort of lesson from the 1960s Baikal-inspired campaign which had led to such a quickening of public interest in industrial pollution. New legislation made it impossible for anyone to publicize any facts or figures on industrial development within the extended Baikal region. Even in post-Soviet Russia such facts and figures are hard to find and seeking them can be dangerous. The new mongrel authorities (foreign corporations crossed with indigenous mafia) quite often turn rabid.

We were too far offshore for photography but many pictures remain engraved on my memory. For hundreds of miles mountains rise from the water; some are sheer, multicoloured cliffs, bare of vegetation, many are taiga-clad and steeply sloping, others are weirdly chaotic – almost menacing – stretching inland at right angles to the shore, the crests of their long, thin, naked rock-walls wind-sculpted to resemble rows of spears. Then came a dramatic smooth-faced, level-topped bastion of dark granite, several miles long, so perfectly regular in its formation one could scarcely believe it to be the work of nature.

Briefly we moored off the island of Olkhon, lying close to the shore – forty-five miles long, the largest of Baikal's twenty-seven islands, its lichen-covered cliffs bulging over the lake, its regal 3,900-foot Zhima Peak surrounded by expanses of grey-green steppe. Three fishermen from Olkhon's village, Khuzhir, were into the cash economy, receiving roubles for their 15kg wooden boxes of omul, grayling and cod. As they bargained, a young man was rowing his wife and son from the mainland. By then the wind had strengthened, Baikal was getting stroppy and I admired the young woman as she judged the precise moment for a safe leap on to the platform from a wildly rocking boat. Her blond five-year-old son – beaming, eyes bright with excitement – was then handed up, to be followed by two formidably heavy milk churns of fresh fish and a very young but very large puppy of inde-terminate breed.

As the *raketa* went on its noisy way I retreated to the cabin to warm up; that wind was cold and had brought low, dark clouds – there would be no more sunshine. The pup's bloated belly and dull coat indicated dire worm infestation; his owner wrapped him in a sweater and settled him on the seat next to her son. I bought beer at the kiosk, which also sold fizzy drinks, horrible snacks, excellent chocolate, tol-erable biscuits and a dozen brands of cigarettes, the cheapest $US 0.25.

As I drank, the pup farted – potent farts which at first provoked only laughter and comically expressed disgust. Then, as they increased in volume and frequency, filling the cabin with asphyxiating fumes, the consensus was that he should be exiled. Tears gathered in the little boy's eyes. But I had finished my beer, and thawed, and was returning to the platform where the pup could sit on my lap because Baikal's wind would disperse his wind. When I had found the most sheltered corner he gazed up at my face with a puzzled expression. No doubt I smelt wrong, foreign. Soon he struggled to be free, loudly relieved his bowels behind a milk churn and thereafter farted no more.

An hour or so from Port Baikal, where the mountains withdraw slightly from the shore, a few horses and cattle grazed on level strips of lakeside pasture and small flocks of sheep dotted the overlooking steppe slopes. Occasional villages appeared, some with recent additions – two-storeyed, balconied houses, their shiny tin roofs and fresh golden timbers too conspicuous beside the weathered grey of squat, shingle-roofed *izby*. In these southern parts of Buryatiya, Russians and Buryat have lived in neighbouring villages for generations.

The Buryat – related to nearby Mongolia's Dzungars and Khalkhas – were in the seventeenth century the dominant indigenous inhabitants of this comparatively fertile region of south-eastern Siberia. When the pioneer colonists arrived (Cossack troops and fur traders) these numerous and wealthy nomads put up more resistance to the Russians than was common east of the Urals. Their wealth depended on enormous herds of cattle and horses and on the exaction of tribute from vassals, the much smaller and less sophisticated Nenet and Ket tribes. They possessed a written language, firearms and metals, prodigious physical stamina and shrewd military leaders who in times of crisis could assemble a 2,000-strong army.

What are known as the Buryat Wars extended over more than thirty years, starting in 1631 when the Cossacks built their first fort on Buryat territory, in the Bratsk area. A few years later the Buryat slaughtered that garrison, burning the fort. Rapidly it was replaced and better-armed garrisons survived prolonged attacks in 1638 and 1658. The Buryat Wars really amounted to a sustained guerrilla campaign: raids on the camps of exploring Cossacks, ambushes of traders' boats from river banks, sieges of hastily-built forts. The Russians coped cleverly with this obstacle to expansion. Given the distances involved and the resources available, there could be no question of eliminating these hostile natives. Instead, they were subdued by negotiation, the invaders offering their leaders exemption from tribute, freedom to graze over specific areas, grand titles with an impressive ring to them and eventually, in 1762, permission to raise their own regiments of 'native Cossacks' to patrol the border with Mongolia, then Chinese-ruled.

Most Siberian tribes dwindled in numbers soon after the Russians and their diseases came on the scene but the Buryat increased as they became Russified. The Russian settlers, and those Buryat who had given up their nomadic way of life, exchanging livestock-dependency for crop-cultivation, coexisted peaceably, even participating in each other's traditional festivities. During several transitional decades, former nomads relied on the Russian newcomers for advice about arable farming and the settlers needed Buryat advice about how to survive the Siberian winters. I can think of nothing comparable within the Western European imperialists' colonial history. In Asia and Africa even the least educated whites normally regarded themselves as 'superior' and entitled to live apart from the natives, both physically and mentally. But then, many of Siberia's settlers were escaping from serfdom, relishing their freedom despite its accompanying hardships and certainly not regarding themselves as superior to the always-free and economically better-off Buryats.

The early 1950s brought both an enlargement of collective farms to increase production (notoriously, enlargement had the reverse effect) and the enforced unification of Russian and Buryat villages to complete the Russification of the Buryat. This outside intervention awakened animosities dormant since the early eighteenth century – and still awake today, able to provoke spasmodic friction. However, both communities are united in their angry but ignored opposition to a recent development, a direct result of the automobilization of the New Russia. Although no roads as yet exist, two coves along Baikal's shore are accessible to car-campers from Irkutsk and more than a thousand visit each site during summer weekends. Already much damage is visible; indiscriminate tyre tracks criss-cross the steppe slopes, causing rapid erosion and the loss of that pasturage on which the locals remain largely dependent. Those cores incorporate Buryat and Russian sacred lands, still regularly used for religious ceremonies (Buddhist and Orthodox) and also for family reunions when people come by boat from Irkutsk and elsewhere to picnic, dance and swim. Now locals feel excluded and, most distressing of all, hillocks of garbage and swathes of broken glass desecrate their sacred sites.

One village's new blue-domed church looked toylike by the water's edge. This, I later learned, is Bolshoye Goloustnoye, the oldest Russian settlement on Baikal's shore, founded in 1677. Its 200-year-old church was razed in the 1930s, rebuilt with foreign aid in the 1990s, then destroyed by fire soon after its consecration. A state-appointed conservation officer had recently arrived in the village and quickly antagonized the locals who accused him of being a city man, knowing nothing about his job and colluding with a coterie of Orthodox clergy keen to circumvent logging and hunting regulations. One day a request for his resignation was faxed to all relevant government offices in Irkutsk and Moscow and that night the church went up in flames. A month later the officer was promoted to an urban post within the conservation bureaucracy. A year later the church was ready for reconsecration. The arsonist(s) remained undetected. 'And so are problems solved,' said my informant, 'in the rural recesses of our new Russia.'

Cold heavy rain and dense low cloud reduced visibility as we turned into Port Baikal at the mouth of the Angara river, a small derelict harbour sheltered by forested mountains. We moored by a crumbling quay where all around rusting ships loomed forlornly out of the gloom, some with mobile cranes still poised over their holds, more sad memorials to the suddenness of the Soviet Union's economic collapse. Here most passengers disembarked and the rest of us changed to a smaller *raketa*. As no one competed with me for the front seat in the all-window 'prow' I enjoyed unimpeded views during the final stage of our journey.

Although 336 rivers and streams flow into Lake Baikal, only one flows out of it: the mighty Angara, which drives the turbines of the Irkutsk, Bratsk and Ust'-Ilimsk hydro-electric stations. Pre-dam-building, the Angara flowed so swiftly that it never froze top-down, like other Siberian rivers. Instead, giant ice-chunks formed on its bed, then rose to the surface as sometimes mobile icebergs capable of shattering bridges. The Irkutsk dam was needed to provide electric power to the builders of the record-breaking Bratsk dam, of which much more anon. Begun in 1955, it was producing 660,000 kilowatts by September 1958 – at considerable cost to Lake Baikal, whose level had been raised almost three feet. A trivial modification, one might think, but in time this disturbance of species habitat caused incalculable and irreparable damage to migratory birds and spawning fish. The flea on the mammoth . . .

From Lake Baikal the Angara escapes through a mile-wide gorge where, in midstream, the famous Shaman Rock (now spray-painted by vandals) commemorates an ancient Buryat legend. George St George, who spent most of his childhood in Siberia, recounts it thus:

> Baikal was a miserly widower who doted on his only beautiful daughter, whom he kept in a virtual prison surrounded by mountains. He collected water from the many streams pouring in but never let a drop out. His daughter, Angara, was very unhappy in her father's prison where an evil old shaman guarded her. From birds she learned that far away there was a handsome giant, the Yenisei. Angara fell in love with this hero sight unseen, and decided to escape and join him. One night, in a howling storm, she pushed aside the mountains and broke out. The evil shaman was not quick enough to stop her, but did manage to awaken old Baikal and handed him a big rock. Enraged, Baikal hurled the rock after his errant daughter, but it was too late – Angara was on her way to Yenisei, the rock landed harmlessly in the stream, and so it rests there now as a silent memorial to triumphant love.

This legend, I was to notice, is one of the most popular bedtime stories for small Siberians.

As we passed the Shaman Rock, with untouched taiga reaching to the water's edge on our left, the clouds suddenly lifted and ahead was a vast glimmering sky of faint pinks, high grey-purple streaks, shreds of muted gold, green-tinted flecks near the horizon. For thirty miles we were skimming towards this ever-changing sunset across what is now an artificial lake, the dam having raised the Angara's level by 98 feet. Soon, to starboard, newish settlements could be glimpsed amidst the taiga and little fishing boats were rocked by our wake, some oar-dependent, others sporting sails. The dam's ugliness and 'developed'

Irkutsk – sprawling factories and high-risery – come into view together. Miles away on the Angara's east bank, above its confluence with the Ushakovka and the Irkut, stands the old city. Hereabouts the Angara is so wrigglesome that I found myself topographically confused when the No. 16 minibus from the *raketa* terminal took me across a river I thought I had left behind.

Natasha and Lev (the 'Tourism Development' students met in Severobaikalsk) had recommended a B&B – 'easy to find, near the Hotel Angara where the minibus puts you down'. As thousands of flats are near this central hotel I was now up against the non-Russian-speaker's main difficulty, finding private addresses. Clutching a scrap of paper with Raisa's name and address written in Cyrillic (but no telephone number), I entered the Angara to seek guidance; this previously Intourist hotel must surely have an English-speaker on the staff. In contrast to its Soviet Utilitarian exterior, the foyer was glitzy-turned-shoddy: enormous, ill-lit, almost empty, the décor wavering between British late Victorian and Sixties Scandinavian. In one corner a cramped bar (imitation English pub) permitted smoking as a concession to foreign potential investors who might be rubbed up the wrong way by nicotine deprivation. Both teenage barmaids looked dual-purpose and though neither spoke English their one customer did. A smallish, fortyish Muscovite, representing Tetropak and designer dressed, he impertinently asked why an Irishwoman should want to stay in a B&B when everyone knew Ireland had become one of the richest countries in the EU. He then asserted that post-Soviet Russia was also prospering – look at the demand for Tetropak, people wanted hygienic and convenient liquids, not milk sold out of some bucket in a dirty market or fruit juices needing labour in the home. When I castigated the hotel for selling only expensive foreign beers, he dismissed Russian beers as inferior, brewed unhygienically. This unpleasant little man was among the few Russians I met who did not loyally defend everything Russian. But no doubt free market Moscow is breeding many such mutations.

The bar-girls, who did not know the way to Raisa's B&B, conveyed that the sooner I stopped distracting Mr Tetropak the better they'd be pleased. By then the throbbing of my right leg (carrying even a light rucksack didn't suit it) was tempting me to squander $50 on an Angara room. At that crucial moment a handsome young couple joined us – also Muscovites, speaking fluent English, staying overnight in Irkutsk after a fortnight's sailing around Lake Baikal. Immediately they volunteered to find Raisa in the telephone book and went to their room.

Mr Tetropak now took off with one of the bar-girls – they had been not very subtly competing for him – and I moved to sit near the reception desk where two young women were doing crossword puzzles, sharing a sofa opposite the entrance, quickly glancing up each time the door swung open. The peroxide blonde wore a low-cut fishnet blouse, a red and black microskirt and lime-green tights; her brunette companion favoured an ankle-length shiny blue skirt, slit high up the sides, a short scarlet jacket and a wispy spangled stole; both wore pencil-thin high heels and lots of rings and bracelets. A certain aura of patience-cum-alertness, and often cheerfulness disguising unhappiness, marks their profession. In our day, when so many of both sexes regard casual sex with an acquaintance as a normal part of social life, attitudes to prostitution should logically have changed. But in Russia, it had been made clear to me, the oldest profession retains its stigma. The Soviet ethos contained elements of Puritanism still operative – and, given the AIDS epidemic, post-Soviet Russia needs them.

Soon my rescuers returned. The B&B was literally around the corner, three minutes' walk away; they would escort me there and Raisa would be waiting at the entrance. By then it was dark, and our path over drainage channels and around mounds of rubble was only faintly illuminated, but out of the darkness came a welcoming shout. Before I had time to thank them adequately the young couple had handed me over to Raisa and vanished.

My hostess greeted me like a long-lost friend, then pushed open a small metal door and led the way up a wide, dimly-lit, stone stairway strewn with cigarette ends and smelling of past meals and decaying masonry. On each long landing of this 115-year-old 'mansion block' high wooden double doors were set in iron frames – the floor level bits easy to trip over in the poor light, as Raisa cautioned me. On the fourth of five floors she unlocked a heavily-padded, leather-coated door and we entered a large unfurnished hallway shared by two flats. Each had two doors close together, the outer requiring one key, the inner three keys. I never discovered why security was so tight; Irkutsk didn't feel like a lawless city yet when Raisa handed me the guests' bunch of six keys she emphasized that all were to be used at all times.

This was a luxury flat, recently renovated: spacious, bright, the windows wide, the floors of gleaming golden parquet, the kitchen Ideal Homes-equipped and separated from the living-room by a spotlit US-style food-bar. The hallway alone was as big as many Soviet era flats, likewise the three bedrooms, a state-of-the-art bathroom and a utility room where I must feel free to use the washing machine. Raisa looked incredulous when I conveyed my inability to use such gadgets and sought permission to launder clothes in the bath.

In Raisa's youth, this flat had accommodated her extended family of seventeen: three generations. Now she shared it with B&B guests (treated as friends) and with Polya, a twenty-one-year-old niece of startling beauty about to graduate as a biologist and hoping for a job at the Limnological Institute near Port Baikal – but its funding had been so reduced her hopes were not high. Both she and Raisa were indefatigable users of my mini-dictionary and here I discovered that under pressure I had begun to understand a few phrases of Russian, while remaining unable to articulate anything comprehensible.

In instalments, over the days ahead, Raisa told me her life story, the dictionary being supplemented by bulky photograph albums dating back to the 1890s. The many snapshots taken abroad between 1965 and 1985 (in Japan, Cyprus, China, Italy, Singapore) suggested that Raisa's parents and in-laws had been senior Party officials who never, as my grandmother used to say, dirtied their bibs.

Born in Irkutsk in 1960, of a Ukrainian Jewish father and a Korean mother, Raisa looked entirely Korean. (At first glance, on the twilit stairway, I had assumed her to be Buryat.) Such mixed families were usual enough in this 'crossroads city', an important trading centre which attracted many foreign entrepreneurs long before the free market became official. The nineteen-year-old Raisa married a Tatar Party official, now a very successful businessman, and their recent divorce had been painful. Raisa's face hardened as she recalled how her husband had emptied her ancestral flat of all its furniture as repay-ment of a loan provided in 1993. Raisa, by profession an economist, was then setting up her own Financial Advice Bureau. This explained why the renovated flat didn't feel like an old family home.

Raisa's distinguished-looking and multi-talented twenty-two-year-old daughter closely resembled her Jewish maternal grandfather; of Korean genes there was not a trace. Now living in Stockholm with a Swedish musician husband and twin sons, she had already established herself as a fashion designer: the photographs were there to prove it. Her only sibling, Denis, a charming nine-year-old, lived with his father, visited his mother frequently, spoke inaccurate English confidently and took a precocious interest in world affairs. 'Why,' he asked, 'do Irish people in America give so much dollars to Irish people in Ireland to kill other sorts of Irish people?'

The second B of Raisa's B&B was fortuitously geared to my eating habits. At 7.15 a.m. she delighted in serving substantial three- and four-course Korean meals which at 7.15 p.m. would count as dinner. While I ate by spotlight, perched on a high stool at the long food-bar, my hostess retired to dress stylishly and expensively before hurrying away to open her bureau just across the street. After the 1998 crash, 80 per cent inflation had forced her to close it and move with Denis to Seoul where for a year she acted as overseas consultant to a small firm of toy exporters. In 2000 it seemed worth returning to Irkutsk because her clients valued her, but business wasn't thriving…

Siberia was explored and exploited, and decisively secured for the czars, by a few generations of daring, ruthless adventurers travelling in smallish groups because the terrain could not sustain large numbers. Astonishingly, it took only sixty years to reach the Pacific across those 3,000-plus miles of pathless, treacherous, almost uninhabited territory between the Urals and the coast. In 1641 Cossacks under Ivan Moskvitin were carried by the Okhotka river to the Sea of Okhotsk and thus the Russians gained an outlet to the Pacific long before they enjoyed any access to either the Black Sea or the Baltic.

Twenty years later another Cossack leader, Yakov Pokhabov, was hired to subdue and collect tribute from the Baikal Basin Buryats. He soon saw the strategic possibilities of a site at the confluence of the Angara and Irkut rivers, only forty-five miles from the lake, and added another to the many 'Czar's forts' then dotted about Siberia. By 1686 this fortification had been moved from the island at the confluence of the rivers to the right bank of the Angara and Pokhabov's small settlement quickly developed into a garrison town. The 1689 Treaty of Nerchinsk, which stabilized relations between China and Russia by fixing the frontier, immediately stimulated trade with China via the Mongolia route south of Buryatiya. Merchants who had previously used the northern route, passing through Yakutsk on the Lena river, now turned towards the new town on the Angara. Irkutsk also became the base for numerous expeditions to the unknown far east and far north. Its Institute of Geography predates the American Declaration of Independence by several years and from it set forth some of Russia's greatest explorers, having been well equipped, both intellectually and materially, by an experience-hardened staff. In 1784 an Irkutsk trader, Grigori Shelekhov, landed in Alaska which subsequently became known to the Russians as 'the American district of Irkutsk'.

In 1695–96 the Buryat again took up arms and once during that futile campaign Irkutsk was besieged. Otherwise nothing happened to halt its growth and from all over Eastern Siberia, a territory much larger than the whole of Europe, came boatloads of mammoth ivory and pelts then more valuable than gold. From China came silk, porcelain and tea by the ton. (The Russians vie with the Indians as the world's most insatiable tea drinkers.) By the eighteenth century Irkutsk was a famous trading post and an important centre of imperial authority, though distance protected it from too close scrutiny. In time it acquired the flavour of an independent merchant city whose large colony of wealthy Chinese introduced some of the refinements of life to the rough-hewn Russian population: explorers, miners, soldiers, brigands, traders, plus versatile chancers from Western Europe and Central Asia.

Catherine the Great (1729–96) was eager to plant many more Russians in southern Siberia and took a special interest in the Baikal region. But the institution of serfdom was unknown in Siberia and there existed no socio-economic foundations on which it could be built. This inhibited Catherine. How to establish free peasant communities, whose new lifestyle would be immeasurably better than they were used to, without risking unrest in European Russia? Catherine failed to find a humane solution to that problem.

In 1753 Russia abandoned the death penalty for minor misdemeanours like illegal tree-felling; it made more economic sense to populate Siberia's empty spaces. Soon tens of thousands of serfs (some genuine criminals, the majority guilty of taking snuff or fortune-telling) had embarked on a life sentence of hard labour. According to reliable estimates, more than a million convicts arrived in Siberia during the nineteenth century, often accompanied by their families though many couples were forced to leave behind any children under the age of ten.

Not all were serfs or peasants. In July 1826 the first batch of Decembrists (eight aristocrats, all veterans of the 1812 campaign) were put in chains in St Petersburg and began their thirty-six day journey, by horse-cart, to Irkutsk. (Peasants of course had to walk, dragging their chains.) These men had been among the 121 army officers who on 14 December 1825 intervened, with reckless courage and insufficient planning, to prevent the coronation of Czar Nicholas I. Their demands included a constitutional monarchy, the abolition of serfdom, freedom of the press and certain other not unreasonable reforms. Five of their leaders were hanged. The rest, among the most cultivated and thoughtful of Russia's liberal minority, were exiled to Siberia where traces of their influence remain discernible in Irkutsk. Many of their wives voluntarily followed them in defiance of official disapproval. Governor-General Levinsky of Eastern Siberia proposed that those women, married to state criminals, should be treated as accomplices, stripped of their titles, forced to do hard labour and made to forfeit any babies born in Siberia for rearing as state-owned serfs. Happily the Russian Chief of Staff, Baron Dibich, knew many of those élite regiment 'criminals' and was able to restrain Levinsky.

Forty years later the Poles arrived in bulk: 18,600 had been exiled as punishment for their 1863 rebellion against Czarist rule. During the next half-century a fascinating cross-section of unruly elements – nihilists, anarchists and socialists including Stalin – involuntarily took up residence in the Irkutsk region.

As the capital of Eastern Siberia and the seat of the Governor-General, late nineteenth-century Irkutsk had a reputation for cultural ambitions and extravagant living – though being at the hub of the world's largest penal colony detracted somewhat from its grandeur. A rather disarming frontierland form of egalitarianism allowed the miserable hovels of destitute exiles and released criminals to be built in the very shadow of spacious mansions occupied by rich merchants and the Czar's high officials.

Irkutsk, like London and Moscow, was reshaped by a Great Fire. In July 1879 flames reduced most of its 3,500 wooden buildings to ash and its 200 stone buildings to mere shells. Out of a population of 30,000, 24,000 were left homeless. But not for long. The speed of Irkutsk's reconstruction astonished observers, given the city's pre-Trans-Siberian inaccessibility. Its controlling magnates, always prone to flaunting their wealth, now did so to good effect. Within a few years Irkutsk was being referred to as 'the Paris of Siberia' – another of those absurd analogies, like Rwanda being 'the Switzerland of Africa', which are intended to flatter but in fact demean. Everywhere is *itself*, nowhere is the 'X' of 'Y'.

If you're not expecting a Parisian ambience and feeling let down by its absence, Irkutsk is very agreeable in autumn. Tall fountains sparkle in hot sunshine, municipal flowerbeds glow red and orange, stretches of river (the Angara or the Ushakovka) appear unexpectedly, frost-tinted leaves drift down from the mature poplars and maples that line long streets, their more vigorous roots wrecking pavements. Irkutsk's three aspects – Czarist, Soviet, post-Soviet – don't add up to 'beauty' but they do make this a city of surprises. Throughout the centre monstrosities like the Hotel Angara are obvious enough yet never dominant. Around almost every corner the streetscape changes utterly and many two-storey dwellings, built of massive tree trunks, are dispersed amidst stately stone or brick administrative and commercial buildings, or dwarfed by adjacent 1890s mansion blocks such as Raisa's. Some wooden houses' boulder foundations have sunk so deep into the ground that the thresholds are below pavement level and out-of-kilter windows give the façades a raffish look. Shingle roofs show alarming dips and many gable walls have bulges suggestive of imminent collapse, yet photographs from the 1980s and 1970s show those same dwellings in the same condition.

The Irkutsk city fathers value their inheritance and on the main shopping street, the mile-long *ulitsa* Karla Marxa, several dignified late nineteenth-century edifices have been restored with care, and converted to free market uses, instead of being razed to make way for corporate glass towers. Their exteriors contrast with the dismally neglected though potentially equally handsome mansion blocks in the background. A reincarnated Mr Marx would surely not approve of this *ulitsa*'s sleek competing banks, seductive boutiques, luxuriously appointed Italian and Korean restaurants – or of the exclusive hyper-market to which I was refused admission because I wouldn't entrust my small carrier-bag to an insolent security officer wearing a comic-opera uniform.

That bag (more prudent than a trendy, mugger-tempting day-pack) contained my journal, camera, binoculars and an unusual amount of cash. I had just changed money and received a minor shock when the bank clerk rejected at a glance fourteen of my $10 bills. No explana-tion was given by this ill-mannered young woman who went on to scrutinize the acceptable bills, on both sides, under her forgery-detection machine. (Exceptionally talented counterfeiters are prolif-erating in Russia.) As those sensitive machines don't work with worn notes – Raisa later explained – half my dollars were by Russian stan-dards obsolete. I was given no time to count my roubles; the clerk stuffed them into my passport and handed it over while beckoning the next customer. But that didn't bother me; one doesn't expect to find dishonest bank clerks in Siberia, however churlish they may be.

The post-Soviet rich/poor divide is much more apparent in Irkutsk than in the BAM towns – partly, it is said, because a far higher per-centage of BAM folk can grow their own food. Every day numerous Central Asian women, usually with babies on their laps, sat in niches along Karla Marxa and *ulitsa* Lenina, rattling begging boxes into which few coins were thrown. In a bar opposite the Antey bookshop I watched two dirty, dark-skinned little boys, with infected eyes and shredded sandals, urgently begging from customers before being angrily banished by a barmaid brandishing a grass broom. These are 'economic migrants', in our jargon, and most Siberians despise them, their contempt often tinged with fear.

In the student districts of Universitetskij, Sudgorodok and Akademgorodok it worried me to see so many unhealthy-looking youngsters with rotting teeth, splitting fingernails, dark circles under their eyes and facial sores resembling boils rather than acne. One couldn't judge their hair condition; most young males were crew-cut, most young females had for years been using cheap tints or dyes.

Those districts across the Angara, forming the newer Irkutsk, have that incoherent quality common to Soviet developments which involved housing and servicing the greatest number of people in the shortest possible time with minimal regard for 'visual impact'. The best that can be said for trans-Angara Irkutsk is that it feels uncrowded; the featureless block estates, numerous university institutes and dead or dying factories are interspersed with eye-soothing expanses of taiga parkland.

Irkutsk's two bookshops lacked anything in English apart from schoolbooks. But then Alexei, one of my new student friends, pulled a string to enable me to use a Faculty of English bookstore and there I bought everything available: J. Meade Falkner's *Moonfleet*, Conrad's *Lord Jim*, Lawrence's *Women in Love*, Aldous Huxley's *Chrome Yellow*, Eric Segal's *Love Story*. Alexei complained about this limited choice and about recent price rises. Soviet subsidies being no more, it was usual for four or five students to club together to buy one copy of a text.

Throughout Russia the beginning of the new academic year, for all age groups, is celebrated on 1 September, designated Education Day by the Soviets. In 2002 it fell on Monday 2 September and at lunch-time both bookshops were thronged with parents and children, some of the former looking rather tense as they totted up the cost of text-books and other educational equipment. Many grandparents fidgeted in the background, offering advice that frequently provoked arguments.

From 1917, education was kept near the top of Moscow's agenda. On Education Day parents if possible take time off work to accompany their young into the new classroom; and for the parents of the seven-year-old First Day pupils free time must be possible. The little boys wear neat new suits and saucer-sized white rosettes in their lapels. The little girls wear party dresses and high crowns of white ribbons, variously designed. At noon the sun shone hot and bright, after a foggy morning, and the city centre pavements seemed strewn with white blossoms. Irresistibly I was reminded of Irish seven-year-olds on their First Holy Communion Day, wearing the same expressions of half-scared self-importance, aware of being special and indulged, posing shyly or boldly for photographs that in 2050 will be proudly shown to their grandchildren. This resemblance is not entirely fortuitous. In *Night of Stone*, a most moving and illuminating study of coping with death in twentieth-century Russia, Catherine Merridale quotes a 1960 Party memorandum:

> What is needed is a carefully worked-out and thought-through complex of measures to disseminate new Soviet traditions, customs and practices; and also the revival and strengthening of some folk customs and practices, when they have been purged of religious overtones.

Soon after, as Catherine Merridale explains:

> The propaganda specialists designed a cycle of Soviet rituals. Traditional rites of passage – marriage, for instance, and the birth and naming of a child – were on the list, and so were new ceremonies to mark the first and last day at school, the acquisition of a passport and the receipt of a person's first wage packet.

(The passport in question was necessary for movement within the Soviet Union; it did not permit travel abroad.)

Through Rashit's network of friends I contacted Bruno and was invited to his flat in Studgorodok. A fifty-ish American, of slight but sufficient independent means, he had first visited the Soviet Union in 1982 as leader of a group dedicated to reducing tension between the US and the SU by giving 'ordinary people' an opportunity to make friends. At that date Reagan's 'evil empire' rantings had increased tension and Bruno recalled the astonishment with which he and his friends were welcomed. He also recalled their own astonishment on finding the Soviet population adequately clad and fed, not living in extreme poverty as an ineluctable consequence of Communism. Even more disconcerting, the average Soviet citizen seemed better informed about world affairs than the average American citizen. It took Bruno only a day to fall in love with Irkutsk, and only a week to fall in love with a young woman of that city where he settled in 1988, working as a voluntary fire warden in one of Lake Baikal's Nature Reserves. When on duty he lived in a mixed (Russian and Buryat) village where communal friction has been provoked by developers bribing one group while the other continues to strive to defend the environment.

A No. 3 minibus took me from the Kirov Square terminus, outside Hotel Angara, to Studgorodok. Irkutsk enjoys an excellent public transport system; one rarely has to wait more than a few moments for a trolley-bus or minibus taxi. The former (4 roubles for all distances) tend to be so overcrowded during rush hours that visibility is nil. The decrepit minibuses (5 or 6 roubles) are restricted to seventeen passengers and on-the-spot fines punish overloading. In nine days I witnessed four finings, possibly because underpaid policemen need little supplements.

That morning I had walked a few miles, stubbornly ignoring The Knee – which now began to take its revenge. Limping away from the Studgorodok bus stop, I abandoned my afternoon's plan to become acquainted with New Irkutsk on foot, rambling to and fro, going nowhere in particular, just getting the feel of the place. In a nearby park-cum-sportsground I sat amidst vandalized benches; seven out of ten had been dismantled. Here were disused tennis courts, their umpires' seats rusting, and a football pitch glittering with broken glass, its goal posts collapsed. Beside a plantation of birch saplings (also vandalized) a few young couples or solo babushkas were pushing buggies or leading toddlers by the hand or applauding skipping granddaughters. Thus far it had been an 'Irish September' day, sunny with a slight cool breeze. But now dark clouds suddenly gathered and drenching rain sent me back to the bus shelter where a friendly English-speaking law student was bewildered because I didn't have a guardian travel agent. The 'independent traveller' still puzzles Siberians.

My companion smiled rather sourly when I enthused about Tynda and Severobaikalsk, while commiserating with their present economic plight. Then he said, 'Those places are too sorry for themselves. You must stay in *real* Russian towns, west of the Urals, same size places. *There* is poverty to shock you. The BAM towns seem forgotten by Moscow but even now they're privileged. Those people got so many concessions they have advantages their children and grandchildren are still living off. Though maybe for not much longer, if all our railways are efficiently privatized.'

The downpour soon stopped, the sun shone again from a deep blue sky and I took a No. 3 onwards to Akademgorodok, disembarking when an open-air bar appeared beside a strip of pine forest. The big kiosk sold drinks, snacks and ice-cream, to which Siberians of all ages are hopelessly addicted at all seasons. A score of battered plastic tables and chairs stood on a patch of stony wasteland under a sagging canvas canopy. Only two tables were occupied, one by a couple of unshaven old men sharing a large can of *pivo*, the other by a pallid, undersized young woman wearing jeans and a fraying T-shirt and trying to light a cigarette off a butt. Passing her table, I realized that she was a prematurely aged adolescent and close to tears – eyes brimming, chin trembling. As I brought my diary up to the minute I became aware of her staring at me, fixedly, so I laid down my pen and smiled at her, asking if she spoke English. She shook her head and made a beckoning gesture, then began to sob convulsively, her hands covering her face. As I went to her side one of the old men shouted at her, abusively, while the other glared silently at me. Just then a small boy, aged nine or ten, came hurrying towards us from the bus stop. Obviously he was her little brother – the family resemblance was strong – and I withdrew to my table. An angry argument began between the siblings, conducted *sotto voce*. The old men stood up and departed, muttering to each other. The boy raised his voice, shrilly demanding something and showing his sister a tiny slip of folded paper. She hesitated, then took a hundred-rouble note from a neck-purse beneath her shirt and exchanged it for her next fix. At once the boy raced away and his sister, avoiding my gaze, slowly followed. One hundred roubles is big money in Irkutsk and the average price, I later learned, for a single fix of not very pure heroin.

Back on Bruno's *ulitsa*, row after row of long, nine-storey blocks confronted me, built on rough ground sloping gradually down to the invisible Angara. In vain I sought No. 126/5/18 Kln. I would have to ring Bruno, begging for rescue. Irkutsk has many free public telephones but all three in the shopping area were dysfunctional. (These shops are basic, no Karla Marxa affluence here.) I was by then in considerable pain and must have looked rather desperate as I returned to the blocks because a young woman, walking home from the shops with two small daughters, asked if I needed help. When I showed her Bruno's address she went far out of her way to lead me to his entrance.

Now, reading over my journal, I realize that for three months I benefited almost every day, in ways large or small, from spontaneous
Siberian kindness.

Bruno's three-roomed flat was book-filled and smelled of herbal
teas. We bonded instantly, as members of an increasingly rare species:
citizens of the West who have never owned a motor car. Bruno
lamented the rocketing increase in private car ownership during the
previous few years and the extent to which this has changed the whole
pattern and pace of life in Irkutsk. Now his teenagers were urging him
to get with it, transport-wise, and his resolve to stick to his principles
seemed not conducive to domestic harmony.

Bruno also held strong views about foreigners' campaigns to ban all
hunting of Lake Baikal's unique seal (the nerpa). He argued, 'For centuries small lakeside communities have been dependent on the nerpa.
They know how to keep the balance, commercial hunting and pollution are the threats. Without seal-hunting those people will be
destroyed themselves, as distinctive communities.'

Ironically, given his original motive for visiting Russia, Bruno
shared my Tynda friends' reservations about American/Russian
student exchange programmes. Adolescence, he opined, is the least
appropriate age for such an experience. 'I'd like to see programmes for
graduates in their mid- to late-twenties, people with their own cultural identities established. Then they'd be able to learn a lot, analyse
values, choose what's worth bringing back in their minds and hearts.
Most Russians are miles more enterprising than us about survival
methods – all sorts of survival, physical and emotional. Yet we're supposed to be the brilliant guys, inventive and individualistic! But life's
gotten too soft for our Haves. And our Have Nots are either ignored
and hopeless, like in the US, or given enough hand-outs to stifle
initiative, like in the EU. Russian kids getting a taste for our Haves'
lifestyle come home undervaluing their own folks' survival skills.
That's bad! Here they're going to need them, for an awful long time!'

I asked how Bruno interpreted the new Russia's compulsive vandalizing. 'Not that the West is short of vandals,' I added, 'but here it
does seem off the scale.'

Bruno shrugged. 'You should go look at America's cities! Russian
kids are only amateurs – but I guess they all have the same thing going

on inside them. The backgrounds are different, the reactions the same. Here it's a cry for help from confused young males with no moral or material framework, nothing to replace what went before. They've no personal memories of the Soviet system, but they know their parents' and grandparents' world has fallen apart. That change was supposed to bring benefits that haven't got to them. It's all gone crazy in a new way. Before it was crazy with those kids' parents employed in factories that were an economic black joke but gave workers a sense of security. A false sense, breeding corruption and hypocrisy, but while it lasted it felt *real* for those workers. And day-to-day it *was* real, they got fed and clothed and sheltered and educated and medicated. Then suddenly it was gone. And poor kids in a vacuum, what do they do? They get angry and vandalize. It's not about Russians being "brutalized by their history" – you know that theory? Last week I met an American diplomat – senior guy, influential – who said at this dinner party, "All Russians are vandals by nature. They've never been civilized." I said nothing. If I'd said anything it would have been too much and embarrassed our host!'

We were talking in the tiny neat kitchen, drinking tea and eating freshly picked forest berries, in appearance like redcurrants but much sourer and with a distinctive flavour.

Bruno's children had been to Siberia's only Waldorf School and when I mentioned that my granddaughters were flourishing at the Scariff Waldorf school, in Co. Clare, he invited me to visit the Irkutsk version on the following Friday. Initially he had had some doubts about choosing what is, in its own outré way, an élitist educational system setting children apart from their contemporaries. 'Then my wife pointed out that kids with Waldorf-inclined parents are coming from homes out of tune with the way we live now. So being schooled someplace *in* tune with family life must make up for being socially set apart. Anyway here it's only a kindergarten, three teachers and twenty pupils. Ten years ago a German woman started it, planning to expand. But I figure it's too soon after Communism, not many can accept the idea of a school funded by parents with no state support.'

That heroin purchase I had witnessed was a not unusual sight in AIDS-afflicted Irkutsk where discarded needles lie around in many districts. Visualizing children picking them up, I collected at least two a day for disposal with Raisa's kitchen rubbish, which was dropped into a grinder.

One evening Raisa told me that her neighbour's fourteen-year-old son and a school friend had been attacked that afternoon by skinheads in a street just off Karla Marxa. Money was demanded, Vlady had none and his friend claimed to have none – then handed over 30 roubles when both boys' scalps were cut with broken bottles. Raisa condemned the police for being too slack about such crime, 'so *new* in Irkutsk!'

According to my student friends, Irkutsk's police (like some of their colleagues in many countries) were worse than 'slack', being themselves implicated in the drugs trade. Also, for a month before recent local elections one candidate for high office announced that he (but only he) could deal with this problem. The supply of all drugs then dwindled dramatically – until after the election, when that candidate had secured his seat and 'normal' trading was resumed. Or so the anecdote went; true or false, it reflected the cynicism aroused by politicians of every stripe.

In between doing some of the things a tourist should do in Irkutsk, I visited a rambling, ramshackle two-storey building in the grounds of an enormous half-restored church encased in dodgy cedar-trunk scaffolding. This former monastery housed a group of men who at their local polyclinic had completed a methadone course (as controversial here as in Ireland) and were being helped to 'stay clean' by Father Grigori, a small, slight young man with wavy auburn hair, a trim little beard, a short straight nose, shrewd blue eyes and an engaging smile. His relationship with his fifteen protégés seemed easy; one felt he was offering them supportive friendship rather than authoritarian guidance. In age they ranged from eighteen to forty-four and some of the younger men had been brought to Father Grigori by near-despairing parents.

We sat in a long narrow refectory-cum-chapel where during meals a deacon read from *The Lives of the Saints* as in Roman Catholic monasteries – and in my convent boarding school during Lent in the 1940s. Several icons occupied one corner, a cluster of tiny candles flickering before them. My answer to Father Grigori's predicable first question

– 'Do you believe in God?' – made him look sad but not censorious.

None of the men spoke English but all were fascinated by the foreign babushka and astonished to hear that the Irish, too, have 'a drugs problem'. In their view, explained Father Grigori, addiction happens when poor people who can't get a job are lured into the 'happy' escape of heroin. So why, they wondered, did affluent Ireland have drug addicts? Giving even an over-simplified answer to that question took half an hour. My listeners exclaimed incredulously on hearing that Ireland's comparatively poor minority feels as desperate as they do, not because of equal poverty but because we associate status with possessions to a dangerous extent, making them *feel* equally deprived.

The image of rich drug addicts seemed still more bewildering – what could they be escaping from? Father Grigori's answer was 'spiritual poverty': without faith, without God in their lives, how could riches make anyone happy? He added, 'Seventy years is not much time – our atheist era. A thousand years is a long time – our Christian era. The older men who come here grew up with no faith, in times when believers didn't do so well. But our faith didn't go away, it's there now when people need it and most Russians do. Even people who know nothing about it need it emotionally. Russia as a nation was formed 700 years ago by the Orthodox church – the Tatars destroyed everything else Russian but they couldn't damage *Holy* Russia! I've borrowed from Bruno a book called *Empire* by a part-Russian called Dominic Lieven – that's a famous name in our history. He doesn't understand about Holy Russia's power, he says even by 1914 we weren't really a nation because we'd no cultural links between educated people and peasants. He thinks we're confused now about our post-Soviet national identity, as if it mattered that the Russian Federation is only four-fifths Russian. Our very old nationalism is strong enough to deal with one-fifth non-Russians and non-Christians.'

I said nothing, sensing Father Grigori's reverence for his own version of Holy Russia. But that last sentence had slightly chilled me; in another setting I might have fished for his views on Chechnya.

Meanwhile tea had appeared, accompanied by plates of buns, biscuits and toffees, set in a symmetrical row down the centre of a long pine table. Three of the older men – shabbily dressed, with gaunt faces and gentle manners – wanted me to hear their similar stories. Each had sought out Father Grigori as atheists newly aware of 'an empty inner space'; believing friends or relatives had persuaded them that this priest could help. The youth in charge of the samovar felt certain that his schoolmates' prayers had saved his life after a near-lethal shot of contaminated heroin. A thirty-year-old with an ominous facial cancer reckoned that miracles still happened, were not only biblical events. Clearly all these men were gaining hope and strength from their conviction that praying would bring God's help, preferably in the form of a permanent job. Pinned to the wall beside the icons was a list of eight former residents who had relapsed and died and were prayed for every day. The relapse rate, said Father Grigori, was closely linked to a failure to find work. Before leaving, I lit eight candles on the appropriate tray.

Institutional Christianity is not guaranteed to bring out the best in its adherents and many Russian Orthodox, clerical and lay, hate (not too strong a word) the Roman Catholic Church. Yet on first reading Maxim Gorky's *Childhood*, half a century ago, I noted a certain similarity between Russian Orthodoxy and Irish Catholicism. Some of Gorky's peasant characters enjoyed a consoling, comfortable, almost social relationship with God and God's Mother and their favourite saints, a phenomenon familiar to me in childhood. Here in Irkutsk I was again glimpsing that fervent belief which both sustains the misfortunate and resigns them to their fate. When I mentioned this to Father Grigori he smiled faintly and wondered, 'Did Gorky mean you to see it like that?'

On the way out we passed through an office where I observed shelves of those inexpensive Bibles printed by the million when *perestroika* encouraged the hierarchy to call for Russia's reconversion to Christianity. The bishops had Gorbachev's support. Although an unequivocal atheist, he agreed to the celebration in 1988 of one thousand years of Russian Orthodoxy (as controversial a dating as St Patrick's conversion of the Irish in 432 but just as widely accepted). Two years later Gorbachev went further, stating that contemporary communism would do well to absorb some of the philosophical values of the world's great religions – which inspired groups of elated babushkas to pray publicly in Red Square for his health and safety.

Daily at 5.30 Father Grigori collected his three-year-old daughter from her crèche; his medical student wife had an evening job in a supermarket ('to pay for her textbooks') and rarely got home before nine. We drove to the city centre in a large 1964 Soviet-made car which had never yet let Father Grigori down despite being twelve years his senior. En route he revealed his ecumenical aspect, angrily denouncing the recent burning in some town centres of literature distributed locally by foreign Protestant missionaries who, as it happened, were famously open-minded and open-hearted. They had been preaching co-operation on a practical level that appealed to Father Grigori, urging Orthodox, Protestants and Catholics to form teams for helping the sick and the handicapped, isolated old people, homeless orphans and refugee children.

My companion felt less fraternal towards what he described as 'competitive sects', imported self-styled 'Churches' with names like The Living Word, The Light of the Gospel, The New Life, The Spirit of Life, The Cornerstone. 'Such proselityzers, they know nothing of Christianity. Here their anti-heroin centres are only doctrinal brainwashing. And they bribe people to join with promises of free trips to the West.'

Even more troubling to Father Grigori were the open divisions among the Orthodox leadership. Some of the higher clergy – men known to have been KGB informers and/or appointees – have for long been inclined to condemn all Protestants as heretics and order the burning of scholarly tomes by such esteemed 'reformist' Orthodox theologians as Father John Meyendorff and Father Alexander Schmemann. As we stopped outside the crèche Father Grigori declared, 'This is the way to suffocate Holy Russia, not revive her! My generation wants a Mother Church sure enough of herself to allow debate – even encourage it. We want to protect all the old beauty, music, icons, vestments, jewels, buildings. We don't want churches looking like factories full of girls in shorts singing pop songs on Sundays. But we do want new *thinking*...'

Before returning to Raisa's flat – a no smoking area – I relaxed with a *pivo* at my favourite open-air café. The sun was still hot and cheerfully chatting 'after-workers' in summery attire strolled up and down a long plaza, overlooked by dour 1970s office blocks and lined with improvised bars, food stalls and kiosks. A canal-like concrete 'water feature' stretched the length of this plaza with variegated litter floating on its surface and fountains feebly playing. Pigeons and sparrows competed for crumbs beneath café tables. Here were several of those Irkutsk citizens who most disturbed me: my contemporaries, old women at the end of respectable, hardworking lives whose pensions had evaporated in the heat of capitalism. They never begged but scavenged desperately with downcast eyes. Empty beer bottles were especially coveted and watchfully they lingered around the tables, then seized each empty bottle to add to a little collection which, when sold, would enable them to buy a loaf of bread. One babushka paused at the just vacated table beside mine to gather a few crisps left in a saucer and dusted with cigarette ash which she blew off before relishing this treat.

Bruno and I took a trolley-bus to the Waldorf school, a wooden building behind a high picket fence up a rough laneway in an 'undeveloped' district of old Irkutsk. We found four-year-old boys playing in the yard with sand and interestingly shaped tree branches. Nearby, on the verandah, sat one of the teachers, Anna, and three little girls, being creative together with pine cones and sheep's wool. We sat with them for a time and I found the atmosphere pleasingly familiar; here was a benign aspect of globalization. The Waldorf/Steiner ethos is not to everybody's taste but surely small children can only gain from being educated in an uncompetitive atmosphere. And it makes sense to exclude garish plastic, slick computer games and battery-run toys while pupils discover what simple beauty they themselves can create using wood, wool, water, clay, sand, grass, leaves, beeswax, candlelight. When one four-year-old hit another over the head with quite a substantial branch Anna intervened gently but firmly while Bruno wondered if the human young of all races are naturally red in tooth and claw. (I think not: but just now we mustn't digress along that path.) Waldorf schools don't lack discipline; a child's individuality is respected and fostered but self-expression is never encouraged at the expense of others. For this tightrope act teachers need special talents, in addition to the skills acquired at training colleges.

Inside, a large L-shaped room served as classroom, gymnasium, dining-room and kitchen. A team of six-year-olds was competently at work preparing lunch: chopping vegetables, washing lettuces and slicing bread which they had already helped to mix and bake – part of their training for a healthy lifestyle independent of the food industry. Another teacher stood by the stove, frying fish, and – inevitably in Siberia – we were invited to stay for lunch. Equally inevitably, there was a cat on the scene: Leo, a superb long-haired ginger tom, placidly amenable to being carried around. Although carrying him was a privilege, he wasn't quarrelled over but gently passed on to another pair of arms at a slight signal from a teacher.

We sat on child-sized stools around a child-sized table and enjoyed an excellent lunch, followed by tea and jam. For both pupils and teachers it's a long day – 8 a.m. to 6 p.m. – but everyone relaxes after lunch when for an hour the children lie down (or sit up) in an adjacent room equipped with three-tiered bunk-beds. All the furniture had been made by fathers, who also re-roofed and re-floored this building.

When I asked for the loo Anna looked a trifle embarrassed; though odourless and spotless, it was very much part of old Irkutsk. As Bruno and I walked to the trolley-bus stop we scoffed at the West's hygiene paranoia. Said Bruno, 'Americans abroad go sick so much because Americans at home have no way to build up immunities. We don't trust our bodies any more, to handle everyday challenges. We see remote possibilities as immediate threats and dodge even the smallest risk.'

That prompted me to recall a fragment of family history. When my daughter was aged three an American friend, visiting our home in Ireland, went rigid with shock on observing Rachel experimentally eating a scrap left over in the dog's dish. Mary was even more shocked by my reassurance: 'That's fine, she's just building up her immunities for when we travel beyond Europe.' Thirty years later I reminded Mary that throughout several journeys on three continents, eating whatever was put before us, Rachel had never suffered from tummy bugs.

At dawn on 7 September, as I waited for the Golovin family outside the Hotel Angara, a dense silvery mist enshrouded Irkutsk. Sophia

Golovin had interviewed me the day before – she edited a literary magazine – then invited me to spend that Saturday 'at the dacha' some forty miles west of Irkutsk. Small, sturdy and efficient, with cosmopolitan interests, she looked like the mother of her grandchildren – Sasha, a tall, athletic sixteen-year-old, and Lydia, an ebullient but perfectly mannered six-year-old. Her husband Anton, a retired geologist specializing in meteorite craters, was large, gentle and shy. He had retired early when the new Russia lost interest in meteorite craters and forgot to pay his salary for eighteen months.

In Britain and in Siberia 'a cottage in the country' means something very different. The dacha is no refuge from urban pressures, a place to relax after the week's work. However tiring that work, whole families, including small children, must slave in their dacha throughout summer weekends, only taking time off to collect berries and mushrooms in the forest. This self-sufficiency is so important, nowadays, that when observing a city crowd one can guess who must buy all their food and whose family has a dacha.

The Golovins arrived on time in their 1988 Zhiguli which smelt more like a farm wagon than a motor car. The mist lifted as we drove past the dam on a wide tarred road, then followed a narrower road across undulating farmland scarred by collective farm buildings and enormous plastic tunnels. In one large village a handsome old wooden church had survived decades of use as a Soviet barn and plans were being made to restore it.

Seen from the air, in springtime, this region's privileged position is obvious – so said Anton. Within a radius of 200 miles or so of Lake Baikal the thaw comes a little earlier than usual, in mid-May, owing to the lake's storage-heater effect. Hence a comparatively long growing season, until the end of July when night frosts resume. By then all cereals must be harvested and all vegetables gathered by mid-September, at the very latest.

For three centuries, explained Sophia, Siberia's settlers were mainly dependent on food transported slowly and expensively from European Russia. Then in the 1960s Irkutsk plant-breeders, despite minimal investment and encouragement from Moscow, produced fast-maturing varieties of wheat, oats, millet, maize and vegetables. Simultaneously the most fertile and accessible river valleys were being deforested and converted to arable. This revolution made livestock farming possible (cattle, sheep, pigs, poultry) though numbers are limited by the brevity of the grazing season.

Suddenly Lydia began to bounce up and down, her face glowing. We had topped a rise and ahead lay a wide green valley, between low forested ridges. Lydia turned to me, pointing towards the distant dacha – a mere dot beyond a score of farmhouses with long gardens running up the lower slopes of their sheltering ridge. This was a 'natural' hamlet, not a horrid concrete leftover from collectivization. Soon we were bumping along a dusty track, the 'main street', which ended at the Golovins' dacha, built three years previously by Anton and his two sons, its half-hectare enclosed by a high picket fence. Under this five-roomed, tin-roofed house – sparsely furnished but cosy, its long enclosed porch forming a sixth room – enough firewood was stacked to keep three stoves going throughout the winter. A generator provided electricity and raised water from the fifty-foot-deep well.

At once the grandchildren and I were despatched to fetch milk from a neighbouring widow who lived with her unmarried grown-up son (he looked like a vodka victim), their two cows and a loudly ferocious Alsatian guard-dog, tethered near the gate. I had by then realized that the Siberians' devotion to their domestic animals does not extend to guard-dogs who must endure a loveless life, forever chained, feared by all but their owners.

This prosperous homestead had delicate fretwork around the windows, freshly painted blue and white. An imposing twelve-foot cedarwood double gateway (its intricate herringbone design must have whiled away many a winter's evening) was surmounted by a carved birchwood arch. In the neat yard, tall potted plants flourished on the sunny side. Opposite the gateway were stables and a cow-shed and in the dairy to the right Mrs Gavrilovna made soft cheese and butter for local consumption. Both the *banya* hut and the earth closet were beyond the outbuildings, in the back garden, surrounded by potatoes and cabbages.

Mrs Gavrilovna asked if the foreign babushka would like to see a *kulak* home, then led me through the kitchen-living-room with its big tiled stove and small electric cooker, through the parlour with its nylon-covered sofa and cabinet of cut glass, through two bedrooms with icon shrines and miniature candle trays in wall recesses. All the pine floors were highly polished, all the walls and low ceilings painted dazzling white. Viewing them from outside, one imagines such *izby* to be cramped and rather gloomy; in fact many are quite spacious and bright, each room having two or three comparatively large windows and colourful (not to say gaudy) floor rugs and tapestry wall-hangings. Siberian windows were double and triple-glazed long before ours and every room has one window with a hinged pane eight inches square, to be occasionally opened in winter for brief periods. These panes are essential; from November onwards, insulation sealing renders the main windows unopenable.

It is impossible to escape unfed from any Siberian home and while her son filled our milk bottles Mrs Gavrilovna sat us down to hot homemade bread, fried mushrooms and salted omul, accompanied by a refreshingly tangy juice made from those sour forest berries.

Back at the dacha, work was in progress. Siberian hospitality is agreeably informal, strangers being absorbed into a family circle without ceremony, and no polite protests were made when I joined Sophia in one of two hellishly hot plastic huts, not tunnels but huge oblong structures. There a prodigious crop of tomatoes of every conceivable variety had ripened within the past week, red, yellow and green, very big and very small, round and long, smooth and ridged. Within minutes my clothes were sweat-soaked and I looked forward to each walk to and from the house where a glossy mountain was growing in one room. Meanwhile Lydia was diligently picking runner beans in the open air, within chatting distance of Anton and Sasha as they dug potatoes, making their own earthy mountain in another room.

Before lunch we washed our hands under an ingenious contraption, an upside-down jerry-can hanging at a convenient height from a pole surmounted by a little tin roof. When a nail was pressed upwards, water trickled out. I had expected a picnic lunch but the fast-working Sophia produced crisp potatoes fried in bacon fat, a tomato and cucumber salad made fascinating by unfamiliar herbs and braised Bush's legs. Sasha could scarcely conceal his joy when I passed my leg on to him. Presumably the Russians know nought of the sinister mix of chemicals injected into these tortured birds. For dessert

we had gigantic slices of water melon, syrupy sweet, delicately flavoured, copiously juicy, imported by rail from the Caucasus. 'It looks
crazy,' said Sophia, 'sending cargo so bulky thousands of miles to sell
it so cheaply. But the growers have a big surplus, rotting on the
ground.'

Leaving Sophia to wash up (her choice), the rest of us drove off
to the forest to uproot, with great effort, a young juniper bush. For
this expedition Anton and Sasha, who had been wearing only shorts
all morning, felt it necessary, despite the midday heat, to don slacks
and shirts. In some respects the Siberians are curiously prim and
proper.

Our search took us deep into the taiga, here not as dense as it
looked from afar and already touched by the first tints of autumn:
crimson and gold. Underfoot was a wealth of mosses, lichens and
small creeping plants which, when they flower in springtime, make
the forest floor – said Anton – look like an artist's palette. He and Sasha
were carefully comparing several possibilities before choosing their
juniper. As they began to dig, I wandered on alone and came to an
open slope, deforested generations ago and now covered with dog-
roses and crowberries. From the top I could see, far below, wide fields
in which teams of men, women and children were harvesting potatoes for transport to Irkutsk in every sort of vehicle, including an off-
duty No.16 minibus.

Back at the juniper, I found a sad Lydia, verging on tears. Anton
translated: she felt the struggle involved in uprooting this bush meant
it didn't want to leave the forest. I marked her then as a promising candidate for Irkutsk's small but vigorous environmental movement. To
console her, she was allowed to choose the exact spot for the juniper's
new home. We drove back slowly, the bush balanced precariously on
the roof, and saw the hamlet again in action after its lunchtime lull.
'This is the eleventh hour,' remarked Anton. 'Our climate gives us
drama.' Yes indeed – on 7 September the noon sun was too much
for me yet within a week or less night frosts would kill anything not
harvested.

While replanting proceeded, Sophia and I pulled mega-carrots, up
to two feet long and flawless. Siberia's temperatures discourage those
bugs which plague more benign climes and potato blight is unknown.

However, the cabbages – six and seven feet in circumference – are regularly ravaged by pigeons. Like all the dacha gardeners I met, Anton boasted, 'Everything is organic, no chemicals here!' The almost black soil was powder-fine, a sensuous treat for bare feet as I spent the rest of the afternoon collecting carrots, beans and onions.

At 5.30 Sophia summoned us to tea with bliny. (Siberian pancakes are like no others: food for the gods.) Then Lydia went on strike – enough of picking and shelling beans, she wanted to show Dervla the river. So off we went, past the loo hut in its far corner, through a wicket gate in the fence, on to pastureland where a narrow shallow river meandered quietly. For an hour we sauntered across fields that might have been in Ireland; even the coarse steppe grass, growing in hummocks, closely resembled bog grass. An enormous flock of un-aggressive geese lumbered away in noisy terror when pursued by Lydia. A herd of black and white horned cows, with normal udders, was being rounded up for milking by a small boy on a chestnut gelding – a communal herd, Anton later explained. No one in the hamlet owned more than two cows. Despite the language barrier that was a companionable interlude, Lydia and I enjoying together, in our differ-ent ways, the evening's tranquillity. As we sat for a little time on a single-plank 'bridge', dangling our legs in the cool river, I watched through my binoculars hand-won hay being stored in a high wooden barn.

Post-harvest, families must work day and night to pickle and pre-serve their perishables. On our journey home I learned that men take a particular pride in pickling mushrooms, salting them down with garlic, herbs, spices and vinegar. 'But,' said Sophia, 'vinegar kills vita-mins so we don't use it with cabbage or beetroot. I chop the cabbage and salt it down and all winter we have it in soup or as a salad with sunflower oil. The tomatoes take most time, for a month after bot-tling them I don't want to see a tomato ever again!'

'We should change our school dates,' said Anton. 'Families need all hands in the kitchen in September.'

But for the weather forecast, we would have been spending that night at the dacha and tidying up and fertilizing next day, to leave the ground ready for instant action when the thaw came. 'It's important,' said Sophia, 'to waste no hour of growing time.'

Back on the main road, the sunset traffic consisted mainly of bat-tered Soviet-era lorries piled high with potatoes, their exhausted pickers sprawling on the sacks. Lydia amused herself by counting them – a total of twenty-three in ten miles.

I awoke to hear heavy rain pattering on the maple trees outside my window and their branches creaking in the wind. Raisa was discon-solate; she had been looking forward to a day's sailing on Lake Baikal. I, too, was disconsolate; all that enjoyable dacha activity had not suited The Knee. Raisa proposed that we should cheer ourselves up by visiting Irkutsk's Art Museum, just around the corner on *ulitsa* Lenina, and we walked there at noon, sharing an umbrella, our breaths visible. The museum's third-rate collection of Chinese por-celain, nineteenth-century Russian painting and 'native' art is uncheering but a dozen genuinely ancient Tibetan *t'ankas* justify the 70 rouble ticket.

A minibus took me across the Angara to Irkutsk's station, con-ceived as one of the glories of the Trans-Siberian Railway. Its vast-ness is truly Siberian, its proportions are perfect, it had recently been restored and repainted but was three-quarters non-functioning. I wandered bemused through a series of empty vaulted halls, all gilt and marble with magnificently carved cedarwood doors. Then, back on the street, I identified the functioning one-quarter beyond a closed restaurant resembling (I peered through windows) a czarist banqueting hall. Fifty minutes later I had secured my *platskartny* ticket for Ust'-kut, departure 10.50 on the following evening.

Apart from ticket-buyers, the station was almost deserted. Outside, an empty Trans-Siberian, due to depart for Moscow at 6 p.m., stood locked by the mile-long main platform. It looked much posher than the BAM, its two restaurant cars lavishly decorated with fresh flowers, its gleaming coaches tastefully two-toned – pink/blue, green/yellow, blue/white, fawn/pink. At the platform's end I paused to watch its engine being attached – a three-man job – and marvelled in my non-mechanical way at the relative smallness of the hitching device. Then, looking up and down the track, towards Moscow and Vladivostok, I saluted the sheer efficiency of this most famous of railways. So many thousands of miles of intricate electric cables, so many millions of minute connections that could go wrong, all perfectly maintained throughout all seasons in a supposedly collapsed country. Could it be that that judgement is too facile?

My last day in Irkutsk presented a feline crisis – physically minuscule, emotionally large. It was a chilly damp morning and in the middle of *ulitsa* Lenina, with traffic zooming to and fro, crouched a grey and white kitten, its fur drenched, its eyes closed, stiff with cold, much too young to have voluntarily strayed so it must have been dumped. When picked up and stroked, he didn't react. Putting him inside my shirt, where he felt like a wet sponge, I hastened back to the flat, glad that the house-proud and hygiene-conscious Raisa had gone to work. The waif seemed unweaned, didn't know what to do with a saucer of warm milk, sat immobile beside it, eyes now half-open – and I noticed that they were infected. I considered the grim Angara option and wondered why my karma includes so many of these harrowing duties. (In Bosnia I had to drown a week-old litter of starving motherless pups.) However, I was expected within half an hour at a tourism development conference, where a group of local Greens were anxious for me to reinforce their arguments. Having dried the waif, I dressed him in a woollen sock and added him to the contents of my carrier-bag. He weighed only a few ounces and I forgot about him on my way to the trolley-bus stop, preoccupied as I was by tourism's threat to the Baikal Basin.

Eight hours later the sun was shining as I took a minibus to Studgorodok; Bruno had organized a seven o'clock farewell supper party. At a shop near his block I bought a fishy contribution to our meal and left my carrier-bag on the floor while paying. Then came a startled exclamation from the customer behind me. Out of the bag had hopped a fluffy, red-eyed kitten, mewing eagerly as he looked in the general direction of fish. He had simply needed time to thaw. Exulting, I picked him up, sat with him in the sun on a nearby coping and fed him tiny shreds of omul. He ate from my fingers, so ravenously that his needle-like teeth penetrated even my tough skin. If he hadn't been weaned before, he was now. When replete he looked up at me, closed his eyes in a happy way and purred – that ridiculously loud kitten purr which seems so disproportionate to the size of its source. I was almost at the entrance to Bruno's flat when I realized that the omul, having been torn *by* my fingers to feed an infected kitten *with* my fingers, had lost its gift status. I ate it myself, on the train to Ust'-Kut.

Fifteen minutes later Bruno's children had been charmed by the former waif and were busy warming milk and organizing a draught-free bed. End of story.

# 6

## In Search of the *Blagoveshchensk*

In Irkutsk's crowded railway station waiting room I wrote:

*10.15 p.m. 9 Sept.* My journey has become a Mystery Tour of Siberia, played by leg rather than by ear. Where will I be this time next week? Possibly on the steamer approaching Yakutsk. Or a *raketa* may have taken me to some little intermediate riverside town. Here everyone looked blank when I enquired about the downstream service from Ust'-Kut. No one knows when it sails, or if it's likely to have space for an unbooked passenger – or if it's still sailing, so late in the season. But this dearth of tourist info is a small price to pay for Intourist's demise. I've just noticed that our Ust'-Kut train is described as 'local', the journey lasting a mere twenty-five hours.

My *platskartny* was enlivened by fourteen happy ten-year-old boys who had been representing their Bratsk school in a folk-dancing competition and were proudly wearing First Prize rosettes. In cosmopolitan Irkutsk they had expanded their English vocabulary but seemed unaware of the new word's grammatical limitations. Four of them sat in a row on the upper bunk opposite mine, swinging their legs vigorously and gleefully chanting 'Fuck, fucker, fuckest! Fuck, fucker, fuckest!' Their minders, three stern young women teachers, unbothered by notions about 'children's rights', ignored the chanting but stopped the leg-swinging. They were cheerfully obeyed; one sensed affection beneath the sternness. And around midnight, when the boy in the bunk below mine developed a tear-inducing toothache, he was gently mothered until the painkiller, provided by me, took effect.

According to two of my contemporary friends in Severobaikalsk, the Soviets' anti-swearing legislation was more effective than the czars'. But now the Federation's youth is regressing towards the 'many vile and loathsome words' that so offended Adam Olearius in the

1630s. As a member of the Duke of Holstein's embassy to Muscovy, Olearius made four journeys among the Russians and reported, in what became an international bestseller:

> Little children who do not know the name of God have on their lips 'fuck you', and say it as well to their parents as their parents to them. Recently this foul and shameful swearing was strictly forbidden upon pain of knouting. Certain secretly appointed people were sent to mix with the crowd and with the help of streltsi [the Czar's bodyguard] and executioners were to seize swearers and punish them on the spot by beating but they soon gave it up as a bad job.

Olearius normally resided in the ivory tower of Leipzig's Faculty of Philosophy and was one of those travellers (they are still with us) who derive a complacent satisfaction from listing the 'barbarities' encountered abroad.

> After a meal, Russians do not refrain, in the hearing of all, from releasing what nature produces, fore and aft. Since they eat a great deal of garlic and onion it is rather trying to be in their company. Perhaps against their will these good people fart and belch noisily ... So given are they to the lusts of the flesh that some are addicted to the vile depravity of sodomy not only with boys but also with men and horses. People caught in such obscene acts are not severely punished. Tavern musicians often sing of such loathsome things, while some show them to young people in puppet shows.

Olearius also observed that the peasants were confined to Russian territory 'so that they might stay tranquil in slavery and not see the free institutions that exist in foreign lands'. However, his last embassy to Moscow in 1643, bearing special greetings to the Czar Mikhail Fedorovich, cheered him up.

> The present Grand Prince is a very pious ruler who, like his father, does not want a single one of the peasants to be impoverished ... And if someone is sent in disgrace to Siberia, even this disfavour is mitigated by providing the exile with a tolerable livelihood. Magnates are given money, scribes positions in the chancelleries of Siberian cities, soldiers given places as soldiers ... Moreover there have been instances when such disgrace worked a great advantage, namely when the exiles' professions or trades were more fruitfully pursued than in Moscow.

At sunrise no sun was visible and light rain fell from low clouds. While breakfasting I gazed out at sparsely forested flat land, then came rolling steppe where thin cows and fat goats grazed together. Here were many more villages than along the BAM line, most founded as the Trans-Siberian was being built and all looking poverty-stricken. On my 'dacha day' I had realized that cycling through Siberia's cultivated regions would be quite a harrowing experience. The Golovin hamlet was an oasis of modest prosperity in a desert of dereliction, a fragment unnoticed when Khrushchev, in the early 1960s, was attempting to create 'agrotowns' by obliterating traditional villages and forcibly merging their populations. (Many then fled, illicitly, to the cities, leaving the *kolkhoz* undermanned.) The Soviets' unwavering determination to replace agriculture with agribusiness, never mind the cost in human suffering and lowered productivity, has left rural Russia grievously wounded, not only environmentally but psychologically – a point made by Raisa Gorbacheva in her much praised though not widely read dissertation, *The Way of Life of the Collective Farm Peasantry: A Sociological Study*.

From Day One (1917) a fantasy obsessed the Soviet planners. Discarding reality, they insisted that the Soviet Union was destined to be a thriving heavily industrialized country mainly inhabited by city dwellers rejoicing to have shaken the soil of Mother Russia off their boots. Yet the urban population remained in a minority until 1957 and in 2000 38 per cent of Russians were still country dwellers and 15 per cent of employed adults worked in agriculture.

The collectivization-induced (or aggravated) famines of the 1930s, in which millions died, affected Siberia much less than Kazakhstan, the Ukraine and southern Russia. But the territory's more accessible western regions felt the full impact of Moscow's insane annual quota system which demanded a fixed amount of grain, meat and vegetables from each *kolkhoz*, to feed the townsfolk – leaving the peasants hungrier than even their serf ancestors. It seems the Kremlin never forgot that the 1917 February Revolution had an urban food shortage as one of its mainsprings. Then, in the middle of a World War, the peasants, feeling cheated of a fair price, simply refused to bring their crops to market.

Unsurprisingly, for farmers the first post-Soviet decade has brought about only hesitant changes and minor improvements, the latter too often outweighed by a general worsening of living conditions throughout the Federation. Agricultural production and distribution are no longer state-controlled and state subsidies for machinery, fertilizers and fuel have been drastically reduced or abolished. Peasants are free to sell their produce wherever they choose, but the farm labourer earns less than a third of the factory worker's wage (itself inadequate). Most of the 'denationalized' collectives have remained intact and been relabelled agricultural co-ops but usually these are managed by the corrupt chairman who always ran them – or, nowadays, by his nepotic successor. Yeltsin wanted to see the co-ops replaced by small independent family farms and the province of Nizhny Novgorod became a laboratory for this experiment. More than 250,000 homesteads had been set up by 1996 but when subsidies ended so did the enthusiasm for family farms. Very few could afford even minimal inputs and already it was known that the pilot projects had been, thus far, unprofitable. Knowledge and skills soon wither when not passed from generation to generation. Moreover, there was orchestrated opposition, from local government officials, to the break-up of co-ops in which many officials or their cronies had long been lucratively interested. A new network of bureaucratic tripwires was quickly invented to discourage would-be family farmers. Without ever admitting defeat, Yeltsin averted his eyes from the countryside and talked of other problems.

Our first halt was at the big logging town (or little city) of Zima, its stolidly handsome railway station newly painted white and umber. Beside the track, over a couple of miles on either side of the long platform, thousands of numbered pine trunks were stacked high – a melancholy sight, for these had been towering monarchs of the taiga. This was a brief halt, during which three men from my *platskartny* hurried to the station entrance where stood a battered farm lorry. Few words were spoken as they exchanged synthetic blankets, imported from China and wrapped in sellophane, for large sacks of potatoes.

Soon after we were in the cloud-blurred, uninhabited, roadless foothills of the Western Sayan mountains – gentle hills, clothed in a seamless garment of forest. For hours on end we saw only larches, spruces, pines and silver-firs, almost within touching distance on both sides. Here was the longest stretch of taiga I had yet traversed, at least in daylight, and its extent and uniformity had a soothingly hypnotic effect. But also I felt very conscious of the Trans-Siberian as still an intruder. The Western Sayan are not really uninhabited although passengers rarely glimpse their population of marten, ermine, squirrel, chipmunk, weasel, kolinsky, otters, foxes, wolves and bears. Some of these species are seasonal migrants, moving south in autumn from the open tundra to the sheltering taiga. Twice we passed clusters of kennel-like wooden shelters – railway workers' camps – and the orange-jacketed teams stood back from their track-checking and waved at us. Momentarily I envied them their opportunities to observe the above-mentioned species in which they doubtless take an interest not confined to observation.

When we pulled into Taishet at 10 a.m. most passengers bought food from platform hawkers while other hawkers came aboard. Two comely young Tajik women, their smiles revealing an astonishing investment in gold, displayed for my benefit Kashmir-soft pale grey shawls and scarves of the sort described by Chekhov and Turgenev. Then suddenly the schoolboys were jostling around both young women, jeering and grimacing, grabbing at the shawls. At once the golden smiles vanished and the Tajiks, seeming scared, retreated to the platform. I glanced towards the teachers, expecting sharp reprimands, but they were looking the other way.

East of Taishet the clouds lifted and tried to break and when occasional gleams of sunlight touched the taiga its autumn tints flickered gloriously – but soon dimmed.

Four hours later, around Bratsk, there were no autumn tints, only dead trees witnessing to the terrible toll demanded of Nature by Soviet industrialization, its irrationality nowhere more evident than in this region. A hilly region, unusually fertile, it became in the mid-seventeenth century a base for the pioneer colonizers of Eastern Siberia and the Russian Far East, centred on a crudely fortified settlement with a transient population of trappers, traders and explorers. (This, you will remember, was a target for Buryat warriors.)

Modern Bratsk was officially founded on 21 December 1954. The temperature was minus 52°C when the first work-gang arrived, the vanguard of those 54,000 'heroes' (mainly Komsomol-chosen) who spent the next thirteen years damming the Angara and building this infamous industrial complex. The pioneers pitched their tents near the Padun Rapids, generally regarded as impassable, which then raced between 300-foot cliffs through a gorge 500 yards wide. In preparation for dam-building, virgin taiga had to be violated, gigantic quarries blasted into existence, roads gouged out when the thaw came, an airstrip laid, power transmission lines brought from Irkutsk, a communications network set up. Soon one of Siberia's most dramatically beautiful landscapes had been degraded for ever.

The Bratsk High Dam is of course dramatic in its own way, the most ambitious of the many mad schemes ill-conceived in Moscow to prove the Soviet Union's technological potency. Everything in Bratsk is 'Russia's largest', if not 'the world's largest' – the dam itself, the reservoir (2,112 square miles), the aluminium smelter, the cellulose factory, the fertilizer factory, the timber industry complex covering 278 hectares and so on and on. Yet the Soviet planners, always disastrously obsessed by BIGNESS and arrogantly confident that everywhere Nature could be made to serve their purposes, were in fact humiliated by what became the Bratsk débacle. A misjudgement of the reservoir's filling speed meant that 70,000 peasants from 249 villages had to be evacuated long before Bratsk's apartment blocks were habitable. The rapidly rising water drowned immense forests of valuable mature larches which should have been felled. The region's food production was reduced by 75 per cent when most of the fertile land disappeared. And then the dam generated far more energy than could possibly be used in remote Bratsk. According to The Plan, all those designed-to-be-record-breaking industries would need all that electricity. Not so, however. The industries, being themselves impracticably big and complicated, failed to operate consistently or consume energy at the planned rate, and the Bratsk High Dam has never been required to generate more than half the electricity it could produce.

Laurens van der Post visited the dam while it was being built and wrote:

> ...we turned due north and left the new world and railway quickly
> behind ... It seemed less and less credible that we could be on the way
> to what the Russians say is the world's greatest hydro-electric project.
> Other doubts too assailed a lay mind like mine. Could it be wise and

indeed economical to create so great a source of power in such empty
land, so far from the main centres of demand and supply? All I knew
was that some thousands of Russian scientists at a great conference in
Irkutsk had decided that it was ... Sixty-nine different nationalities
from all over the Soviet Union worked on the scheme: the Chief
Engineer was a Jew, his deputy a Tatar. They said emphatically that the
only sorts of workers they did not have at Bratsk were 'slave workers'
... It seemed incredible to me that these two men did not know that
until very recently Siberia was full of concentration and forced labour
camps ... one of the biggest situated not far from Bratsk at Taishet.

(*Journey Into Russia*, Hogarth Press, 1964)

From afar the toxic haze is visible above Bratsk – not really a city
but a string of hilltop settlements, some twenty-five miles long, semi-
encircling the northern shore of what is locally known as 'the Bratsk
Sea'. Here dwell 280,000 unfortunates in serried ranks of high risery
interspersed with smokestacks even now uncontrolled. The most
lethal fumes come from the fertilizer factory; frequently it malfunc-
tions, releasing clouds of nitrogen gas. To deal with this the municipality has installed on the streets loudspeakers through which citizens
are warned to 'Stay indoors!' Yet the army chose to build four health
sanatoria for its personnel on the reservoir's shore, confirming the
Soviets' 'in denial' attitude to environmental danger.

At Padunskie Porogi, Bratsk's main station, each prize-winning
schoolboy was greeted by proud parents and relatives bearing huge
celebratory bouquets. The dancers were replaced by two elderly
couples, several Buryat women traders and a quartet of Yakut miners
on their way back to the diamond-mining town of Mirny in western
Sakha. The couples soon fell asleep, the Buryats got out their knitting
and crossword puzzles, the miners settled down to their novels –
science fiction, judging by the covers. Then Ludmilla arrived, breathless and dragging a sackful of something too heavy to be carried. She
was aged forty, of Ukrainian parentage, with very short blonde hair,
pale blue eyes behind thick spectacles, not a word of English and an
impulsively generous nature. Soon she had decisively adopted me, dis-
missing mention of Ust'-Kut's hotel with a gesture of disdain. I must
be her guest, she would help me to find out when/if the steamer
departed and where to buy my ticket.

The BAM crosses the dam, a 400-foot high wall of concrete half a mile wide and two and a half miles long. Beneath the railway is a motor road, invisible to train passengers. 'The Bratsk Sea' seems an apt name for this apparently illimitable expanse of water at which everyone around me gazed with a sort of reverence. Then they looked towards the foreigner, expectantly smiling, awaiting expressions of amazement and admiration. I didn't disappoint them. At that moment I could only feel amazement and admiration. The construction of the Bratsk High Dam was achieved despite unimaginable (to us) climatic handicaps in winter and in defiance of the world's most tormenting insects in summer.

Near Ust'-Kut the 2,750-mile Lena is joined by the 255-mile Kuta and at their confluence, in 1631, Yerofei Khabarov founded a fortified settlement. (Few of the men who took possession of Siberia for the czars were kindly but Khabarov's extreme cruelty puts him in the Stalin category.) Soon this settlement had expanded into a trading port which for 250 years supplied most of Eastern Siberia with food and equipment. Officially designated a town in 1954, it is now an agglomeration of several settlements and oversized inefficient industries (population 70,000).

At midnight Ust'-Kut was very dark, very wet and rather cold. By then Ludmilla had discovered that one of the elderly couples (not people she knew) lived on the edge of her district – so they mustn't take a taxi, there would be room for them in the car. As their numerous pieces of luggage wouldn't fit in the small boot Ivan, Ludmilla's husband, had to brave drenching rain while roping everything to the roof-rack. This however seemed to be taken for granted; it was an obvious thing to do, by way of sparing pensioners the considerable taxi expense. Ust'-Kut is all over the place and that was a ten-mile drive, into a hilly area where the tarred road was replaced by a maze of muddy tracks.

In the Tarkovskys' single-storey wooden home we were enthusiastically greeted by two handsome cats, one a long-haired black with lamp-like orange eyes, the other a symmetrical Siamese/tabby cross: cream body, chocolate head, tabby legs and tail. At once I displayed my flea-bag and pointed to the sofa in the living-room. But no, moments later a sleep-dazed fourteen-year-old daughter came stumbling from her room. *Maya* must sleep on the sofa, *I* must sleep in a bed. I didn't argue; Siberian hospitality is implacable. Then I was shown the big loo-bucket in the porch, for everyone's nocturnal use because the earth-closet in the garden was so far away. The cats flattered me by choosing to remain on Maya's bed. They purred and kneaded and as I drifted into sleep I thought, 'In Siberia even the cats are welcoming.'

At dawn I woke to see three teddies, a velvet monkey, a knitted tiger and two china dogs balanced on a wardrobe top. Shelves packed with picture-books, children's poetry anthologies and textbooks were flanked by samples of artwork and school photographs, Maya's position indicated by a red ink arrow. On the desk were a homework file, crayons, a geometry set, a neat circle of multicoloured Lake Baikal stones, a fascinating collection of old coins and a stick of chewing-gum.

Opening the curtains, I saw a sodden mist-veiled world. Despite her late night, Ludmilla was already up, pickling cucumbers and bottling tomatoes. The Tarkovskys' four-roomed house (plus a porch-cum-store bigger than any of the rooms) had been built in 1995 by Ivan, with the help of Ludmilla's father, and two of his nephews. Although solid enough, it showed signs of having been put together by men too 'industrialized' to be at ease working with wood. This district was without running water, buckets were carried from a communal well.

Father and daughter disappeared at 7.15; Ivan would drop Maya at her school gates before going on to his furniture factory job, as quality control supervisor. Ludmilla had varnished chairs in the same factory until 1992 when suddenly half the workers were dismissed. Since then she had been a self-employed market gardener. All this was conveyed in sign language with the aid of pencil and paper (for numbers) and that hardworked mini-dictionary. Ludmilla reinforced my impression that many Russian women are both more dynamic and better organized than their menfolk. As we breakfasted (eggs fried in the middle of a slice of bread) she outlined our programme for the day. First, to the Osetrovo River Passenger Station to, if possible, book my ticket. Second, to her semi-invalid mother who lived alone and needed daily assistance. (Her father had died in 1996, aged fifty-six; a startling number of Russians, especially men, die in middle age.) Third, go home, cook a meal, show me round the garden. Fourth, visit the Tarkovskys' good friend Tamara Revtova who very much liked meeting foreigners.

We walked downhill through light rain to the minibus stop, crossing the BAM line en route, and I saw that this was a semi-rural suburb of *izby* in large gardens and a few new red brick two-storey homes, known as *kottedzhi*. It's where I'd choose to live, if stranded in Ust'-Kut; most of the town's twenty-five-mile-long agglomeration is visually charmless. Yet people look surprisingly cheerful for all the evidence of decline: street surfaces and pavements broken, spacious public parks weedy and unpruned, minibuses that seem to have been exhumed from some motor cemetery, hospital and school façades neglected. An exception is the Osetrovo station on the Lena, an imposing pre-Revolution building, recalling the era when Ust'-Kut's importance as a port fostered affluence – even a touch of opulence. Recently repainted (Jersey-cream yellow and sea-green) it stood in solitary grandeur and was apparently empty.

Our voices echoed in a bare, barn-like space, one wall lined with shuttered kiosks. Several doors led out of it but only one was unlocked. Venturing in, we climbed a flight of steep narrow stairs, wandered down a few dusty silent corridors, then saw an open door and an elderly man hunched over a desk, fumbling through files. Grumpily he disclaimed any knowledge of the steamers' movements or of the ticket office's location.

Behind Osetrovo, I had my first sight of the Lena – olive green under a low grey sky, here in its youth yet already a quarter of a mile wide and powerful. Only two men were visible on the high embankment, pensioners exercising their dogs. No, they couldn't help; nor could we find any informative notice-boards around the landing-stage. Ludmilla was beginning to look worried on my behalf: perhaps the sailing season was over? Then some cheering thought occurred to her but couldn't be shared with me: this wasn't the moment for slow-motion dictionary communication. Next stop – her mother's flat in an area of ten-storey blocks, their bleakness softened by lofty plane trees, some branches touching balcony railings. During that half-hour walk we passed five schools with gables and/or façades covered in comical, well-executed murals appropriate to the age of the pupils – but now the bright colours were fading.

Mother was a memorable character: small, fat and jolly with strangely flecked eyes (blue-green-grey) and a carefully tended (by Ludmilla) chestnut chignon. Although handicapped by arms that ended at the elbow, where each hand had only two fingers, she was a prolific weaver of exquisite, intricate tapestries, an art acquired in the 1950s when she attended a special school for the disabled. Her flat was comfortably furnished, with overcrowded bookshelves covering half the sitting-room walls.

Ludmilla at once rang Tamara, a businesswoman who regularly shipped goods to Yakutsk. The terms 'businesswoman' or 'business-man' have gained common usage among non-English speakers and are often uttered in tones of mingled puzzlement and envy. Putting the phone down, Ludmilla clapped her hands – Tamara would appear later on and solve all my problems. Then, at 11.15 a.m., a bottle of brandy was produced to accompany the Siberian notion of elevenses: salami, cheese, tomato and cucumber salad, homemade bread. I had long since accepted that slimming cannot be part of one's Siberian experience; a foreigner who declined to partake would be seen as ill-mannered.

When we went shopping for Mother I acquired a bag of goodies to be left in the Tarkovskys' fridge. Then Ludmilla shopped for herself; she needed new curtains. My attempt to pay for the material gave umbrage and in retrospect this *faux pas* made me squirm. I had failed to take my cue from Ludmilla's insistence on paying her guest's minibus fares though by my standards it should have been the other way around.

We returned home in a packed minibus with alarmingly loose seats; the fittings that should have attached them to the floor were missing. By then the forenoon's chilly gloom had given way to hot sun and beyond our suburb I could see a forested conical mountain rising above many lower taiga ridges.

The Tarkovskys' half-hectare garden sloped gradually down to a hidden stream and its fence was low, a sign that hereabouts neighbours are trusted. Ludmilla urged me to photograph the two enormous hot-houses, the wired hen-run in one corner (the hens lived under the dwelling during winter), rows of raspberry canes and currant bushes, three beehives, scores of cabbages soon to be picked, banks of shoulder-high asters and chrysanthemums flaring festively amidst the autumn dullness. We were ten yards from the nearest hive when I was stung on the left cheek, a pre-emptive strike by a solitary bee. If the old wives' tale is true, and the degree of pain is related to the bee's emotional state, this bee was frenziedly enraged – perhaps felt threatened by my foreign smell. The immediate agony was extreme and my heart seemed to miss a beat before racing so fast that momentarily I felt dizzy. By the time we got back to the house my cheek and lips were so swollen that I had to explain what had happened – which, predictably, gave Ludmilla guilt. Quickly she fetched from a herbal medicine cupboard some ancient shaman's remedy and smeared thick, red-brown liquid all over the affected area. Instantly it relieved the throbbing though for eight days my cheek remained swollen and tender to touch. But then, Russian bees have a long-established reputation for ferocity. Olearius, on his first journey to Moscow, passed through one village where

> the horses began to wince, stand upon their hinder feet and beat the ground as if they had been bewitched, whereof we could not imagine what should be the cause till that, having alighted, we found them covered all over with bees, which were beginning to fall upon us and prosecuted their animosity so far as to force us to keep them off with our cloaks and to go and take up our quarters in the fields. We understood since that it was a stratagem of the inhabitants, who had incensed the bees purposely to prevent our lodging in the village.

Many of the villages on Olearius' route had recently been pillaged by abruptly disbanded Scottish and English mercenaries: hence, perhaps, the inhabitants' xenophobic mood.

I found Maya doing her homework with one cat on her lap and the other sitting tidily tucked up on a corner of the desk. Eagerly she opened her atlas, already marked at the 'Ireland' page, and asked to be shown my home town which, rather surprisingly given its size, was plain to be seen. She then read out other place names, pronouncing them perfectly when the English spelling was phonetic (Cork, Clonmel, Limerick) but being defeated by Armagh, Youghal, Portlaoise. She claimed to speak no English but when coaxed proved well able to read fluently from an unfamiliar text. Before I had time to test her comprehension Ludmilla called her: water was needed from the well.

Ludmilla served a late lunch in the kitchen where special stools were provided for the cats. Throughout the meal they sat upright, never laying a paw on the table, politely awaiting the titbits passed to them by mother and daughter. Ivan didn't reappear until much later; his devalued wages compelled him to do a second, more menial job six evenings a week.

As Tamara the businesswoman knew no English the dictionary became pivotal when she arrived to organize my onward travel. A brisk, plump little woman, with rosy cheeks and large dark eyes, she had gone to considerable trouble, during the day, on my behalf. I was lucky, the *Blagoveshchensk* would be sailing next morning at an hour to be decided by the captain. Moreover, as he and Tamara were friends she had arranged for me to take up residence in my cabin that evening. This plan displeased Ludmilla and Maya, who urged me to stay another night, but Tamara insisted that it made sense, given an uncertain departure time. Nikita, her husband, would drive us all to the port towards sundown. Nikita was large and laid-back, a man of few words but many chuckles. Recently he had retired early from an ill-paid clerical job to become his successful wife's driver.

A check cloth had been spread on the living-room table and now another meal appeared – salami, two sorts of dried fish, cheese, peanuts, cucumber, tomatoes, sweet biscuits, toffees, wild strawberries, the usual tower of thickly cut bread, a two-litre bottle of *pivo* and milk for Nikita because he was driving. Two hours earlier I had enjoyed potatoes creamed with lots of butter, tender braised beef liver and a bean salad. But I *must* try the fish – and the salami because Ivan's mother had made it – and only in Siberia could I eat such strawberries ...

That morning I had spent an hour entranced by one of Maya's books, a collection of hundreds of photographs of Lake Baikal with bilingual captions. As we all gathered on the verandah for a farewell photograph, Maya presented me with this volume, lovingly inscribed to 'the Irish babushka'. A 1986 Moscow publication, it was probably irreplaceable and certainly, in the new Russia, unaffordable. Ludmilla nodded approvingly at her daughter. I almost wept.

En route to the port we visited the Revtovs' spacious four-roomed flat in a new five-storey block opposite the conical hill. They had only recently taken possession and in spirit this seemed very much *Tamara's* home. When Nikita and I were left alone in the sitting-room he glanced around with a quizzical expression, then looked at me almost conspiratorially and grinned and shrugged. The contrast to the comfortable but all-on-a-shoestring Tarkovsky home could not have been greater. Here were obese purple and yellow armchairs (the yellow bits forked lightning), an ankle-deep carpet of singular flamboyance, embossed wallpaper depicting scarlet dragons against a star-spangled background, a monster TV set hanging from the ceiling and an array of ferns and cacti taller than Nikita.

Tamara had been wearing a smart navy blue trouser suit, but that was businesswoman's attire. Now she changed into a clever brocade gown that made her look almost svelte, definitely not plump. She and Ludmilla reappeared carrying large trays, offering tea or coffee, light or dark chocolate slabs, a plate of shiny iced biscuits, a piled bowl of gaily wrapped toffees, a gigantic water-melon dextrously carved by Nikita. Can any tooth be sweeter than the Siberians'?

Although the *Blagoveshchensk* is a passenger ship, many of its passengers run one-person (or one-family) trading enterprises and at sunset their cargo was being taken aboard. From the top of the embankment two wide flights of broken concrete steps led down to the gangplank and as Nikita went ahead, carrying my rucksack, it annoyed me to notice how badly I had packed it; I rather pride myself on being a champion packer of pannier-bags and rucksacks. Then came a hiatus: the *provodnitsa*, keeper of the cabin keys, was missing. I insisted that that didn't matter, I could sleep on one of the padded benches in the first class corridor. But Ludmilla and Maya were determined to see me safely into my cabin though the Revtovs had to leave at once: Tamara was expecting an important business call at 5 p.m. Moscow time. Vigorously I protested – they must *all* go now! How long would it take Ludmilla and Maya to get home, after dark, by Ust'-Kut's dodgy public transport? My protests were of course ignored; mother and daughter sat by me for forty minutes until the *provodnitsa* came aboard. She was requested to cherish me, my cabin was surveyed and approved of, and after tight bear-hugs (substitutes for all I wanted to say but couldn't) I parted from friends whose kind-ness I shall never forget.

When the Revtovs left us Maya had swiftly taken charge of my rucksack, sat close beside it, carried it to my cabin. Now I discovered why. Appalled, I stared at the contents. All those goodies left in the fridge had been furtively packed, plus six mini-yoghurts and a two-litres bottle of *pivo* – and I thought I had won my argument with Ludmilla, had persuaded her that this Irish custom must be upheld. Here was more food than I could eat in a month: I would surely become popular with my fellow passengers.

# 7

## Very Slowly Down the Lena

In Irkutsk I had been informed that it is now polite, not merely polit-ically correct, to refer to the 'Sakha' people rather than to the 'Yakut' and to call their republic 'Sakha' instead of 'Yakutiya'. It seems the indigenous people of this territory have always used 'Sakha' and 'Yakut' was a seventeenth-century adoption by Russians of the Evenk word for 'horse people'. The new Republic of Sakha is the old Yakut Autonomous Soviet Socialist Republic (Yakutiya in czarist times) and its name change carries an emphatic political message. In 1994 the Sakha government, led by the half-Sakha former Party boss Mikhail Nikolayev, made plain its intention to be much more autonomous than before, without formally seceding from the Russian Federation. Then, as the republic was being renamed, someone decided that to change the capital's name would involve too much clerical work so Yakutsk remains on the map.

Mutterings about independence have been heard in the back-ground but as Anna Reid points out in *The Shaman's Coat* (an enthrall-ing history of Siberia's natives, as witty as it is erudite):

> In practice, Sakha independence is hard to envision, even if, as is cur-rently unimaginable, Moscow were to consent to it ... Sakha's mineral wealth is less significant than it seems since the republic depends on Russia for imports of food and consumer goods. Its only non-Russian border is along the barely navigable coast of the Arctic Ocean.

The Nikolayev régime soon flaunted its autonomy by imposing Soviet-style visa regulations on foreigners. However, visas could be obtained only within Sakha from the Ministry of the Interior who required the listing of every town and village to be visited, AIDS and hepatitis certificates for anyone staying more than thirteen days and the payment of $75 – or so said my *Lonely Planet Guide to Russia, Ukraine and Belarus*. My more clued-up *BAM Guide* disagreed, mentioning a possible fine of $2.50 for not having a visa. According to the government, this regulation is essential to discourage visitors who demand too much of Sakha's limited supply of food and goods. I was offered a more convincing explanation in Yakutsk: visa constraints help the authorities to keep foreigners' commercial activities under surveillance.

The Sakha place of origin is uncertain. A Turkic branch of the Ural-Altaic stock, they speak a Turkic language written in Cyrillic script, supplemented by a few extra symbols to cope with peculiarly Turkic sounds. Some of their folk tales and traditions indicate that in the distant past they moved north from the Trans-Baikal/Mongolia regions. Later they shared the Buryat fate and were absorbed into Ghengis Khan's almost unbelievably extensive empire. In 1922 Sakha made up 85 per cent of the population and Russians 11 per cent, mainly based around the Aldan gold mines and in Yakutsk. The other 4 per cent were the remnants of tiny tribes: Chukchi, Yukagir, Even and Evenk. Then the Soviets 'relocated' many thousands of Russians – prisoners, miners, factory workers – and now the population is officially 40 per cent Sakha, some of those being mixed race citizens who feel closer to their homeland than to the Federation.

Sakha stretches 1,560 miles from east to west and 1,250 miles from the Arctic Ocean to the Stanovoi Mountains. It is among Russia's richest regions, producing an abundance of hydro-electric power, strategic metals, fur, coal, diamonds and gold; the largest nugget so far found weighed 21lb. The total population is just over one million, of whom (in 2001) 228,000 lived in Yakutsk and 108,000 in the new coal-mining city of Neryungri, leaving not very many to inhabit more than one-sixth of the Federation's total area, a republic bigger than India. For nearly four centuries the Lena has been Sakha's main link with the outside world; even now 80 per cent of all its imports are shipped from Ust'-Kut during the four ice-free months. Seen from outer space Russia's second-longest river (after the Yenesei) forms the biggest 'S' on our planet while winding its way from the mountains west of Lake Baikal to the Arctic Ocean.

It is still not possible to travel from Ust'-Kut to Yakutsk by road but the obstacles presented to road-builders by Siberia's terrain and climate are compensated for by many very long navigable rivers. Of these the Lena was once most important of all because its tributary links opened the way to the Pacific and elsewhere. It was 'discovered' during the first decade of the seventeenth century when Evenk allies of the Muscovites were boldly seeking pelts in unknown territory beyond the Yenesei. Cossack pioneers then prepared to embark on an unwitting expansion of empire such as the first of the Romanovs, Czar Mikhail, could not begin to imagine.

Those pioneers used decked, one-sail wooden boats some 30 feet long, able to carry eight or ten men and 6–7 tons of cargo. Their oars were often needed, even going downstream; Siberia is not very windy. Being flat-bottomed, such vessels could, with much exertion, be hauled over portages by their crews. A little later, for voyages all the way to the Arctic or Pacific Oceans, ships up to 60 feet long, with a keel and two or three sails, carried 34–40 tons. When the most practical portage routes had been discovered, through many trials and errors, things were so organized that travellers could change boats and needed to haul only (only!) the cargo. And astonishingly soon, usually within a few years, an inter-river pack-horse network had been established.

And now, fast-forward to the passenger vessels of today, described thus in the *BAM Guide*:

The *Krasnoyarsk* and the *Blagoveshchensk* have paddle-wheels amidships, powered by twin horizontal single-cylinder steam-driven oil-powered engines. Built in Hungary in 1959, with length 71.4m, breadth 15.2m, height 10.5m, and draught 1.6m, they carry 148 passengers with bunks and an unbounded number of passengers without bunks.

I had at first been taken aback to find myself in the only single cabin (Tamara's decision) but soon I came to appreciate this isolation. One needs an occasional break from communication through the media of sign language, a dictionary and school textbooks. My luxury cabin, some five feet by ten, was painted off-white and duck-egg blue with golden-brown woodwork and royal blue curtains on the wide window; to our *provodnitsa*'s disapproval, I never used the slatted wooden 'security' shutter. A tiny table below the window served as my desk and the sofa converted effortlessly to a bed, with a long shelf above it. Cold water came from the wash-basin tap, 25 roubles bought a hot shower in the first-class *banya*. My ticket cost $130 and, if one reckons on spending an average of $15 a night on lodgings, this fare comes to only $25, given seven nights aboard. Good value for a 1,270-mile voyage down one of the world's greatest rivers.

At 7 a.m. a thick chilly mist hovered above the Lena. Its embankments were deserted, all important cargo having been taken on the previous evening, and as I explored I seemed to have the steamer to myself. Down at steerage level, I peered into the malodorous dusk where raucous snoring startled me: two young men, evidently adenoidal, lay asleep on the floor wrapped in nylon sacking. They were, I later discovered, working their way to Yakutsk as porters.

Sitting in the prow with my morning tea, I watched the mist dispersing and passengers arriving by car, taxi and truck. They looked an interesting mix, many apparently all-European, many others obviously not. Nowadays some Sakha tend to boast about their rich genetic pool to which Cossacks, merchants, convicts, peasant settlers and aristocratic political exiles so generously contributed. The typical pure-bred Sakha is thickset, black-haired and brown-eyed, with an ivory complexion (until tanned), broad cheek-bones and a rather low forehead. About 15,000 remain nomadic to this day, having escaped both industrialization and collectivization. But will they escape globalization?

I now re-read *The BAM Guide*'s 'Lena Facts':

The 4,440km Lena river is the ninth longest river in the world.

High water is in June, when its water level is 10 to 18m above the winter level.

Its June temperature ranges from 14°C to 19°C.

The Lena freezes on average ten days after its tributaries and provides ice-roads from December to March. It is usually ice-free from May to September. Vladimir Ilyich Ulyanov chose the Lena as the basis for his revolutionary name – V.I. Lenin.

In the Yakutian language, 'lena' means 'very big river'.

An abnormally quick freeze-up sometimes immobilized the exploring Muscovites. No statistics record the consequent fatalities but we can surmise that those who lived to see the thaw were dependent in a big way on local advice. This was so not only in emergencies. Siberia's natives had devised nothing more cold-excluding than the Muscovite *izby*, for which building materials were available throughout the taiga, but when it came to clothing, and the finding and preparation of food, the newcomers had to learn fast from those of the tribespeople who were not intent on killing them. Within a few generations, varying degrees of 'Yakutisation' were observed among the *Siberyaki* (Russian settlers), in contrast to the partial Russification of the Buryat down south.

At 9.30 the *Blagoveshchensk* hooted ceremonially and a scruffy little tug bustled up to turn her around and get us started. Soon we were under the BAM bridge, then sailing past Ust'-Kut's run-down cargo port and oil depot, its expanse of semi-derelict ship maintenance yards and what looked like a row of abandoned factories. On either side the hulks of long-dead vessels, jagged where sheets of reusable metal had been wrenched away, stuck out of the water at awkward angles, having been pushed around for years by ice-blocks. After the Second World War much was invested in this port when Moscow decided to supply some of Siberia's remotest areas *downstream* from within the new BAM Zone rather than *upstream* from the Arctic Ocean.

Now a brisk breeze was blowing, the sun shone hot from a clear sky and within half an hour every trace of urbanization had been left behind. On both banks low forested ridges wore autumn patchwork quilts of old gold, pine green and crimson. So close to Ust'-Kut settlements are quite numerous, some neat and evidently thriving, others seeming to consist mainly of squalid shanty-town shacks. Near one village a cemetery stood just above the bank, set amidst pines, the railed graves resembling rows of babies' cots painted blue and white. Hereabouts the Lena is shallow in September and we had to weave cautiously between small buoys topped by white triangles recording the distance from Yakutsk. All day I remained on deck, only moving from my unshaded prow seat at noon when the heat became intolerable.

Each of the steamer's four classes has its *provodnitsa*; steerage passengers are left to their own devices. Our Katerina was a lean six-footer who smiled only on special occasions, could impose law and order with one syllable and every day swept, mopped and polished the cabins and corridor floors and windows. A youth scoured our upper deck, not forgetting to scrub the railings. As most people ate in their cabins the litter-bins placed at strategic points soon filled up and were promptly emptied – not into the Lena, I was relieved to observe. On this sailing the oval forward saloon, its walls mostly glass, and the first-class restaurant were closed because of a passenger shortage. Why give Katerina unnecessary work?

I've recently been collecting other people's mental images of Siberia and a fuzzy composite picture emerges: awesome, yes, in the sheer extremity of its extent and climate – but more than slightly sinister, having been a place of punishment for 500 years, and mind-numbingly monotonous with either too many trees or too much snow. That last misapprehension compelled me to break a rule and show photographs to my friends, especially photographs of the Lena. Its course being so sinuous – rarely can one see more than a mile or so fore and aft – it was never possible to guess what the next hour might reveal. Perhaps high slopes, their taiga touching the water's edge – or rough multi-coloured naked cliffs – or a gentle foreground of irregular hills with towering ranges in the background – or on one bank level emerald grassland dotted with miniature hayricks and sleek cattle. Countless little waterfalls sparkled down the steeper slopes, despite the regional lack of rain. And towards evening the river became a tranquil sheet of blue, flawlessly mirroring its low forested banks – here pure gold.

Ornithologically the Lena is more rewarding than the BAM line or Lake Baikal. Within a few hours I had seen black and white duck, herring gulls, kestrels and even a few lordly eagles circling high and slow above the taiga. I also listed the day's traffic: five oil-tankers, four vehicle ferries, two small hydrofoils serving Kerensk, two coal barges returning empty to Ust'-Kut and another colossal barge packed with scores of BAM freight wagons.

At 8.10 the sun set, leaving a sky tinted peach to the meridian and the Lena suffused with rosy ripples in our wake. And then, suddenly, the air was cold. Some time during the night we would arrive at Kirensk, our first port of call, founded by Vasili Bugor and his posse of Cossacks in 1630.

That evening I got very drunk very quickly on only two litres of *pivo*. Conveniently I was already settled on my bunk, writing, so I could gracefully keel over where I sat; a footless babushka would not have amused Katerina. Next morning the label told me that Ludmilla had provided top quality 'alc. 8 per cent' instead of the standard 'alc. 4 per cent' – and one shouldn't drink 'alc. 8 per cent' quickly. I'm still puzzling over the last barely legible and totally irrelevant lines of my diary for 12 September. 'Being an o.a.p. does have lots of advantages, to compensate for certain disadvantages.' What can those advantages be?

I have difficulty mentally dissociating Cossacks from garish Duffy's Circus posters, displayed all over my home town in the 1940s. No doubt wartime shortages had cleared the ring of wild animals and instead we were being lured by wild men, dark-skinned and shaggy, astride over-muscled rearing horses, brandishing long swords. 'New to Ireland! See for the First Time the World's Most Daring Horsemen, the Cossacks from Faraway Caucasus!' Clearly the reality was less impressive than the posters; I remember nothing of those 'Cossacks'', performance in the ring.

It is scarcely an exaggeration to say that Siberia could not have been settled (or not until much later) without the daring Cossacks who willingly went where most Muscovites feared to sail or row. Yet the genetic background of these irregular forces remains obscure; we only know that it was thoroughly mixed. They first stepped on to history's stage in the Middle Ages as mercenaries protecting Kiev, and later Moscow, from the south. 'Cossack' is supposedly derived from the Turkic *kiz* or *kez*, meaning 'to wander', and for long periods nomadic Cossacks certainly did wander over the steppes and up and down the river highways where brigandage was their main source of income. As considerable numbers of fleeing criminals and deserting soldiers joined them, they cannot be described as an ethnic unit or tribe. Then the sedentary life began to appeal to some and by the mid-sixteenth century the Don Cossacks formed a community whose particular identity had been generally recognized. From them emerged an ambitious and not at all sedentary group eager to help collect pelts far beyond the confines of the known world. These were the first Russian government agents encountered by the native Siberians and their drunken orgies shocked all tribes – shocked even their Muscovite companions, not themselves known for sobriety.

Between a Cossack and his czar there was what I hesitate to call a gentlemen's agreement – but something of the sort. In exchange for certain privileges, the Cossack devoted most of his adult life (nineteen to twenty-five years) to the service, being ready to fight anywhere at any time and usually being able to get himself and his horses and his weaponry to the battlefield without help from cumbersome military logistics departments. In Siberia there were of course no fixed battle-fields but the Cossacks proved well able to adapt to other conditions, until these became boring.

As time passed, local *Sibiryaki*, including traders, hunters and fugi-tives, were recruited to the service. Yet in Sakha there was not much for a Cossack to do, once the territory had been explored and 'pacified'. (On the whole, pre-Russian north-eastern Siberia had been a peaceful place, free of firearms; but all imperialists used this early example of 'spin'.) The service was not hereditary, yet few boys failed to follow in Dad's footsteps and so this obsolete community went on steadily increasing.

During Peter the Great's reign (1696–1725) Eastern Siberia's Cossacks were divided into southern frontiersmen operating along the Chinese border, skirmishing with the Kirgiz or Dzhungarians, and northern 'Town Cossacks' charged with policing and maintaining lines of communication. As there were then very few law-breakers, and equally few lines of communication, this did nothing for Cossack morale and degeneration proceeded apace. Was Moscow's failure to recall the force a symptom of extreme inertia?

In 1786–88 a member of Billing's expedition, which employed Cossacks as interpreters and guides, complained about 'these hardly animated lumps of clay, lazy, faithless and sly'. At that date the pay of a Town Cossack was minuscule but he also received annually 854lb of grain and owned forty acres of grazing land.

Things were different in European Russia. By the end of the eight-eenth century the Cossacks, no longer seen as unruly though often useful brigand/warriors, had been integrated into the Imperial Army as light cavalry. In the Civil War (1918–21) most of them fought with the White Army and the Kuban and Don Cossacks were the first to be deported *en masse* by Stalin. Then, as Dominic Lieven recalls in *Empire*,

> a separate Cossack identity was effectively destroyed, partly because Russian-speaking Cossacks deported from their villages ... had fewer cultural defences against Sovietization than Muslim Chechens or Tatars. It is true that during the Second World War and afterwards the Soviet régime manufactured ersatz Cossack traditions, dance troupes and even military units. These had a roughly similar link to authentic Cossackdom as the tartan-wearing German consort of Queen Victoria had to the clans who charged at Culloden. The failure of any genuine Cossack traditions and units to re-emerge in the wake of the Soviet Union's collapse underlined the extent to which any authentic Cossack identity had been broken.

At dawn I awoke, none the worse for my 'alc. 8 per cent' mishap, and through a drifting mist glimpsed fragments of Kirensk where we had moored an hour earlier. Until the 1970s, the *BAM Guide* explains, this town occupied an island at the confluence of the Lena and Kirenga rivers. Then the Kirenga was dammed, transforming the island into a promontory, to prevent it 'from taking the short cut to the Lena, upstream from the town, thus creating havoc in the bottleneck at the downstream end of the island'. Blocks of ice forcing their way through this bottleneck in springtime used occasionally to tear houses apart.

No one was around when I took my mug down to the samovar taps beside the engine room to make tea. (The engine boils the water.) The day before, a group of tough-looking young Tajik traders had been strolling around the upper deck, trying to sell me 'ancient Russian coins' which may or may not have been ancient When I politely declined to buy they became slightly impolite, until Katerina appeared in the distance. Now I saw three of them in the corridor near the engine room, sleeping on bare wooden benches using their arms as pillows – looking defenceless, the way sleeping people do. That gave me guilt. My first impression may have been accurate enough but who was I, writing in my luxurious cabin, to condemn them for trying to prey on the rich?

Sipping my tea on deck, I watched Kirensk (population 12,000) swinging into action. We were moored off the right bank's stony slope. Nearby, tall trees shaded a few three-storey blocks from which workers were commuting by ferry to Kirensk while others commuted from the town to shipyard jobs. A few took small aged cars on the ferry, returning with them at lunchtime; such car-addiction in a virtually roadless Siberia depressed me. Several dogs came to see people off, received good-bye pats, went about their business, then at noon were back by the water's edge to greet returning owners. Only the Tajik traders disembarked here: ten young men, accompanied by a stalwart young Buryat woman. The *Blagoveshchensk* was tied to bollards on either side of a primitive landing stage and her steel hawsers impeded the traders as they struggled to drag unwieldy heavy loads up a steep, gravel-skiddy hill, then down to where the flat-bottomed little ferry ran aground. Their meagre profits were being hard-earned.

Our cargo for Kirensk consisted of twenty gigantic sacks of salt obviously meant to be mechanically moved; three men had difficulty hoisting them on to the open back of a farm lorry with sagging springs. There was no other activity on the long, wide beach, or around the little jetty on the Kirensk side. In Soviet times this port was much busier. During BAM building, materials and machinery were shipped from Ust'-Kut to Kirensk, then up the Kirenga to what is now the BAM settlement of Kirenga. Also, cargoes were transferred here from smaller to bigger boats, the Lena being quite shallow upstream from Kirensk. Now Russia's economic collapse has so reduced freight traffic that small boats can carry everything all the way.

The formidable Katerina had my welfare at heart. There was time to go ashore, she assured me through the medium of our wrist-watches; we wouldn't sail before noon. By then (nine o'clock) the ferry was uncrowded, most of the passengers stylishly dressed women carrying briefcases or trendy shoulderbags. The two-rouble fare, trifling to a visitor, must seem burdensome to regular commuters. I felt myself being furtively inspected and nobody smiled. In general the townspeople showed little of that friendly open curiosity I'd come to expect of Siberians. They seemed awkwardly, almost defensively shy, as if afraid even to attempt to cope with a foreigner who couldn't speak Russian. Fair enough, given their residence on an island in the middle of the Lena in the middle of Eastern Siberia.

Despite that dam-bridge, Kirensk still feels like an island. A short walk in any direction, along curving broken streets of one- and two-storey tin-roofed wooden houses, brings you to a river bank – Lena or Kirenga. Two brick buildings had been, respectively, a church, now towerless and home to a TV transmitter, and a vodka factory used as a Soviet prison. In its basement more than eighty bodies were found buried in 1991, some mummified and easily identifiable, all murdered on one day in 1938. As nobody had authorized these executions, skulls were smashed instead of guns being fired.

Disappointingly, Kirensk's diminutive museum would not be open until noon. I had hoped its curator might direct me to the site of Vasili Bugor's *ostrog*, if that is known. Few traces remain of the numerous Cossack frontier fortifications, from which are descended almost all Siberia's pre-Soviet towns. However solidly built, the *ostrogi* were as vulnerable to fire (deliberate or accidental) as any other mainly wooden construction. In size they varied greatly but the design was standard: a rectangular towered fort containing barracks, secure storage spaces, houses and a mini-church. In the eighteenth century, when forts were no longer needed, *ostrog* came to mean 'prison' for the obvious reason.

Kirensk's only café was also closed, and there is no restaurant, nor any canteen in the market where I came upon the Tajiks sitting on their loads, sharing a loaf of grey bread while their Buryat friend boiled water on a camping-gas stove. It seems Kirensk has been very hard hit by the new Russia; most market stalls were vacant and those occupied had few customers.

By 1640 there were hundreds of fur-hungry Russians sailing down the Lena and as a well-defended island Kirensk soon attracted settlers. However, things turned nasty in 1641, after Yerofei Khabarov's multiple crimes were punished by the confiscation of all his enterprises around Ust'-Kut. At once he made for Kirensk and started again – both his farming (less lucrative here) and his sadistic torturing and gang-raping. When the governor of Yakutsk sent a few hundred peasant convicts to try to grow desperately needed crops around Kirensk, Khabarov killed most of them before departing in 1649 to explore and ravage the Amur region, further east.

During the following century Kirensk expanded rapidly, its devel-

opment directed from Yakutsk, and in 1775 it became a 'town' by official decree. Many famous though not necessarily successful expeditions
used the island as their base and many idealistic political exiles lived
here, turning the place into a breeding ground for revolutionaries.
Some of those activists must on one level have enjoyed their exile, grim
though it is to be forcibly uprooted. As members of the educated élite
they were free, in Siberia, to make a (subsidized) home, take a wife (if
desired) and be discreetly revolutionary, something they had found
they could not be in European Russia. When Lenin was banished to
an Eastern Siberian village for three years, having served fourteen
months in a St Petersburg prison, he received a monthly government
allowance of 7.40 roubles – enough, in the 1890s, to pay for a comfortable bedsitter, good food including lots of mutton and milk and a
washerwoman. He wrote cheerfully to his mother about his new dog,
Jenka, and the excellent fishing and hunting – 'there are even wild
goats in the woods' – and about long swims 'in a broad tributary of the
Yenesei with the snowy Sayansk Mountains in the distance ... So even
from an artistic viewpoint there is something to be said for our place.'
By correspondence he played chess with a distant friend and he also
proposed marriage by letter. When his beloved Nadezhda Krupskaya
arrived in Shushenskoe the couple collaborated on a translation of the
Webbs' *Theory and Practice of Trade Unions*.

No doubt a similar lifestyle, agreeably combining physical and intellectual exercise, was available to Kirensk's political exiles. Having
curbed their trouble-making potential, the central authorities forgot
about them and the Yakutsk authorities didn't take them too seriously.
Moreover, they now lived in a world where the legacies of serfdom
they so detested were unknown (apart from the Orthodox Church's
estates) and where in practice peasant convicts – many only convicted
to furnish unalluring Sakha with manual labourers – were respected for
their agricultural skills.

Limping around dejected Kirensk, where few householders could
afford a pot of paint, I tried to imagine it a century ago when the
exiles, getting a whiff of the revolution simmering in European
Russia, were looking forward to a liberation that never came, that
was displaced by a tyranny under which political prisoners did not
live tolerable lives. But at the dawn of the twentieth century, in

Kirensk, there were surely several open cafés abuzz with hopeful speculations.

Post-1917, Kirensk became the centre for three *gulag* transit camps, one stocked mainly with Christians of various low church denominations. A majority of these were Baptists, though immediately after the Revolution the authorities had treated them leniently, perhaps because they were so severely discriminated against under the czars. The Soviets even condoned their setting up a Baptist collective farm. But one of the Baptists' main duties is to spread their faith and a 1929 decree prohibiting evangelism left them subject to arrests and deportations by the hundred. During the 1930s the Stalinist régime regarded them with loathing and perhaps some fear. They had a considerable following in Western Siberia's recently built industrial cities, where Orthodoxy was weakest and unlike the Orthodox Church they encouraged Bible reading, which made them popular among people new to literacy. Also, they preached sobriety, self-discipline, hard work and mutual aid – as did the Bolsheviks, but the Baptists' practise of those virtues was very much more obvious. However, they redeemed themselves in Soviet eyes by using their influence to good patriotic effect during the Second World War, after which there was a reconciliation of sorts with the Kremlin. In Severobaikalsk I had noticed the little wooden Baptist church in the Old Town attracting sizeable congregations – to the impotent (so far) disapproval of the Orthodox clergy.

In fact I could have visited the museum; we didn't sail until 4.10 because our refuelling tanker arrived late and filling us up took three hours. Leaning over the top deck rail, I closely studied this process as it happened directly below me. The fat rubber pipe linking the two vessels looked way past its use-by date and was giving a lot of trouble. Two frowning tanker men squatted beside it, doing complicated things while chain-smoking. On the *Blagoveshchensk* passengers and crew were allowed to smoke only on deck and I wondered when the captain (or the invincible Katerina?) would put a stop to this recklessness. But during those hours no crew member appeared.

Within thirty minutes of sailing we dropped anchor, in midstream, for no apparent reason. This did not displease me. Here, to starboard, the Lena flowed at the base of immensely high cliffs, their sandstone turned to ruby by the slanting sunlight, and one could see where the rough rock had been smoothed throughout aeons by ice chunks jostling downstream. On the other bank, in dramatic contrast, flat green land – part pasture, part taiga – stretched away to a faint smudge of dusky blue hills. A mile or so downstream the Lena disappeared, curving around a massive bastion of golden rock, the pines on its crest standing out darkly against a deep blue sky.

At 5.50 we hooted – what did that mean? It meant the approach of another oil-tanker to provide what had leaked from the dodgy pipe. Not until 7.45 did we sail on past the bastion, its reflection quivering slightly on a Lena now catching the sunset afterglow – streaks and swirls of lemon and carmine.

Opening my diary and a bottle of *pivo* I realized that it was Friday 13 September: the captain's unlucky day.

Improbably, the engine room mesmerized me. It was open to view from the second-class corridor, being not really a room but the exposed guts of the ship where any terrorist could have had his/her way unhindered. Whenever I took my mug to the samovar taps I had to stop and gaze at those mighty wheels, slowly and quietly revolving almost within touching distance, surrounded by giant bits of mysterious (to me) machinery. I never saw anybody in that space: one could fantasize about the wheels being autonomous, transporting us down the Lena of their own volition.

The hot-water taps overhung long earthenware sinks in which third-class and steerage passengers could wash themselves and their clothes. Beyond was the shop, selling teabags, tinned milk, cigarettes and the usual range of vile snacks. Beer (no vodka) was stacked in one corner and sold only between 5 and 7 p.m. The adjacent second-class restaurant, beside the kitchen, catered for the crew and those few passengers who weren't self-sustaining.

During the night we had anchored again – but where? A dense surrounding mist, still and silvery, isolated us from the visible world. Silence enveloped the *Blagoveshchensk*: no one else was around at my morning tea-making time. Not until 9.15 did the mist stir, just perceptibly. I hurried out on deck; given the variety of the Lena's landscapes it was impossible to guess what might now be revealed.

Gradually the mist thinned. Then, like the slow raising of a theatre curtain, the sun lifted it above a river that had doubled in width since last I saw it. Downstream, this expansion was accentuated by the flatness of the taiga on both sides. Suddenly, here, space seemed infinite. But then, turning, I realized that we were scarcely thirty yards from a logging settlement, a score of identical new huts and a solitary two-storey brick house standing close to the stony beach's high water mark. Just behind them rose a partially deforested ridge where the birches had survived and were all aglow. Soon the Lena was reflecting a cloudless sky – and also small cargoes of red-gold cedar logs, neatly stacked by the water's edge. Three rowing boats lay on the stones but there was no one in sight. I assumed the loggers lived independently of the *Blagoveshchensk* and were at work, so why did we not weigh anchor until 10.30? The language barrier occasionally irked me.

Early that afternoon our pilot had to negotiate several tricky stretches. Most memorable is a half-hour navigation test where the Lena, confined between 600-foot red-brown rock walls set at awkward angles, narrows and quickens and surges, compelling vessels to veer repeatedly from side to side with (seemingly) only yards to spare. Where the river again widened, we had to skirt long midstream gravel banks – very slowly, a young man standing in the prow wielding a measuring pole, then shouting to our pilot far above. Here, too, were a few humpy islands, miles long and vividly green: coarse grass, bramble bushes, stunted alders. From one rose an alarmed flock of Arctic geese, migrants having a refuelling stop. On this mid-September day a frisky breeze tempered the sun's heat and the clarity of the light was incomparable – or only comparable to a frosty winter's day on the Aran Islands.

Later we sailed close to the left bank, for many miles. On its lowish cliffs dwarf pines surrounded isolated silver limestone crags, soaring towards the intensely blue sky, each crag so fancifully eroded that one seemed to be viewing an open-air sculpture park. Human heads were discernible, and raised arms, and circular windows in a slim, wall-like slab, and a canoe balanced between the two sharp points of a split crag. Briefly I toyed with the notion that men *might* have created these shapes, countless thousands of years ago. After all, Siberia's Palaeolithic and Neolithic artists produced petroglyphs and rock drawings (humans, horses, elk, reindeer) rivalling France's cave paintings. These were discovered, in 1941, on a two-mile stretch of high cliffs above the Talma, a tributary of the Lena. And so died the theory that Stone Age culture first evolved in Western Europe.

On this third day there were no stops as the Lena wound through uninhabited territory, carving out what geologists call 'a true valley of erosion'. We met only four empty oil-tankers, going upstream at speed, and three mega-barges, laden with BAM wagons and army trucks, going upstream very slowly. Somewhere in this area, in 1926, the first Soviet geological expedition to Siberia got lost in the taiga and almost died of hunger. By chance they came upon a gold-miners' settlement and their report noted that 400 grammes (12oz) of salt cost four grammes (0.14oz) of gold and one kilo (2.21lb) of meat cost 40 grammes (1.4oz).

Leaning over the prow, revelling in this human-free zone, I again wondered how the pioneering Cossacks felt as they looked down-stream, not knowing what awaited them around the next bend – either topographically or anthropologically. They were not a literary species, given to recording their impressions for posterity, so we can only speculate about their individual reactions to the dangers, hard-ships, tensions and beauties of journeys that sometimes lasted years, with question marks all along the way. On two of my own mini-journeys, with pack-animals in roadless and sparsely inhabited regions of Ethiopia and Peru, I was an explorer only in the personal sense yet there were also daily question marks, most of which enjoyably stimu-lated me. But no doubt the physical effort to survive dominated the Cossacks' voyages, discouraging introspection – even had they been so inclined, which is unlikely. Of one thing we can be fairly certain: the wild and wondrous beauty of the Lena's course would have left them unmoved – their Western European contemporaries didn't respond positively to the Scottish Highlands or the Alps. Yet the survivors (there were always casualties) must have felt a glow of triumph when at last they reached a site where it was possible to build an *ostrog*, contact the natives and bully them into providing furs.

Most Cossack leaders were literate enough to send factual reports to Moscow every few years, commonly written on birch bark. In *Russian Settlement in the North*, Terence Armstrong quotes the literal translation of a typical report, addressed to Czar Mikhail Fedorovich by Petr Beketov, the Cossack who founded Yakutsk. Having described his profitable adventures 'below Bratsk rapids', and up and down various tributaries of the Angara, Beketov continues:

And in 1630, Sire, I, your slave, was sent on your royal service from Yeniseyskiy Ostrog with service men [Cossacks] to the great river Lena. And from below the Lena portage I went up the great river Lena and reached the Buryat lands and those of other peoples. And these Buryat people, not wishing to pay fit tribute to you, righteous Sire, collected together and surrounded me. And with service men I was besieged in my Buryat lands. And near these Buryat people, Sire, lived Tungus [Evenki] of the Nalyaskiye lands, and they gave fur tribute to the Buryat people. And I, your slave, brought the Nalyaskiye lands under your exalted rule, and again collected your fur tribute, Sire, from the Tungus, and at that place, the Nalyaskiye lands, the Tungus pay fur tribute to you, righteous Sire.

And from the Bratsk lands, Sire, I went, your slave, to the Lena portage, and at the Lena portage I wintered. And from the Lena portage I, your slave, sent out service men to collect your royal fur tribute along the tributary rivers Ilim and Kirenga, and obtained more fur tribute for you, Sire, than in former years. And in the spring of that year, Sire, when the ice went out, I, your slave, and the service people sailed down the great river Lena, and having arrived at the Yakut lands, built an *ostrog*, and made all necessary defences for the *ostrog*.

And at Yakutskiy Ostrog I, your slave, spent a year with the service people, and for your royal contentment brought under your exalted rule many Yakut princelings and their villagers ... and for you, righteous Sire, collected much fur tribute from the Yakut lands and Yzhiganekh, and from the Tungus on the surrounding streams. And I, your slave, at that time collected again for you, Sire, on the great river Lena 6—[text deficient] roubles in ship tax. And before me, Sire, no one spent a year on the great river Lena, and no one built an *ostrog* anywhere on the Lena, nor collected ship tax, nor tithes from service and trading people...

And while in your service, Sire, in distant parts, I shed my blood for you, Sire, and suffered hunger and every sort of hardship, and defiled my spirit, and ate Mare's meat and roots and fir bark and all kinds of filth, and many times had scurvy.

The Cossack leaders were venturing down the great river Lena, and all those other rivers, for personal gain. But what of the nameless service men without whom they could have achieved nothing? Not many roubles rewarded their endeavours; most of the big bucks went to Moscow. So did they in their way enjoy exploring, relish the excitement of the unknown? Despite the standard grovelling tone of Beketov's report, the Cossacks were nobody's slaves; as irregular troops for hire, they didn't have to make a pact with the czar. It might seem that by any standards, whatever motivated them, their courage was extraordinary. Yet evidently they felt quite confident of being able, except in the most unfortunate circumstances, to defend themselves with guns against tribes using bows and arrows. Of course they were well aware of the multiple risks inherent in their adventuring. But maybe they were simply an optimistic, fearless breed, not needing courage – just lots of stamina.

Thus far my excess food had remained a problem: how to distribute it tactfully? As an odd-bod foreigner, an inexplicable babushka speaking no Russian, I could hardly thrust smoked omul, salami, caviar, cheese and bottled olives into the hands of total strangers. However, three Sakha families had embarked at Kirensk and, unlike most of the passengers, they spent hours on deck, having small children who needed exercise. One couple's eleven-months-old daughter took her very first step on the *Blagoveshchensk* to the acclaim of all present. She then took many more steps, wobbling between her jubilant squatting parents while the rest of us photographed this unremarkable yet always thrilling event. After that everyone produced their portable family albums, mine containing more animals than granddaughters to the delight of the older children. Meeting someone who couldn't speak Russian hugely amused them and by sunset, after some arduous dictionary work, I felt free to distribute my surplus supplies without causing offence.

Overnight the weather changed abruptly, a cold wind replacing the breeze, heavy layers of low cloud replacing the early mist. On both flat banks, strips of grey alkaline soil separated the taiga, here much thinned by loggers, from the Lena.

When Lensk became visible in the distance its few ten-storey blocks seemed shockingly incongruous. This is the only port between Kirensk and Yakutsk, built to serve Sakha's diamond mines. From it a motorable track runs through taiga for 145 miles to the lavish diamond deposits discovered in 1953. These inspired the rapid jerry-building of Mirny – a town I do not yearn to visit, now the administrative and industrial centre of Western Sakha. In 1963 Lensk's construction began on the left bank of the Lena. Overlooking the port, a twice-life-sized mural on a school's gable end celebrates some seventeenth-century (judging by his headgear) hero – perhaps Petr Beketov? Then I noticed a tiny wooden church, grey-brown with age, its two towers asymmetrical, standing alone above the water – a relic of the early nineteenth-century settlement of Mukhtuya, founded to accommodate postal couriers. It is alleged that during the summer months czarist Yakutsk enjoyed a more dependable postal service than twenty-first-century Yakutsk.

In May 2001, after the coldest winter for fifty years, a slow thaw downstream caused severe flooding in both Lensk and Yakutsk. Lensk was almost swept away and many of its 27,000 inhabitants had to be evacuated to Mirny. Afterwards there was talk of the town being rebuilt farther inland but it seems the majority of the population prefer to live by the Lena – which I can well understand. That river does have an extraordinary magnetism.

We anchored by the wide landing-stage, below a steep gravel slope, at 7.35 – twenty-one hours late. Hectic activity followed, supervised by a young Sakha policeman whose unpleasant expression caused me a tremor of visa alarm; during the night we had entered the Republic of Sakha. I counted forty-six sacks of onions being unloaded – and many more sacks of flour, sugar, salt, garlic – and gallons beyond reckoning of beer, fruit juices, tinned milk – and crates of bananas, grapes and water-melons for the well-paid Mirny miners – and sealed boxes, cartons, bags and bundles by the score, these last causing obstacles on the landing-stage, making access difficult for embarking passengers. Their shouted complaints to the policeman were ignored; he was now standing near me, signing chits of paper presented by young men in exchange for a small fee. Only half a dozen disembarked here, among them a handsome young *Sibiryak* couple whose joyous reunion with their small son and large hairy hound was touching to behold. In the over-excitement of the moment the dog's lead was dropped and he went bounding away up the slope, then raced back, woofing happily. The couple's luggage suggested that they were moving house; it included two carpets, three six-foot potted plants and ten enormous crates needing two men apiece to carry them.

When the *Blagoveshchensk* hooted a score or so of Mirny miners hurried aboard, discarding empty vodka bottles. All day they swaggered about the ship drinking too much beer and frequently provoking Katerina's wrath. One was accompanied by a cowed-looking wife and three tiresome sons who made quite a nuisance of themselves until Katerina decreed that they must remain in their cabin.

Beyond Lensk the Lena flowed much wider, browner, faster and deeper between low banks. To the west, in the middle distance, an interesting layered cloudscape of varying shades of grey stood above the long crests of smooth hills. Hereabouts, riverside fields of not very fertile alluvial soil allow enough cultivation and pasturage for a few small settlements to survive. In autumn their cattle look like prize animals; in spring, I'm told, they look otherwise. Far from the settlements we passed five herds of ponies – dun, piebald, chestnut – grazing close to the water. Two mares had newborn foals which, given winter's imminence, seemed like bad family planning. In Yakutsk pony meat is considered a delicacy.

For our porters this was a busy day. By noon, when we anchored a hundred yards off Nyuya's sandy beach, cold rain was spitting and a gusty wind had roused the Lena to roughness. For fifty minutes, supplies of sugar, salt and beer were being delivered, sacks of potatoes and cabbages collected. Five little rowing boats with outboard engines needed the assistance of our six-person lifeboat which, for the rest of the day, was left dangling, between stops, over the port side. (In a crisis, what would happen to all but six of the *Blagoveshchensk*'s passengers? But this hope-for-the-best attitude is far healthier than our present neurotic concentration on safety.) From Nyuya twenty-two Sakha passengers came aboard, scrambling up a short ladder into the hold.

Soon the flat land gave way to sparsely wooded cliffs and more grotesquely beautiful rock formations – no longer reflected in the Lena, for now its surface was restless and sunless. Two hours later, when we anchored off Tinnaya, the waves were rough – and even rougher an hour later, at Chapaevo. This big village, one of the oldest on the Lena, was the site of a Decembrist prison, renamed by the Soviets in honour of Vasili Ivanovich Chapaev, a Civil War commander. It is invisible behind a high ridge of shale; I deduced its size from the potato-laden vehicles awaiting us – seventeen aged cars, a minibus, two army jeeps and ten motorbikes ingeniously adapted to carry bulky loads. As the heavy sacks were being taken on board from wildly rocking boats, through doors fore and aft, one boatman fell overboard and screams of alarm came from the shore. Quickly his mate pulled him to safety but he had lost one of his waders – a major loss and I felt for him. Despite being soaked to the skin he made three more trips. The waves breaking on the beach caused problems for oncoming passengers and men in waders piggy-backed children and fat women into boats, their gallantry causing much amusement. One slim young man couldn't cope with an exceptionally stout body and a taller, stronger fellow took over, kneeling while she mounted him to loud cheers.

A few Chapaevo cars used wheeled boat-trailers, a neat labour-saving device. To launch them cars were backed half-into the Lena – then in again to reunite with the loaded boat and off they went up the roadless slope, water streaming from under back doors. Here several passengers who came aboard at Lensk, and most of the Nyuya contingent, disembarked.

Approaching Macha, at sunset, we hooted three times instead of once. The captain had been unable to communicate our much-delayed time of arrival and the crescent of stony beach was deserted. This village, too, is invisible from the river and was a Decembrist destination. In these open prisons exiles had to grow their own food or, if they could afford it, find someone to garden for them.

At 7.30 a young woman carrying a fur-cocooned toddler came aboard, father having paddled their tiny canoe through the rainy dusk from some point beyond the crescent. For another hour we lingered, but no one else appeared.

Descending to the shop, I found potato sacks piled high on both sides of the samovar corridor, necessitating crabwise movement. After dark, Katerina chose not to notice a few steerage passengers slinking up to sleep on the soft sofas of the first-class corridors. But no one even slightly merry – not to say drunk – was permitted this upward mobility.

The hooter woke me in the small hours and much activity followed but the hour was too small for me to be interested. Later, hearing the anchor being winched up, I looked at my watch – 2.30 a.m.

Five hours later a gale was driving sheets of sleet almost horizontally up the Lena. For the first time I needed socks, and a sweater under my windcheater. Yet only four days previously the noon sun had been too much for me.

Soon the anchor was rattling down again, fifty yards off a straggling hamlet of impoverished-looking *izby*. No passengers awaited us and the few boatmen who rowed out wore furry *shapkas* with the ear flaps down. As they took delivery of basic goods the turbulent Lena claimed a precious sack of salt – one of those sacks not meant to be manhandled. Its loss caused consternation but no recriminations. The Lena's turbulence anger is nobody's fault.

Evidently the regional supply of salt has at last run out. By now we've almost forgotten the historical importance of this humble item on our shopping lists which stimulated (among other colonial enterprises) the earliest Russian ventures into Siberia. Towards the end of the fourteenth century the Stroganovs, starting out from their peasant *izba*, got into the Novgorod salt trade through obtaining a government monopoly. Quite quickly they developed several other business interests and became the richest merchant family in Muscovy. In 1517 a royal charter permitted them to mine the Urals for salt and iron. By the 1570s they owned vast estates of arable land and tens of thousands of serfs and could afford to send two salt-seeking expeditions beyond the lower Ob', led by a Dutch employee, Oliver Brunel. To protect the settlements he founded, his employers hired 800 Don Cossacks, led by Yermak Timofeyevich, and in September 1581 this well-armed force set out from one of the Stroganovs' estates on the upper Kama river. By the time Yermak was killed in 1584, fighting the semi-nomadic Western Siberia Tatars, he had occupied a (relatively) small area and ever since he has been popularly lauded as 'the conqueror of Siberia'. His successful campaign aroused an official interest in the

Great Unknown and immediately after his death Moscow sent a force of 500 men, under Prince S.D. Bolkhovskiy, to the Irtysh river. At the confluence of the Irtysh and the Ob', in 1585, the first Russian town was built in Siberia.

(To digress briefly – for 600 years the Stroganovs remained in the foreground of Russian life. By the mid-eighteenth century, when they were ennobled, they controlled many Ural mines and metallurgical industries. In 1814 Count Stroganov was one of two nobles who made legal history by obtaining the imperial assent to entailing their properties. Primogeniture had never before been recognized in Russia, either in custom or in law. An imperial decree of 1845 permitted all nobles to entail property above a certain value – such a high value that only twelve entails had been created when serfdom was abolished in 1861.)

Eventually Sakha was found to contain some of the world's largest deposits of top-quality rock salt. But Boris Godunov and the Romanov czars who succeeded him were much more interested in furs than in salt and Siberia was the native habitat of the sable, a marten-like little animal whose pelt had for centuries been regarded as a far more valuable commodity than gold, never mind salt. Terence Armstrong cites a sixth-century Gothic writer, Jordanes, who mentions Slavs trading with tribes living at the fur-rich Arctic end of the Urals. And *circa* 912 the Arab geographer, Ibn Ruste, refers to a Slav trade in sables, found only in the far north. Novgorod, for long a major centre of the world fur trade, was given a spectacular boost by the 'opening up' of Siberia. Historians reckon that until the beginning of the eighteenth century this trade was second only to agriculture in its importance to the Russian economy and was the main source of foreign currency. Furs also had their political uses, as Anna Reid records:

> In 1595 Boris Godunov was embarrassed by a request from the Holy Roman Emperor, Rudolf II, for military assistance against the Turks. Not wishing to jeopardise trade with Constantinople, he compromised by sending Rudolf the pelts of 337,235 squirrel, 40,360 sable, 20,760 marten, 3,000 beaver and 1,000 wolves. Their display – not counting the squirrel skins, which had to be left in wagons outside – took up twenty rooms of Rudolf's palace in Prague.

Before the Russians' arrival, Siberia's tribes had killed only as many animals as were needed for their own survival – or, in some cases, to pay tribute to locally dominant Buryat or Sakha chiefs who sold the pelts to Chinese and central Asian merchants. When the tribes were forced to kill in an organized way on a massive scale (so many pelts to be delivered in exchange for family members held hostage) a shortage of the relevant creatures spurred the Russians to penetrate farther and farther into the unknown. Along the Lena's course, where fur bearers were not commercially exploited until the 1630s, their numbers had dropped so dramatically within thirty years that traders began to lose interest in the region. This inspired the government drastically to reduce their tribute demands in some areas, to give the various species recovery time, a tactic our twenty-first-century fishing fleets seem reluctant to adopt.

Siberia provides a classic example of that favourite imperialists' ploy, the extraction of a colony's wealth by native labourers (in this case hunters) controlled by very few settlers. The Russians rarely hunted or trapped. Their role was to run the show, first terrorizing the natives while keeping deaths to the minimum in view of their manpower value, then demanding a specific number of pelts to be collected by traders, then ensuring that each trader handed over to the Moscow Treasury the best pelt out of ten in his stock, as tax, and that he sold the rest to the Treasury at fixed (by the Treasury) prices. As time passed these traders took to dealing in other goods, importing iron-ware, tobacco and alcohol (that last illegal) for which novelties the natives soon acquired a taste.

Obviously this system of fur collection could be abused, to the Treasury's detriment, and in 1763 Catherine the Great set up provincial fur-tribute commissions, Sakha's the most important. It sat in Yakutsk (1766–67) and, having closely considered current practices, recommended a changed method of payment and encouraged the acceptance of money, in certain circumstances, instead of furs. A second commission (1827) also promoted the acceptance of cash and urged an increase in the tribute demanded. Fur was still the main commodity traded throughout Sakha but now the natives brought it to annual fairs in various centres, Yakutsk among them. At these efficiently-run fairs, seen by the Russians as the most profitable pelt-gathering method, the natives had to settle for shamefully low prices; many claimed to have done much better when dealing with individual taiga-touring traders. Thus was the roving fur traders' significance diminished and by the end of the nineteenth century only 139 remained in all of Sakha.

We could see the old (1635) port of Olekminsk long before the *Blagoveshchensk* was moored to its floating landing-stage from where hills of coarse sand concealed most of the town. Originally a small Cossack *ostrog*, Olekminsk thrived after the arrival of the Skoptsi in the 1860s. This dotty cult had been banished from European Russia, as the Old Believers were in the mid-seventeenth century to punish them for their rejection of Patriarch Nikon's reforms. But the Skoptsi were far odder than the merely inflexible Old Believers. They lived in communes known as 'ships' and each 'crew' was led by an autocratic 'helmsman'. They were teetotalers, non-smokers and celibates who addressed each other as 'brother' and 'sister'. Salvation, they believed, was conditional on sexual abstinence (were they influenced by France's twelfth-century Cathars?) and caring helmsmen had their male crew members castrated. However, new recruits arrived at intervals and the colony survived for a few generations. Unlike the Old Believers, who could eventually return home if they wished (many didn't), the Skoptsi were exiled for life – perhaps because the authorities appreciated their exceptional farming skills, which enabled them to make the most of the fertile soil around the confluences of the Lena, Olekma and Chara rivers. They introduced new crops to the Olekminsk and Yakutsk districts, planting barley, spring rye, wheat (which did rather poorly), potatoes, turnips and cabbages – all expensive imports in the mid-nineteenth century.

This was the day's main stop; dozens got off, scores came on. From the top deck a steep narrow gangplank led down to the roofed landing-stage which soon became a scene of disorder as crew members, local porters and harassed-looking passengers struggled both ways with sacks, crates and cartons. For half an hour the first mate restrained oncoming passengers behind a rope cordon where large farewell groups, some tearful, were stubbornly contributing to the confusion. When the cordon was dropped a seriously rough scrum developed: much elbowing and pushing, often of women by men and vice versa. A few confrontations led to enraged shouting but roars of laughter were commoner. When one weedy youth was pushed too hard he fell on the crate he was carrying and cracked his ribs; later I saw him white with pain, lying on sacks of potatoes near the engine room. Meanwhile two of our crew – teenage lads – were using the lifeboat to earn tidy sums by paddling passengers and their mounds of luggage to and from little craft that had moored some distance downstream from the landing-stage. An excited-looking Ust'-Kut woman and her five-months-old daughter were thus taken to join a tall elderly man standing by his boat. Through my binoculars I watched the man stretch out his arms to take the baby and look down at her with great joy – surely a grandfather meeting his granddaughter, probably for the first time. Then the three sat huddled in the tiny boat, in that piercing wind, for almost half an hour, awaiting a man who arrived in an army minibus. We overtook them later, several miles downstream, where they were turning up the Olekma river to some remote hamlet.

Not far beyond Olekminsk an odd little episode occurred. When we met an oil-tanker going upstream both vessels stopped and were roped together, sides touching. I was alone on deck, being more resistant to cold than to heat, and with astonishment saw the tanker's captain attempting to board the *Blagoveshchensk* but being shoved back on to his own deck. As a fierce dispute broke out between him and our pilot the latter suddenly noticed me and angrily signalled me to go inside. Did he imagine I was a spy, pretending not to understand Russian but eavesdropping on this mysterious dissension? I obeyed him but from my cabin window could observe the whole scene. Eventually bits of paper (or rouble notes?) were passed one by one – with more arguing between each, from tanker to steamer. Have the mafia reached the Lena? That would hardly be surprising; the Cossacks prepared the way. This tanker was a 'home' vessel with a vegetable-providing plastic hot-house on the cabin roof, surrounded by still colourful flower-boxes, and from the cabin doorway an anxious-looking, weatherbeaten woman had been watching the drama.

All afternoon the clouds – every shade of grey – matched the right bank's low bare cliffs. On the left, thick taiga covered a seemingly boundless plain. Here the Lena was more than a mile wide and for twenty miles or so below its confluence with the Olekma, a river mighty in its own right, the tributary's forceful contribution quickened the Lena's current. This was not sitting weather; I had to keep moving, round and round the deck, wearing a thermal vest as headgear. Four long flocks of migrating duck flew high above us – approximately one an hour – and I wondered about their social organization. Presumably they don't all fly together for logistical reasons. Their transient active presence emphasized that immense Siberian stillness through which the Lena has been flowing for some twelve millennia. (Only twelve because until the last Ice Age the Lena, like all Siberia's rivers, flowed south from the Arctic Circle into Lake Baikal or the Caspian Sea. Or so some eminent experts say: personally I find this quite hard to believe.)

At four o'clock we anchored far off an almost invisible settlement where only two boats and a small lorry awaited us. Five adults and three children came abroad, packed tightly into one boat, its cargo topped by a red plastic potty. This soon slipped into the Lena, causing its owner to wail most piteously; the following boat did a slight detour to retrieve it. Then came a long delay – another communication breakdown, doubts about whether or not sacks of sugar should be unloaded. Eventually three boats had to do six trips each to get them ashore.

The Lena was calm again, under a clear sky, as we sailed on. Then our world was transformed for a few freakishly beautiful moments as the sunset sky, mirrored in the gently eddying water of our wake, created an intricate pattern of long golden curves on a royal blue background, extending as far as one could see and edged by the ebony reflections of the pinewood taiga. Had I not taken a photograph, I might now be asking myself, 'Did I imagine it?'

Overnight the wind rose again and the morning sleet, verging on snow, confined me to my cabin for two hours. When I emerged, the grey-green Lena's wavelets were white-capped and erratic, tossed this way and that by the gusty gale. On the distant left bank stretched a low dark ridge, many miles long and level-topped. Above it ran a ribbon of paleness and above that an immobile cloud mass filled the sky – almost black to the south, gradually shading to iron grey in the north. Amidst this sombre splendour, by some trick of the light, a fringe of burnished birches defined the water's edge – their brightness a mystery, for no sun was visible.

Soon after, disconcertingly, our funnel began to emit dense clouds of foul brownish smoke. Had something gone wrong? Or is this pollution normal on Day Six of a *Blagoveshchensk* voyage that is supposed to take four days? Throughout the forenoon those emissions continued at irregular intervals.

I was brunching when there came a knock at my cabin door and two middle-aged Sakha women introduced themselves as Oksana, a university librarian, and Mariya, a geology professor. Ever since embarking at Lensk they had been observing both my 'lonely' existence and my limp and feeling sorry for me. Neither spoke English but they had enlisted Viki as interpreter, a conspicuously Chinese-looking girl (recalling one of Prince Phillip's more notorious gaffes) who came from a village near Olekminsk. In her second year at university, she aspired to be a teacher of English yet knew only a few phrases and found sign language daunting. She had never heard of Tynda or Severobaikalsk; a steamer took her to and from Yakutsk, or a minibus when the Lena became a winter road, and Yakutsk was *it*.

Given Viki's (and my own) limitations, it was dictionary time and photograph time, once again – until we came to the Lenskie Stolby (Lena Pillars). Then many passengers braved the icy gale to stand on deck for hours, despite their familiarity with Siberia's contribution to the Wonders of the World.

To facilitate Stolby worship, the *Blagoveshchensk* sailed close to the right bank for all those 112 miles. The Stolby are not cliffs in any ordinary sense of the word but columns of perpendicular limestone, some rising 400 and 500 feet above the Lena. Here erosion was/is not a sculptor but an architect – creating domes, arches, spires, flying buttresses, rounded forts, rows of pillars. Elsewhere, below soaring pinnacles, smooth semi-circular 'trays' of honey-coloured rock protrude from grey shale slopes and are precisely equidistant – about 15 yards apart – as though artificially arranged. Also there are free-standing sheets of rock forming square 'rooms' with one wall missing. The predominant colour is pale gold but some stretches are streaked, for many yards, with red and green strata, perfectly horizontal, each about twenty inches broad. Crevices between the 'structures' support dwarf pines or tangled bushes; grassy slopes fill the occasional wider intervening spaces. The Stolby are Sakha's only tourist attraction and someone organizes midsummer weekend excursions from Yakutsk. But I foresee no Theme Park or Visitors' Centre threat.

To counteract the marrow-freezing wind most male Stolby worshippers had recourse to litre bottles of vodka which they generously passed around – hiding them when Katerina appeared, a further intriguing example of the social (not legal) pressures now operating against vodka. However, given the exceptional circumstances Oksana and Mariya gratefully accepted unladylike swigs of anti-freeze and by the end of our Stolby experience we were all feeling jolly.

I was then invited to my friends' second-class cabin to drink *pivo*; they had evidently been observing my patronage of the 'off-licence'. In their congenial company I regretted especially keenly my linguistic handicap. By this stage the average traveller would certainly have learned to speak a little Russian; I had only learned to understand a little.

Oksana offered to give me a lift to my hotel next morning; her daughter Tara, an English teacher, would be meeting the *Blagoveshchensk*. Mariya volunteered to show me round her university department and introduce me to English-speaking students; two days hence she would collect me from the Hotel Kolos. Both women apologized for not asking me to stay – heartfelt, shame-faced apologies, as though hospitality were a wandering foreigner's right. I later discovered that their flats were overcrowded with student lodgers because of the depreciation of their irregularly paid salaries. (To anticipate: Oksana's plan didn't work. When Tara came aboard to help with luggage she seemed flustered on meeting me and her very poor spoken English being exposed to her mother made for embarrassment all round. Saying hurried goodbyes, I easily got lost in the confusion of the disembarking crowd.)

On that last evening of our voyage the *Blagoveshchensk* was in festive mood. A sing-song began in the corridor (many *pivo* bottles being shared, Katerina looking disapproving but not intervening), and we joined the happy group. There were folk songs in praise of the taiga, the tundra, the Lena, Lake Baikal – Oksana the lead singer, her rich contralto voice reminding me of my mother's. Finally she and a young man sang a lament for the victims of Hiroshima and Nagasaki, a lament so poignant it still echoes in my memory. Robert Service, reviewing the first post-Soviet decade, has written: 'The music and dancing of old Russia has lasted better in the countryside than in the towns. Folksongs retain a strong appeal, strong enough to outmatch the "light entertainment" offered by television and radio.' Perhaps, in this context, remote Yakutsk counts as 'countryside'.

Before I retired, half a dozen people presented me with minuscule gifts most skilfully made of mammoth ivory and seal fur, for my granddaughters.

# 8

## City of Pipes

Sleet and mist obscured the Lena's six-mile width as we approached Yakutsk's port, large but no longer busy. A twin of Osetrovo Station overlooks the steamers' quay and I was halfway up its steps when the sleet became snow: tiny flakes, slowly swirling and three weeks early, as though laid on to provide the solitary tourist with local colour.

Siberian hotels are obdurate – no booking in before noon – so I decided to do a recce by bus, toing and froing across the city. On a very decrepit No. 8 I became aware of feeling oddly disorientated and unexcited about visiting somewhere new; it didn't take long to diagnose Lena withdrawal symptoms. As we left Ust'-Kut I had changed gear without realizing it at the time, allowing that slow river journey, all beauty and calm, to detach me from everyday life both physically and emotionally. Only the present had mattered; both past and future became irrelevant and a deep contentment took over. This is innocent escapism, a brief release into an undemanding Paradise. And now Paradise was lost.

My recce showed Yakutsk at its worse – a sullen sky squatting over everything, the feathery snow quickly turning to slush on cratered streets. Here was an ill-planned (or unplanned) and blatantly impoverished city, despite Sakha's mineral wealth. Jumbles of old wooden dwellings in untidy yards were overshadowed by gaunt residential blocks with broken balconies and crumbling plaster. Miles of gigantic heating-pipes needed repairs. Long lagoons, sometimes spanned by elegant wrought-iron footbridges, had lids of green scum. Cloudtouching cranes swung slowly above bleak building sites. Ailing minor industries languished around the edges. In the centre a few stately 1890s public buildings had been well restored. Startling 1990s architectural extravaganzas (mostly banks) erupted in unexpected places.

And around every corner, to celebrate Yakutsk's 370th birthday, flags, banners, posters and placards bore such legends as '1632–2002' and '370 aet' – those Roman letters seeming off-key. The *BAM Guide* refers to Yakutsk as 'an ancient and fascinating city' which is rather like describing New York or Cape Town as 'ancient'.

The air still felt raw when I left the bus in Lenin Square not far from the Hotel Kolos, one of a row of grim six-storey blocks set back from a quiet street. Two Sakha crossword-puzzle addicts over-womanned Reception and this being 'a Russian hotel' (according to the *BAM Guide*) both were unfamiliar with Western travel documents. I held my breath while the younger woman, Anna, frowned at my passport. The older woman then made a suggestion and Anna took it off to be scrutinized and photocopied by some person or persons unknown. For a tense half-hour I sat on a stained sofa with broken springs; the foyer was otherwise unfurnished. Several huge canvas-wrapped bales were delivered by unkempt youths and their owners followed: two incessantly argumentative Chinese traders, allotted the room next to mine. Then Anna returned, smiling reassuringly, and I unwound.

A gloomy young man wearing a crumpled gold-braided uniform interrupted his window-cleaning to lead me up a bare concrete stairway to the fourth floor; wide gaps yawned between the top step of each flight and its landing. My large room ($12) contained two single beds, a table and three chairs, a refrigerator, a telephone and two TV sets, one atop the other. A few small cockroaches, the palest I've ever seen, lived under the non-functioning fridge. The clothes cupboard was as big as the bathroom where a shower over the hip-bath provided only a trickle of cold water; the city's winter heating system had not yet been switched on. Directly opposite my wide window, half a mile away, rose Yakutsk's TV mast – ugly, but useful as a landmark.

By the time I went shopping blue patches of sky had appeared and spasms of sunshine warmed the long, straight streets. A three-storey czarist-era post office (so announcing itself in English on the roof) occupies one whole side of central Ordzhonikidze Square – why? When did Yakutsk's postal activity need so much space? It has an air of solid dignity, in contrast to the new Sakha Theatre facing it across the square, an unsightly concoction of brick and glass, all jarring sharp angles, bulbous extrusions and meaningless gaps. Nearby a commercial building, too many storeys high, has rounded corners and is completely sheathed in scarlet plastic tiles – international capitalism having a frolic in Sakha. Various 'beautification schemes', as Ireland's town planners phrase it, had been devised by a South Korean (it was rumoured) consultant. In Ordzhonikidze Square, a spacious pedestrian area, new paving bricks were being laid and enormous semicircular wooden benches installed. Opposite my hotel an earth track led between a smelly open sewer and a terrace of old log houses (lopsided because of permafrost subsidence) to the edge of a lagoon. There a park was being created on wasteland, complete with wrought-iron railings, seats enhanced by fretwork and a fountain. Horse-manured flowerbeds awaited the spring and birch saplings had been planted in 'cradles' of imported soil. (Yakutsk's extremely saline soil explains its scarcity of foliage.) I wondered if the consultant had said anything about eliminating the lagoon's scum.

Those who don't like Sakha's capital find it easy to explain why. None of Yakutsk is beautiful and much of it is squalid. Its 'places of interest' are not very interesting. Its past is without notable events, its present is uneasy, its future uncertain. (Summed up thus by one young man: 'We're out of the Communist hell but far from the capitalist heaven, so maybe this is limbo?') Yet I soon grew fond of the city – of its spatial eccentricities, its independent air, its distinctiveness as the home of 200,000 people where Nature is implacably opposed to human beings living en masse. Although the inhabitants seem less outgoing than most Siberians, I sensed no lack of goodwill towards the foreigner, only a degree of understandable introversion.

The next day dawned cloudless, a keenly cold morning becoming a hot noon. Yakutsk, too, has an excellent public transport system, though none of its buses would pass their MOT test, and a No. 17 took me all the way from Lenin Square to the Permafrost Institute on the southern outskirts. Here in times past scientists did ingenious experiments and made discoveries without which modern Yakutsk could not have happened, or so the scientists say. The city's first high-rise buildings soon melted the permafrost and had to be demolished hastily before they fell apart. The second generation stood on iron pile sub-foundations, extending far below ground level, but their walls too cracked open, the piles having conveyed heat to the permafrost. With hindsight the solution sounds obvious; leave a six-foot gap between buildings and ground and use wooden piles which do not conduct heat.

The austere three-storey Institute stands alone amidst swampy land, its white walls and green roof visible from afar. In the hallway, yellowing newspaper cuttings hung sideways on a noticeboard and an ancient asthmatic babushka, wearing a woollen cap and shawl, sat behind the reception desk peering towards the sound of my voice with cataract-dimmed eyes. She mumbled what might have been a protest when I went on my way. Here is another victim of underfunding: long corridors silent, most rooms empty, grand staircases dusty.

On the top floor a melancholy middle-aged microbiologist offered me tea and toffees and spoke enough English to express his resentment of 'the men in Moscow'. Beckoning me to a window, he pointed to the baby mammoth replica which I had noticed on my way in. (Why did its maker give it bright blue eyes – or was the original's eye-colour discernible?) To my host, this replica symbolized the relentless exploitation of Yakutia/Sakha by the central government, whether czarist, Soviet or new Russian. The real baby, a perfectly preserved specimen, was taken to St Petersburg though it belonged to Yakutia. *St Petersburg* should have had the replica!

I then discovered the importance of the ivory trade in nineteenth-century Sakha. Some came from the walrus hunted in coastal areas but most came from mammoth tusks. Huge mammoth herds roamed across northern Siberia in Pleistocene times and when the tribes realized how much traders valued ivory they set about tusk-collecting in a big way, delivering an annual average of twenty tons to Yakutsk's market during the second half of the nineteenth century.

Soon two tired-looking women scientists joined us, a young Sakha and a forty-ish Russian who said diffidently, 'I can read English very good but for being without talking practice please you must make excuses I make mistakes'. The Sakha spoke no English but had a lot to say about the proposed extension of the BAM to Yakutsk, the damage that would do to the environment and to what little remains of the authentic tribal way of life – the two of course going together. My heart sided with her, yet my head had to allow that given a city so hamstrung by transport costs the BAM lobby has a powerful argument.

Below the Institute are deep tunnels and caverns needing no supports because of the rock-hard ground. As the permafrost's temperature is constant, at about four degrees below freezing, such 'cellars' (and every traditional house has its own cellar) are the warmest unheated spaces in Yakutsk during the winter. I had hoped to see this subterranean complex but the man with the key was not on duty, was doing his second job that day. Everyone needs a second job in the new Russia...

I walked back to the Kolos; that inactive Lena week had been good for The Knee. Parallel to the Institute's road, a set of five new metal-coated heating pipes, enormous and shiny, runs for miles across the marshland, several feet above its golden-brown expanse of tall tufted reeds. At intervals the set rises sinuously to form 'bridges' above roads or tracks or lagoons. In this open countryside such pipes have their own sort of strange, purposeful beauty – extending as far as the eye can see, all silvery and symmetrical and essential for urban survival.

Now I think of heating pipes as Yakutsk's emblem; although used throughout Siberia, only here do they so dominate the cityscape. Sometimes they cross acres of uneven wasteland (Yakutsk's developers left many such) and where the ground dips one walks under them, tall people ducking their heads. Many ground-level sets separate blocks from their streets and footbridges are provided, usually unsteady little constructions of rotting wood, four or five steps up and down, which gives some idea of the pipes' dimensions. The city-centre pipe 'bridges' are high and long, spanning wide streets and hung with advertisements and '1632–2002' banners. A considerable percentage of the older sets are badly battered, the metal casing having fallen off some sections. Why did the municipality not repair these, before investing in 'beautification'?

Yakutsk's drains, open and hidden, are another 'special feature'. Some resemble dried-up canals, unfenced concrete channels six or eight feet deep, empty in autumn (apart from litter) and also crossed by footbridges. At night, on ill-lit streets, these constitute a major hazard for drunks or newcomers to a district. In springtime, the abrupt thaw turns them into tumultuous torrents.

No less hazardous are the massive pavement slabs from which protrude six-inch-high iron hoops, two or three to a slab, as though the authorities had thought long and hard about how best to trip people up. These hoops are used to raise the slabs when some crisis occurs beneath them to do with water, electricity, sewage – or all three simultaneously. Sometimes slabs are missing, with no warning signs. A pedestrian who happened to be looking at the sunset, or the traffic lights ahead, would soon suffer a fate like mine in Severobaikalsk. To avoid a third accident I kept off all pavements, walking on the parallel humpy earth paths, the humps a permafrost side-effect. As elsewhere in Siberia, badly drained streets and pavements mean that rainwater gathers in deep ponds (on the rare occasions when it rains) and lies around for days to the delight of small children.

That evening a letter was delivered to my room, inspired by a Lena fellow-traveller and neatly written in studiously correct English. It was from Oksana's Muscovite son-in-law, temporarily working in Sakha. Feodor had been delegated to show me around Yakutsk and would collect me from the Kolos at 10 a.m. on the morrow.

Feodor was one of those standard Muscovites (mousy hair, pale blue eyes, blunt features, average height and build) who have missed out on the varied genetic contributions that make many Russians look interesting. But his appearance belied him; he was a thought-provoking companion, much appreciated after my Trappist interlude since leaving Irkutsk.

On Feodor's suggestion, we walked in the park. This was another bright cloudless day but perceptibly colder; overnight the rainwater ponds had frozen solid and hours of direct sunshine failed to thaw them. Just inside the park were mini-trains, bumper cars, climbing frames to suit all age groups, slides, swings and roundabouts – all the fun of the fair, covering several acres, but now abandoned behind padlocked gates. Weeds grew high around this positive aspect of the Soviet régime, the provision of free entertainment. Feodor pointed to a huge new indoor sports complex beyond the park. 'Private enterprise,' he explained. 'Throughout the year people with spare roubles can enjoy themselves in there.'

Approaching the park's forest, we passed an aborted 'development': scores of stout ten-foot-high concrete pillars enclosed a hectare of briar-entangled builders' rubble. Gloomily Feodor commented, 'Who knows or cares what that plan was? All over Russia we have such monuments to failure. Now I want to hear your impressions of Siberia – *honest* impressions, not being polite.'

'In this case,' I said, 'it's possible to be both honest and polite. Siberian hospitality is, in my experience, unique. That's a fact. As for impressions, not speaking the language mine are restricted. But people's resilience seems extraordinary. Thirty years ago I read Solzhenitsyn and was devastated. I thought, "What can be the future for these people? Communism won't last but how long will it take them to recover?" Now I'm among these people and they seem already recovered, at least outwardly.'

Feodor looked pleased and said, 'I suppose you're sort of right, we're survivors! If Germans, French, British had to live through the Soviet time they might have been destroyed for ever. We were made tough by all our history. Tough and also weak. I believe Russia wasn't really in Europe in czarist times. The Soviets couldn't have ruled Germany, France, Britain. The Germans accepted Hitler but he wasn't Stalin, he had another agenda – OK for Germans who weren't Jews or Gypsies. Solzhenitsyn asked why were we *silent* when Stalin's terrorizing started? I argue that was about us not being real Europeans. The serfs were only sort of freed in 1861, they stayed deprived and controlled. Two generations later was the Revolution, too soon for them to have found the confidence to be *not silent* when new repressions came.'

We were walking between the trees, on footpaths carpeted with russet larch-needles and sometimes with hundreds of broken bottles. All morning we met no one though the park has become a popular unofficial dump, 'normal' household garbage being augmented by cracked plastic buckets and rusted milk churns, bits of iron bedsteads and disembowelled mattresses, worn garments and footwear.

Feodor wrinkled his nose in a disarming small-boy way. 'In this quiet forest people could refresh their souls, but it's not respected. Here is a little display of anarchy, a sample of our economic and political mess. And we don't seem recovered enough to get out of it. D'you remember the question Gogol asked at the end of the first part of *Dead Souls*? "Rus', whither art thou speeding?" Still we have no answer. We don't even have what Americans call "a mission statement". We don't know what sort of new Russia we want. Look at Moscow now and you can say we want only one thing, to live the way the West lives – if possible more so and faster! Even though history hasn't made us ready for quickly having Western affluence. That needs a sort of orderliness we don't know about. You must see the black joke, Western orderliness breaking down with Enron-type crimes being found out just as we joined the capitalist world! Our mafia are happy about that, feeling they have colleagues in Wall Street and London and Frankfurt. In 1991 we were told we must have new rules, laws, an honest system to make outside investors feel safe putting their money here. Now we see the West's rules and laws can't protect their own ordinary investors. Like in Russia, small people are losing their money, capitalism unregulated isn't working for them.

'Was Solzhenitsyn right when he said we should go backwards? You remember? He thought it would be good if the Soviet Union lost its European satellites and its empire. So now that's happened, we should be thinking *Russian* – yes? We don't have to be "globalized", we're the biggest country on the globe. With an efficient government we could be independent, producing all we need. Our psychological block is wanting to compete with America. Before, our economy was skewed and ruined by competing about dams and mines and bombs and space adventures. Now we're still messing it up, competing to have an American lifestyle. I'm part of it, I'm working for a US corporation interested in Sakha's development – but the profits won't much help Sakha. For me personally that's the way to go with good pay, good status, good prospects for my children. I could be happy if I could stop *thinking*! Thinking tells me Russia's going the wrong way, but not how I, Feodor, can change things. I'm a trained mining engineer and so good at my job the corporation loves me. I'm not a trained politician who could turn Russia in another direction.

'My father had the same sort of job and was in the same sort of situation. He was a good Party man, not asking questions, getting on with his work in Western Siberia. I grew up with my mother in Moscow, she had her good job there, getting to be a hospital director. My father had enough privileges to visit us often. I don't know if he ever had thinking problems like me. I guess he didn't, that's how my generation is different. We know about other ways of living and that puts another sort of stress on us. For me there's as much corruption in my corporation as there was for my father in the Party – he lived with it, I live with it. Same reasons, our comfortable lifestyle, security for the family. I've a wife and two small children – boy and girl, aged two and five, later I'll show you photographs. My wife works in Moscow for the same corporation and is very happy. She feels this new Russia is OK, she's not interested in talk of going back to the *real* Russia with Solzhenitsyn as guide.'

I interrupted. 'Surely she's right there! His "real Russia" would be a nasty place, authoritarian and patriarchal. But why do you say Russia wasn't really in Europe? What about Peter the Great and Catherine the Great? And all your musicians and writers – they weren't giving to Europe as outsiders.'

Feodor frowned, ran a hand through his hair, was silent for a moment. Then, 'Forget Peter and Catherine the German woman, people everywhere know about them because they're not typical. Same with our musicians and writers, the Russians the West relates to – mostly *they* didn't relate to the masses, *or* to our rulers. They came out of a thin top layer, maybe three million, and my grandmother says the majority ran abroad just before or after the Revolution. Stalin killed lots more. The rest, like my own family, went along with Communism. My great-grandfather and grandfather believed in it like a religion and I suppose my father did too. He was born in 1940, his father died three years later in what we call the Great Patriotic War. Now my grandmother says, "What was so great or patriotic about it? All those young people weren't given a choice about being killed." She's nearly ninety and was always inside herself a sort of dissident, but not enough to get into trouble and spoil my father's chances.'

I asked, 'When did your father die?' and Feodor's voice tightened as he replied, 'Five years ago after a long time in hospital. He got a blood disease from pollution around his work. We know that but his employers deny it.'

Inevitably, there followed speculation about the afterlife. In a deadpan way Feodor reported that his father, within a few months of his death, had several times communicated with his mother, assuring her that he was at peace, happy, still close to her. And the family cat had been aware of his presence, had behaved as she habitually did when he returned home.

Beyond the forest our footpath joined a motor track winding through miles of golden rushes surrounding three small lagoons. This area was strewn with the skeletons of cranes and tractors, half a dozen cannibalized cars and the contorted wreckage of a two-seater plane. We watched women drawing pails of pale green water from a lagoon and carrying it to a distant row of new wooden houses. I asked, 'Will those homes ever be connected to the city mains?' Feodor shook his head: 'Yakutsk has a very bad water shortage, standing beside the world's ninth-longest river! The authorities wanted fast development – never mind the necessary infrastructure. Now most citizens suffer while office blocks, banks, smart hotels, luxury apartments demand and get unfair shares. Always foreign investors must come first.'

Wearily I nodded. Similar uncontrolled developments have recently been allowed in Ireland, leading to turds floating down the main streets of some pretty seaside villages.

We bussed back to Lenin Square, passing one of Yakutsk's new banks, its thirteen storeys all of coloured glass, its design matching that inane phrase 'post-modern'. Dryly Feodor remarked, 'For certain the architect never spent a winter in Yakutsk.' And then he wondered, 'In 2020, will those palaces still be open for business? Or will squatters have taken over?'

Most Sakha never use such institutions yet this is but one of several new banks, an excess not explained by the Republic's natural resources, fabulous though these are. I said, 'Here's typical disorganized 1990s speculation, completely dissociated from humdrum needs like running water. So what lies ahead for autonomous Sakha, with only one foot in the new Russia?'

Feodor smiled but didn't look amused. 'Maybe it will take the other foot out. Globalization could make it a corporate colony, foreign investors colluding with the Yakutsk government to cheat the people. Or maybe Moscow wouldn't allow that, would fight to keep a share of control. I don't know, nobody knows about the future, it's impossible to foresee or plan when there are no rules, standards, principles. Let's meet again this evening for a drink and talk about nicer things like children and grandchildren!'

That afternoon brought a chance bus encounter with Lena fellow-travellers, now accompanied by their student daughter, Damva. This cheerful Sakha couple – both dentists – had been fascinated by my binoculars and often borrowed them. We met on the way to the Arbat Market – miles from the centre, beyond the airport – and though their home stop came first they insisted on accompanying me, to advise on my purchase of a *shapka*. Damva reproduced a familiar pattern: allegedly an English-speaker, she became tongue-tied when introduced to me and this caused some paternal irritation.

The enormous Arbat market is Yakutsk's out-of-town shopping centre where covered stalls, ranging in size from cubby-holes to mini-emporiums, sell everything from tools and toys to tea-sets and garments, these last often boasting forged designer labels and logos. The Chinese dominate; most games and toys had instructions and baby warnings only in Cantonese and English. Iron handcarts piled high were being pushed at speed along narrow aisles by youths who couldn't see ahead of their loads – causing yelps of alarm as customers retreated to the safety of the nearest stall. In the butchers' department most cabinets were empty and the expensive deep-frozen reindeer joints looked discoloured and unappetizing. Greengrocers' prices were at least double the Siberian average and most of their stock – apples, pears, grapes, bananas, peppers – had begun to go off yet were being purchased without complaint.

Eventually we came to the open-air luxury department: rack after rack of pure fur Siberian *shapkas*, the saleswomen Sakha, the prices from $100 to $150. All proved too small for my fat head, an odd circumstance which enabled me to move downmarket, without loss of face, to a rack of imitation leather Chinese *shapkas*, the lining and ear-flaps genuine rabbit fur, price $36.50. It puzzled my companions to see me veering away from the women's *shapkas* with tinselly bits and coloured beads added, or jaunty pom-poms hanging from the crown. That evening Feodor deplored my choice of a plain working-man's model; it would, he forecast, react to melting snow by exuding purple dye. He was right.

The hotel where Feodor and I met had been extravagantly modernized in 1995 and had since proved a great disappointment to all concerned. The main ground-floor restaurant and its adjacent bar

were only used, Feodor said, for special occasions. Five flights of
concrete stairs, the first two carpeted, led to a small overheated bar-
restaurant where most tables were unoccupied at 7.30. When I suggested eating here Feodor surveyed what was on offer and declined
my invitation. Unlike Siberian home cooking, the region's restaurant
meals rarely excite one's taste buds. During the Soviet era I ate as
well in Moscow market canteens.

Feodor had brought his album and I had brought mine – just in
case, not really expecting a sophisticated Muscovite to be interested in
the Irish countryside, my numerous animals, my three granddaughters and their numerous animals. In fact he was astonished by
the greenness of Irish fields in January, delighted to see dogs and
cats sleeping together on my bed, slightly shocked by granddaughters
romping naked in flowery summer meadows and curious about the
pony and the donkey. 'Do you eat ponies? What is the purpose of Irish
donkeys?' When I explained that the purpose of that particular Irish
donkey was to provide companionship for the pony he looked understandably puzzled. Then he remarked that language-limited foreigners must find photographs helpful on long train journeys. 'Yes,' I said,
'and also when visiting families without English-speakers.'

In all the Siberian homes I had visited (and was yet to visit), two or
three gigantic family albums were brought out of cupboards or down
from bookshelves for my entertainment. Some dated back to the
black-and-white Stalinist era, a few included czarist-era studio portraits of great-grandparents (either prosperous kulaks or intelligentsia)
stiffly posing with or without children. Elsewhere, I admitted to
Feodor, I would have had to conceal boredom while looking through
hundreds of pictures celebrating events and occasions (solemn or
trivial) in the family, neighbourhood, school, college, workplace,
Pioneer and Komsomol centres and camps. But in Siberia I was
riveted by those glimpses of ordinary family life during the seven
decades when we in the West were persuaded that the average Russian
dwelt in a Communist hell, a cold, hungry, cheerless world. Every
album revealed adequately-dressed, contented-looking citizens living
in cramped but comfortably furnished homes, enjoying wedding and
funeral feasts, and jolly birthday and New Year parties with balloons,
crackers, decorated trees – and able to afford cameras and films that

produced excellent photographs. 'Also,' I said, 'there were many shots of youngsters enjoying state-subsidized holidays in St Petersburg, the Crimea, the Baltic coast.' One mother in Severobaikalsk, who visited St Petersburg at the age of twenty, assured me that the three days spent there have enriched the rest of her life. Now, she laments, her own twenty-year-old daughter has no hope of seeing anything beyond Eastern Siberia – ironically isolated by increasing poverty within a generation of the BAM's making it physically more accessible.

'Those holidays,' said Feodor, 'were part of the moulding process. Everyone had to feel proud of belonging to the same great homogenized Soviet Union – no nationalism, all Sovietization. European Russians had Siberian holidays so they wouldn't see the remote land beyond the Urals as somewhere alien. Maybe those photographs mislead you. If you'd grown up in Soviet shackles, not free to write what you thought and roam the world, wouldn't you have felt you dwelt in hell? I believe you would!'

I hesitated, seeing the pitfall of 'patronization' at my feet. Then I took the risk and said, 'Of course you're right, but most people don't want to write books and spend half their lives roaming the world. Please tell me your opinion on two points. One: the post-Stalin Soviets gave most citizens a better education and more material security than previous generations enjoyed. Two: Western propagandists exaggerated the Soviet Union's poverty, while the US worsened it by insisting on an arms race.'

Feodor nodded. 'Both ways I agree. But you should say "citizens who survived purges, famines and war". When Gorbachev came and we learned about international matters people laughed to discover some Party propaganda was *true*! The *so* rich US doesn't house and doctor and school all its citizens as the Soviets did!' However, Feodor went on to explain, Soviet education, though sound in ways, was a crucial part of the moulding process. And the post-Stalin stability and increasing prosperity were in fact, as dissidents like his grandmother well knew, illusory. The Soviets' closed-in world, paralysed by myopic bureaucracy and reeking with institutionalized corruption, was inherently unstable. 'And yet,' said Feodor, 'its sudden collapse left millions traumatized. Even now more shocks are coming because Putin is a cruel man, by temperament a tyrant. You must know about our system of a state holding-company overseeing apartment block repairs, supplying heating, water, gas, electricity, all looked after by local contractors. Always we grumbled about those contractors being lazy and dishonest but everything got done somehow at small cost. Now Putin wants to make people pay *all* charges – but how? With what? He is like American politicians saying hungry cold people must be lazy or stupid if they have less money than they need. Private enterprise must solve all problems but it can't. You see how many little shops and kiosks compete in Yakutsk and other places. Too many! Half the shelves are empty, the selling women get low pay not regularly, sometimes their owners intimidate each other with guns.'

I had noticed that most of those shops proclaim '24 Hours Opening' over their entrances and I asked Feodor why this barbarous custom has been adopted in Siberia, of all places. Who, during an eight-month winter, goes shopping in the wee hours at fifty degrees below?

Feodor laughed, 'Here we think it's part of a "developed" economy. Soon for sure it will stop when traders see it makes no profit to pay staff to wait for non-arrivals!'

Apart from having grown too long, my hair was behaving most peculiarly in Yakutsk, standing upright on my head, which gave me rather an alarming aspect – I only needed a few more limbs to look like the Hindu Goddess of Destruction. Seeking a hairdresser, I met three ex-*Blagoveshchensk* teenage girls who greeted me from across the street (I hadn't in fact recognized them) and were eager to help. 'I want a haircut' is easy in sign-language and they first led me to Hotel Tygyn Darkhan – government-owned, renovated a few years ago at vast expense by a Swiss company and offering a sauna, swimming-pool and weight-room (whatever that may be). Single rooms start at $100, haircuts are probably $50. When I shied away my guides shepherded me along rutted alleyways between externally slum-like blocks, then suddenly turned into one of those, pushed through heavy double doors and smiled at my surprise. We were in a large, tastefully decorated (but it wouldn't be my taste) salon, furnished with state-of-the-art hairdressing equipment and smelling strongly of a chemical cocktail of lotions and shampoos. Three expensively dressed women sat on a couch, studying fashion magazines while awaiting their sessions. The snooty receptionist, viewing my sartorial deficiencies, could scarce forbear to shudder; no appointment would be possible within the next week, not even for a ten-minute trim. An elegant young Sakha woman had volunteered to act as our interpreter and now gave me a quick apologetic glance, realizing that I understood I was being snubbed. Perhaps as compensation, Ksenya scribbled her name and address on a docket and invited me to supper that evening. My young guides looked vaguely discomfited and giggled slightly. They knew of no other salon and we parted outside the State Museum.

I was finding it hard to fulfil my tourist duties in Yakutsk. The day before Feodor had enquired about the *raketa* service to the Druzhba Historical Park on the Lena's right bank, near the site of the first Cossacks' fort. I had planned to spend two nights there, using it as a base for riverside walks, but already it had closed for the winter. Then on my way to the bus station, to book a ticket to Neryungri, I noticed the Literary Museum – its design based on a Yakut yurt – but it was so firmly closed that it looked as though it might never open again. And now I found the State Museum of the History and Culture of the Peoples of the North, one of Siberia's oldest and most interesting museums, also closed – or as good as.

Formerly the Bishop's Palace (late nineteenth-century), it had just acquired a sympathetic extension and the exhausted-looking staff were reorganizing all exhibits which that morning required the improvization of a pulley to winch a mammoth upstairs. No wonder they looked exhausted. Three small rooms remained open, holding insipid tableaux of early twentieth-century Russian Colonial domestic interiors which differed little, give or take a few samovars, from Western European homes of the period. An impassive uniformed male attendant with a lunar countenance – round and pale and shiny – followed me from room to room, observing my every movement and contriving to make me feel absurdly uncomfortable.

On the way out a melodramatic poster alerted me to a special drugs-education exhibition in an annex, aimed at the city's youth and their parents. Gruesomely lifelike waxworks showed young males (why no females?) inexorably descending the slippery slope from glue-sniffing (aet. 8) to cannabis to heroin. The young man on his deathbed had open sores all over an emaciated body, needle-ravaged arms and legs, a tortured face. I once saw several dying addicts in just this condition, lying on deck on a Bombay to Goa steamer in November 1973. My daughter, aged almost five, was with me and these unfortunates are among the few memories she has retained of a three-month journey.

The young woman teacher in charge of this exhibition spoke a little English and became shrilly defensive when asked why AIDS had not been linked to the needles. 'Here is no AIDS! Our government stops it!' Lucky Sakha, were that true!

Ksenya collected me from the Kolos, rightly assuming that I couldn't possibly find her flat in its complex of nine-storey blocks built at odd angles to each other and connected by humpy paths. Not for the first time I noted the eeriness of those dark spaces, under the raised blocks, where between stilts the pipes curve this way and that like monstrous serpents. Ksenya shared a third-floor flat with her munic-ipal worker parents; both were out when we arrived, attending a crisis meeting about Yakutsk's water supply. (My bathroom had then been waterless for twenty-four hours and the cockroach population around the base of the lavatory was increasing.) A 1980 wedding photograph on the multi-purpose cabinet showed that Ksenya took after her graceful, neat-featured mother. On the window ledge a supercilious Siamese sat amidst potted greenery; he flattened his ears and hissed when approached by the foreigner.

Ksenya couldn't understand why I don't have a favourite Irish pop star and footballer, or even a football team to which I owe allegiance. It depressed me to hear yet another shocked reference to TV scenes of Belfast adults terrorizing primary schoolchildren, a shameful image of Ireland now engraved on the minds of millions throughout the world.

'Christians fight too much,' declared Ksenya. 'I am a no god person but I like doing shaman things.' This did not surprise me; for millen-nia shamanism has influenced the Siberian tribes' whole way of being. Officially it was discarded (as were Sakha names) when the early col-onizers arrived, often accompanied by a priest or two, and in time many Sakha found it expedient to convert to Orthodoxy. Also, a con-siderable number of mixed-race Siberians became devout believers.

But the several rag-laden tree shrines I had seen on my walks around Yakutsk's rural periphery hinted that shamanism may retain more influence than one might expect at the dawn of the twenty-first century.

Ksenya scorned my romantic regrets about the Sakha having been 'Sovietized'. Yes, for her great-grandparents' generation it was violent and frightening, they couldn't adjust to being 'collectivized', immobilized, all their traditions so abruptly demolished. They remained sad, suffering, confused people. Yet it was all for the best. Her grandparents appreciated being inoculated against the worst diseases and taught how to read and write. Her parents appreciated being housed warmly in Yakutsk at the State's expense and getting academic qualifications instead of following reindeer herds all over the tundra living in filthy yurts and enduring extreme hardship. Tentatively I suggested that her great-grandparents – who had their own coping mechanisms, based on diverse skills and deep knowledge – might not have regarded that hardship as 'extreme'. But when Ksenya gestured impatiently I said no more.

Mrs Tetskaya returned in time to make bliny for supper. A forceful woman, who had put on some weight since 1980, she seemed to regard recourse to the mini-dictionary as a defeat and communicated through a combination of eloquent gestures, versatile facial expressions and the bold use of a small vocabulary. While the main dish (noodles and tinned meat) was being served, I produced Moldovan wine and Mrs Tetskaya scowled. Awkwardly her daughter explained, 'We have never alcohol, for my father it is a danger.'

Later, as Ksenya guided me back to the Kolos, she suddenly apologized for 'that rude woman in the salon'. I assured her that the incident hadn't bothered me. Russian women of every generation and class attach great importance to dressing well so of course my utilitarian garments were puzzling. Why did this woman from a rich country look like a destitute pensioner? Western fashion magazines used to cost up to $50 on Moscow's black market, now their Russian editions are sold for 60 or 70 roubles – still a lot of money yet a sound investment if one is skilled enough, as many Russian women are, to copy the latest *haute couture* creations in one's own home.

To Ksenya I explained that in my view clothes are mere necessities, to be handed down by friends or bought in charity shops, their only function to cover the body adequately according to the season. I do however enjoy being surrounded by well-dressed women, just as I enjoy other people's beautiful gardens while the weeds grow six feet tall in my own acre of potential garden. Ksenya chuckled and said, 'So you are a lazy person, letting others make beauty for you to enjoy!' Then, as we hugged outside the Kolos, she soothingly quoted an old Russian proverb: 'We meet you according to your dress and see you off according to your mind.'

In Irkutsk, one of Bruno's academic friends, Eva Skurlatov, had given me some insight into this area of the Russian psyche, beginning with the czarist sumptuary laws. Before 1861 serfs could be jailed for wearing noblemen's clothes and Tolstoy's defiant wearing of peasant garb caused a national scandal. Immediately after the Revolution drab garments were imposed on the masses and even a minor flourish of sartorial orginality could land a woman in jail. Generations later, when senior Party officials returned from visits abroad flaunting the latest Western fashions, they and their families and cronies were as readily identifiable, in a crowd, as the nobility of old. It was time to abandon enforced uniformity; by the 1970s 'fashion collectives' were permissible and soon 'artist-designers' could earn as much, selling their models to state enterprises, as highly qualified engineers and top *apparatchiks*.

In the West fashion designing might be seen as a trivial pursuit but in the Soviet Union, explained Professor Skurlatov, it had the reverse connotation, being one of the few professions that not only allowed but required its practioners to study pre-1917 Russian art. Moreover, fluency in one foreign language was essential, an attainment not normally encouraged. Students began their training with a two-year university course, followed by five years' apprenticeship, leading to a tough entrance examination to a Faculty of Fashion Designers or an Institute of Costume Designers. An average of one out of fifteen applicants were admitted to those colleges.

'Before long,' said Professor Skurlatov, 'the labels of our leading designers were successfully competing with Western rivals. But we weren't aping the West, only celebrating our escape from the most oppressive decades. Women then got a new sense of themselves, could feel like enterprising and innovative individuals, creating their own space for beauty. It made healthy competitiveness possible when it wasn't allowed in business or the professions – not officially. People need to compete to keep minds and judgements sharp. But it could be true we've gone a little too far. I've heard foreigners saying our obsession with fashion, our concentration on outward appearance, is found nowhere else in the world.'

When staying with families, I often saw this obsession in action. Before walking to the nearest shop my hostess, or it might be her daughter, would change out of slacks and T-shirt, or skirt and sweater – garments invariably clean and neat – and preparations for that excursion to buy a loaf could take up to half an hour of meticulous attention to clothes, coiffure, make-up, footwear. The amount of energy thus expended does seem disproportionate. Yet given such an ugly environment – all those littered square miles of apartment and office blocks, defaced by time and graffiti – the need personally to look beautiful is understandable.

Around midnight the light being switched on woke me out of a deep sleep. A woman police captain stood in the middle of the room with the Kolos night receptionist – had my visa dodging been detected? Would the fine be $2.50 or $300? Half sitting up, I smiled ingratiatingly and the policewoman smiled apologetically. Then I noticed the holdall on the other bed: Dasha had come to sleep, not to arrest me. I reached for the mini-dictionary and twenty minutes later knew that my room-mate had just arrived by car from Alcan, having been delayed by two breakdowns. Her Rottweiler, Lenin, a professional police dog, was sleeping upstairs in her colleague's room lest he might have xenophobic tendencies. Next day he was to compete in Yakutsk's annual dog show and he had an excellent chance of winning at least one prize. When I expressed an interest in the show Dasha immediately invited me to join Lenin's supporters at noon: we would all set out on foot from the Kolos.

My (now our) window gave a clear view of the next morning's memorable dawn: long banks of scarlet cloud, stacked one above the other, in a cold blue-green sky. As I rejoiced in this spectacle Dasha awoke and soon became tetchy. The waterless bathroom was bad enough; she then discovered that both TV sets were dead and seized the telephone to complain to the management – but it, too, was dead. Pulling a coat over her pyjamas she stormed downstairs and returned within minutes followed by a young man carrying two pails of water (hot and cold) and a bag of tools. Diligently he fiddled with both TVs, finally coaxing one to produce pop group sounds and a blurred wavering picture. At which point I took off for Sunday Mass in the church of St Nicholas.

This is now Yakutsk's main Orthodox church; the brick cathedral, dating from 1708, has long since been converted to a variety theatre. St Nicholas's was built in 1852, used for decades to house Communist Party archives and restored at vast expense in 1995. Conspicuously white, it stands alone on an open space at the high end of busy Oktyabrskaya Street, its small golden cupola visible from afar. A garden surrounds it, equally divided between a flowerbed (marigolds, geraniums and chrysanthemums for the church) and a vegetable-bed (cabbages and onions for the clergy and their families). Inside, one blinks for a moment; someone ran riot with the gilt paint. And the assiduously polished brass candelabra are more than slightly overwrought. Two sixteenth-century icons (who knows what chance preserved them?) hang on pillars at a discreet distance from the uniform rows of new panels on the iconostasis. These treasures had been restored, Feodor informed me, in St Petersburg where nineteeth- and eighteenth-century layers were removed to reveal a Virgin of Jerusalem, and St Nicholas as protector, holding an *ostrog* in one hand and sword in the other. They made the carefully imitative replacements of all those icons destroyed since 1917 seem banal and rather irritating.

During my first visit to St Nicholas's, the previous afternoon, the usual bevy of pious women were busy about flowers and candles, fluttering to and fro in long skirts and headscarves. Within half an hour seven men, mostly young and poorly dressed, came in to light candles (four or six apiece) and pray fervently, crossing themselves again and again, bowing, gazing imploringly at the icons of their choice. The various representations of the Virgin seemed most popular. Here were troubled people, for whatever reason, and I found the intensity of their search for solace both moving and disturbing.

A few energetic Orthodox clergy soon joined the early settlers. By

1664 there were four churches on the Lena, soon after Pokrovskiy monastery was founded near Yakutsk. Throughout Siberia, during the first century of Russian occupation, monasteries were central to the successful colonization of an area. The monks did not only (or even mainly) devote themselves to religion and education. All monasteries owned considerable properties – including serfs until the Church was forbidden to use them in the 1790s – and in the virgin lands all around they became involved in ship-building, fishing, agriculture, animal husbandry, milling, mining and trading. Turukhansk's Troitskiy monastery regularly sent its pelt-gathering crews to riverside centres up to a thousand miles away. In a few regions monks also organized their own defence.

The parish churches played in another league, as elsewhere throughout the empire. Most Orthodox priests had little education, minute stipends and low status. In Sakha they at first avoided missionary work though some natives eagerly sought baptism by way of avoiding tribute-paying and qualifying to marry a Russian, or take a job with the administration. Given this legal framework, proselytizing did not please fur-seekers. But by the 1760s the tribute's importance had diminished, missionaries were being encouraged and a century later all Sakha had, allegedly, been converted. Most of the mass baptisms, not preceded by even the most elementary instruction in Christian beliefs, were unedifying ceremonies, conducted by inebriated priests amidst scenes of inappropriate hilarity around the church precincts.

An exception on this missionary scene was the scholarly monk Ioann Veniaminov who spent forty-seven years (1821–68) in northern Siberia. While Bishop of Kamchatka, the Kurils and the Aleutians, he lived in Yakutsk and translated the gospels and the liturgy into Sakha while organizing the construction of St Nicholas's church. His benign influence was felt long after his death. By 1900 most Siberian monasteries had lost their wealth and power but in Sakha more than a hundred churches were being served by 362 priests and eight monks. The majority of those clergy were Russians; few Sakha cared to join the downtrodden priesthood.

Often over the past two months I had wondered how Orthodoxy can help a people in search of their twenty-first-century identity.

Some of my younger friends had asserted that their church offers emotional security, its survival proof that Holy Russia (a phrase coined, incidentally, by Ivan the Terrible) could not be obliterated by atheist agents of the devil. The country might just at the moment be in a bad way, yet all would be well because Orthodoxy, seen as a distinctively Russian phenomenon (which it isn't) had the power to restore the nation's strength in every sense. But if a resurgent Holy Russia cultivates nationalism and religious bigotry …? This combination crippled the Ireland in which I grew up.

That Sunday morning St Nicholas's was scarcely half full, with few men (again, mainly young) among women of all ages – a minority Sakha. I stood towards the front, the better to observe the rituals, and soon became aware of disapproving stares; no other female was trousered and all wore headscarves. When a pleasant young woman approached me I recognized her as one of the flower arrangers. In a friendly way she indicated, pointing to the bare-headed men, that I should remove my *shapka* which was, as attentive readers will remember, of the wrong gender. On realizing that I was a foreign female she looked bewildered, then flustered and apologetic – and the disapproving expressions around me changed to welcoming smiles.

Two young bearded priests were attended by three adolescent deacons wearing blue and silver brocade robes. The chandeliers looked less pretentious with their fake candles alight and real candles blazed brightly before all the icons, their scent mingling agreeably with clouds of incense. Most importantly, the chanting (the reason for my presence) did not disappoint. Orthodox choirs take one somewhere else – somewhere I like to be, where I can forget about nationalism and bigotry.

Back at the Kolos, our room was full of chain-smoking young policemen in civvies and Lenin was sitting on Dasha's bed, looking dominant. A truly formidable creature, he bared his teeth and glared balefully at the intruder. Yet by 11 p.m., when he and his entourage set out on their long journey home, he had accepted me. I was then privileged to receive two balance-threatening paws on my bosom and a large wet goodbye lick on my face. This farewell gesture was one of his 'tricks', performed when Dasha gave the signal. When she gave another sort of signal, he sank his teeth into suspects' shoulders.

As we crossed Ordzhonikidze Square at noon Lenin attracted much attention from the small crowd assembled to watch the start of a mini-marathon (10 kilometres), organized to celebrate those 370 years. The temperature was minus 7°C and the hundred numbered runners wore woollen tights or long johns under their skimpy nylon shorts. Both sexes and all age groups participated, the eldest a seventy-six-year-old Sakha woman, the youngest a ten-year-old Sakha boy. We paused to watch them taking off as the only uniformed policemen I saw in Yakutsk cleared the streets of motor traffic.

The show arena was a borrowed basketball court with a spectators' gallery along one wall. It formed part of an ungainly multi-storeyed complex including a cinema, a children's theatre, a billiard room, a table-tennis room. And it was blessedly uncluttered by the displays associated with Western dog shows, all those canine foods, treats, shampoos, tonics, medicaments, toys, garments and furniture. As time passed I noticed that it was also free of the tensions provoked at our major shows by breeders radiating detestation of their rivals. This seemed more like a village event, a fun occasion, all the winners being enthusiastically cheered by everyone, even the immediate losers.

Here Siberian toughness again manifested itself. The seating, for 250 or so, consisted of one long, unsteady improvised bench some eighteen inches high; most exhibitors, and their supporters, happily sat on the floor beside the dogs. No refreshments were available and only a few had brought tea and snacks; the majority seemed content to fast for nine hours. Even the judge – on her feet all day – took no more than a half-hour lunch break.

In this atmosphere of disorganized informality the inter-breed dynamics were fascinating, a source of much amusement and some alarm. Several breeds were unknown to me, such as the Russian terrier, not unlike a larger version of the Kerry blue. I had seen them before, around Yakutsk, but assumed them to be handsome mongrels; now I knew better. A Chinese bulldog of medium size and horror-film ugliness had a nose like a football tied to a dog's head. Two hunting hound breeds, like crosses between spaniels and greyhounds, had had their ears clipped at birth; I could scarcely bear to look at them. Another unfamiliar breed had hideously sagging jowls and loose folds of flesh hanging down its legs like ill-fitting trousers.

The poodles, from emperor to miniature, had been clipped in an amazing variety of topiary-like styles, one more absurd than the next, and the undersized fragile shelties couldn't possibly have served their original purpose. There were two griffons with ridiculous mandarin beards; a long-haired chihuahua half the size of a cat; dachshunds with legs so short and bodies so long they looked like enlarged caterpillars; Alsatians with sloping hindquarters and tails almost touching the ground; mastiffs so bulky their legs could hardly carry them; great Danes close to donkey proportions; borzois so narrow-skulled one wondered where they kept their brains; Afghans so frail beneath their silken coats that when I stroked them their spines felt sharp. The obvious missing breeds were retrievers, spaniels, labradors, sheepdogs (apart from the degraded shelties) and whippets.

We could converse with most of the exhibits as they were led past us or parked beside us, though no one tried to be sociable with the rottweilers, Alsatians or mastiffs, several of whom were muzzled until entering the ring. Those breeds longed to get at the tinies, some actually licking their lips as they strained on their chains. But the great Danes, Afghans and borzois were enchanted by the other extreme – wagged their tails, wanted to make friends. Most of the tinies were secure personalities and wagged in response but one chihuahua peed with terror when a great Dane, its head twice the size of the chihuahua, bent down to convey an amiable interest in this strange ball of fluff.

The incidence of English-speakers among the exhibitors was uncommonly high. One woman, the neurotic owner of a nervy French bulldog, apprehensively swept him into her lap whenever one of the slavering biggies came our way. She wanted to know if I had a dog in Ireland. 'Three,' I replied 'What breed?' she asked eagerly. 'Mongrel terriers,' I confessed. 'Very small and definitely terriers but without a label. Their sires are unknown.' She looked as though I had made a bad smell and moved away.

One bouncy wire-haired fox-terrier took a fancy to the foreigner and was happy to be left on my lap while his owner went to the loo. I asked Ivan how the biggies were accommodated, given their owners' limited living space. He laughed. 'In those families the dog comes first, has his own room.' But still my imagination boggled at the thought of a great Dane, or one of those elephantine mastiffs, in the average flat. Ivan continued, 'Their owners have to be rich, with a car, and drive to open spaces, though most big breeds need less exercise than my small one. They are lazy, don't want to run much. They are only show dogs, or police dogs. Police like to keep them without exercise, to make them more angry.'

Later, an Irish setter bitch owned by Vladimir came to rest beside me, her elegance obtained at the cost of bone density and muscle. (At my advanced age I can remember the configuration of such breeds before fanatical manipulation took over.) The bitch's name was Aïda. 'You know why?' asked Vladimir. 'You're a Verdi fan?' I suggested. He laughed and shook his head. 'No – but Lenin was, so he called his Irish setter Aïda. After his first stroke, playing with her every morning was his great comfort. We don't have many of this dog in Russia and I think my Aïda could be a relation of his!'

As we spoke, the contemporary Lenin was being shown so I moved to the ribbon barrier and sent supportive signals to Dasha. She needed them; Lenin was not amenable to pacing sedately around the ring, displaying his muscular magnificence to best advantage. He slouched, glared reproachfully at Dasha, then lunged to escape from the lime-light and almost pulled her off her feet. However, when he came to stand by the judge's cup-laden table her skill brought out the best in him and he struck a potentially prize-winning pose.

Most breeds had only two or three representatives (or one), therefore classes went according to size: small, medium, big. The judge was a middle-aged woman more than six feet tall and broad shouldered, with short dark hair and no make-up – by Russian standards a freak, wearing dark crumpled trousers and a loose faded jersey. In contrast, the young women exhibitors (more numerous than men: is dog-showing non-macho in Siberia?) wore their finest party gowns and some had given thought to the overall effect, clothes matching dogs. All day the judge maintained a grave, almost severe expression except when congratulating winners and commiserating with near misses. In addition to the class prizes – Lenin did win First Prize – there was a Top Dog award, competed for by the nine prizewinners. Here the victor was a miniature Yorkshire terrier almost invisible to the naked eye, and Lenin came second, beating my friend the fox-terrier after much hesitation on the judge's part.

As we returned in triumph to the Kolos the sunset sky seemed to be celebrating with us; cloudlets like flamingo feathers floated above turreted purple embankments fringed with gold. I was planning a *pivo* party in Lenin's honour but alas! there was no time. It's a long, long way to Alcan, as I was soon to discover for myself, and Dasha had to be on duty by 8 a.m. next morning.

That evening I wrote in my diary: 'Dog shows disquiet me, even this laid-back event. What compels breeders to so obsessionally juggle with genes? They lack *respect* for animals.'

In pre-colonial times, in western and south-eastern Siberia, fur tributes had long been levied by Tatars and Mongols and the colonists used their collecting sites. Traditionally, a fixed number of pelts (usually between five and ten) had been demanded annually from every adult male. The Russians, however, tried to extract the maximum number of furs from a given community as often as possible and Petr Beketov's behaviour on his exploratory voyage down the Lena was typical. He killed several small bands of Sakha warriors who were not immediately responsive to his demands – six here, twenty there, nine elsewhere and an uncounted number when Chief Ospek gathered all his followers in a crudely fortified settlement from which arrows were fired at the invaders. The Cossacks promptly set fire to those huts and the three women who escaped didn't get far before being captured. History doesn't need to relate their fate.

Soon after the first sixteenth-century settlements had been staffed by state employees, Siberia became (as it remained) notorious for administrative inefficiency and corruption. Once the exploring had been done, the *ostrogi* built and the natives cowed, the official Moscow attitude towards Siberia's tribes was, by contemporary standards, quite humane. But it was also irrelevant. As the Cossacks and traders told one another, 'God is high and the Czar far away'. He was indeed very far away from Sakha; his fastest couriers spent more than a year travelling to Yakutsk. River boats covered between ten and twenty miles a day and from Yakutsk to the Sea of Okhotsk, following the Aldan and Maya rivers, took another three or four months. Richard Pipes provides some interesting comparisons:

> In Persia of the fifth century BC a messenger of King Darius travelled along the Royal Road at a rate of 380 kilometres in 24 hours; in Mongol Persia of the thirteenth century government couriers covered some 335 kilometres in the same period of time. In Russia, *after* regular postal services had been introduced by Swedish and German experts in the second half of the seventeenth century, messengers crawled at an average rate of 6–7 kilometres an hour; and since they travelled only by daytime, with luck and in the right season they might have made 80 or so kilometres in a 24-hour period.

In Russia's expanding empire, three-year state postings naturally appealed to intrepid, ruthless, uneducated men; throughout Fur-land they could amass quantities of roubles otherwise unobtainable. One of the worst of this species, remembered even now by the Sakha, was Petr Golovin, Yakutsk's first military governor, who arrived in 1640 with 395 Cossacks. The Sakha offered more resistance than most tribes and by then Beketov's *ostrog* had been besieged for four years and many tribute collectors had met an arrow. In 1642, when Golovin's revoltingly sadistic cruelty ignited a large-scale rebellion, forty-two tribute collectors were killed. Golovin then elaborately tortured his secretary and his second-in-command before imprisoning them for two years on suspicion of having incited the locals against him. Those unfortunates can't have needed much incitement; Golovin made a habit of hanging them from their ribs, gouging out their eyes and burying them alive. A colleague of his, at Yesseyskoye Zimov'ye, routinely cudgelled to death Evenk who hadn't produced the demanded tribute because they couldn't find any sable, or who didn't provide enough extra furs, beyond the Czar's share, for the collectors' benefit.

Golovin's torturing of his own Cossack servicemen and their wives drove them to complain to Moscow, begging to be rescued from his tyranny. Two years later he was recalled, only to be replaced, throughout the rest of the seventeenth century, by a succession of lesser tyrants.

The eighteenth-century decline in the fur trade brought about some changes, not necessarily for the better. Siberia became more important as a penal colony and the governors of such places as Yakutsk, in the eighteenth and nineteenth centuries, were often disgraced army officers so badly paid that their exploitation of the natives seemed inevitable. From about 1710 the Sakha had a new task, the maintenance of transportation and postal services – responsibilities reduced towards the end of the century when Russian peasants were 'relocated', as state employees, to care for travellers' horses.

Very occasionally, at the top level of the administration, well-intentioned men came on the scene. Governor-General Mikhail Speranskiy, based in Tobolsk, spent three years (1819–22) devising his 'Statute for the Administration of Natives'. He deplored the traders' callous mistreatment of the tribes and his Statute required servicemen of all ranks to respect native traditions, not interfere with tribal autonomy, insist on fair trading conditions and tax men only in proportion to their resources. It also emphatically reasserted the already 200-year-old ban on giving or selling alcohol to natives and forbade new Russian settlement beyond the districts surrounding the original *ostrogi*, now grown into towns and small cities.

Speranskiy took a personal interest in Sakha where he and an Irkutsk merchant friend tried unsuccessfully to organize a 'fair trading' company. In 1820 he was appalled to read Baron F.P. Vrangel's account of the many outraged protests made to the Baron by Sakha, describing the Yakutsk Cossacks' seizing of 'a woman tribute' in addition to or instead of the fur tribute – by that date meagre. But what to do? As Speranskiy's critics pointed out, laying down the law in Tobolsk or Irkutsk, even with backing from St Petersburg, achieved little for the northern tribes. The Statute made no provision for the detection and punishment of law-breakers; that would have required a more numerous and disciplined state service than could possibly be installed anywhere in Siberia, least of all in Sakha. However, Speranskiy's defenders argued that his leadership had to some extent changed mindsets. In 1825 a forum for the northern nomads, a 'Steppe Duma', was established in Yakutsk. But this positive gesture on the part of the Speranskiy-influenced authorities lasted only a decade; nomads and parliaments don't gel.

In 1854 Gagemeyster's *General Handbook to Siberia* opined that the Sakha were the Russians' equal in 'intelligence, cunning and effectiveness'. By then there were more Sakha than Russian traders in the Lena valley and other outside observers reported that the Sakha were not only the most numerous northern tribe, they were also endowed with a higher average IQ than their Slav masters.

I decided to do a postal experiment before leaving Yakutsk: ten post-cards to my nearest and dearest. The ludicrously enormous post office now houses would-be up-market shops stocking very little (somehow a peculiarly depressing phenomenon), private medical and dental clinics and well-protected foreign investors' offices. This building's two sets of exceptionally thick and heavy double doors, ten feet high with a cubicle of space between them, can be a hazard for the very young and very old; occasionally a child's arm is trapped and broken. In the postal corner I joined a twelve-person queue. Three women sat behind the counter, two ignoring the public while rubber-stamping files, the other haggard and heavily made-up, looking long past retirement age. No doubt 'connections' were enabling her to continue earning. Most in the queue were students, showing passports in the usually unfulfilled hope of collecting letters. I felt sorry for them as they turned away, crestfallen; who knows how far they were from home. Immediately ahead of me, two women despatching parcels to Irkutsk and Moscow had to struggle with grotesque documentation reminding me of Tynda's police station. Then a ponderous search began for the postal rates to Ireland and the UK – less than 50 US cents, but only three out of ten would survive the journey.

My last evening in Yakutsk was spent with Feodor and Oksana in the latter's flat where her lodgers' possessions restricted movement. On Feodor's suggestion, his mother-in-law showed me her collection of dramatic photographs taken by various friends on 21 May 2001 when Yakutsk was marooned by the Lena's flood. Those anti-permafrost stilts could be seen serving another useful purpose and it seems such massive wooden piles, hammered deep into the earth before construction begins, are the best material to withstand periodic flooding; their rate of decay is extremely slow in Sakha's dry climate. Even 2001's freak level and duration of flooding never threatened to melt the permafrost, though some nervous citizens feared it might. The real danger to buildings came from sharp, barn-sized chunks of ice, and uprooted trees and construction matériel, all being swiftly swept along the wide streets. Oksana admitted that she and her friends had begun to feel more than slightly tense when at last the Russian Air Force's bombing of the unthawing ice barricade, some twenty miles downstream, took effect. Then the backed-up floodwaters roared away, that unforgettable sound illogically more frightening than what had gone before. (So bombers do in special circumstances have a civilized contribution to make …) Meanwhile many poor families living at ground level, in small old wooden dwellings, suffered irreparable structural damage and grievous losses of property and were of course uninsured.

As we ate the talk turned to racial integration in Sakha and Oksana (herself three-quarters Sakha) assured me that the Soviets, having weakened the Sakhas' cultural identity through collectivization, showed no prejudice against them as 'primitive people' but valued them as notably intelligent citizens whose co-operation was essential to the Republic's development.

Feodor said, 'Since the Muscovites found Siberia their big problem, not solved yet, has been how to settle enough Russians where food production is so difficult – impossible in many areas. Always this was the main restriction on settlement, more than low winter temperatures. We're all used to snow everywhere and months below freezing, arrivals from European Russia describe this climate as "the same only worse". But I'm sorry to tell you those happy days of Soviet racial integration are over, though some of the older generation don't want to see that. They just want to think of themselves as loyal citizens of the new Republic of Sakha – and superior to anyone else in the Federation!'

Feodor had much to say on our way back to the Kolos. 'My mother-in-law's Sakha family, they were Europeanized more than a century ago, living in fine Yakutsk merchants' houses while most Sakha were still living in yurts, following thousands of horses over the taiga. They weren't caught up in collectivization, they couldn't know or feel the anti-Russian seeds it sowed – much more, I'd guess, than all the czars' bad treatment. The Cossacks treated the Siberians cruelly, back in Russia the Russians treated other Russians cruelly, here many Sakha chiefs treated their own people cruelly. Those were cruel times.

Collectivization was different, I've read books about it. "Cultural genocide", some people call it. My mother-in-law refuses to take seriously fights between Sibiryaki and Sakha though they've been going on for years. She gets annoyed when I say outsiders could use this racism, if it suited them to stir trouble in that corporate colony I can foresee. My hope is Sakha never gets to have a racism problem like Moscow has now. Anyone looking like a Chechen or Central Asian – a Muslim – is resented, distrusted, often attacked by skinheads or the police. My grandmother says that's proof the Soviet Union wasn't a union, we were only brainwashed to accept each other as Soviet citizens, racism being suppressed not cured. I'm a bit muddled about that. If so many different races could genuinely get on by being Soviet citizens together, wasn't that a positive development? Maybe humans need that sort of brainwashing? It can't be an advance that now ex-Soviet citizens are again hostile to one another.'

It was too near midnight for me to prolong our conversation by casting doubt on the blossoming of racial tolerance under the Soviet sun. Before we parted, Feodor gave me his home telephone number. 'Come to eat with us,' he urged. 'In Moscow the food is better. But I notice you prefer Yakutsk.'

# 9

## One Day in the Lives of Thirty-two Bus Passengers

When I mentioned going by bus to Neryungri people frowned, or drew in their breath sharply, or looked sympathetic, or bluntly advised me to fly. Ksenya said, 'Most of us fly, even if we have to borrow the fare.' Feodor gave me a bottle of vodka 'for emergencies'.

By dawnlight I made my way to the bus-station – filthy and gloomy, in contrast to BAM's lovingly tended railway stations. Arriving at 6.45 for an 8 a.m. departure, I hoped to secure a front seat. There was no one else around, apart from a ragged elderly vodka victim aimlessly shuffling to and fro, muttering to himself and gingerly fingering a new cut over one eye. I headed the short queue as the ticket office opened at 7.30 but when boarding-time came four hefty babushkas elbowed me aside and triumphantly settled into the front seats. Every side window was completely curtained so I moved to the rear bench and took a corner seat beside the back door's curtain-free window; the rest of the bench was stacked to the ceiling with huge square striped nylon bags. This vehicle was a bus, rather than a long-distance coach, but it looked quite smart, its bodywork newly painted red and white. The few others lined up to serve nearby destinations were seriously scratched, dented and mud-encrusted. Although the Neryungri ticket had been reduced to $33.50 from the $95 quoted in the *BAM Guide*, sixteen seats remained unoccupied. A day later I understood why.

We left at 8.20 and as Mitya our driver deftly negotiated Yakutsk's potholes and permafrost mounds I noticed loud rattling – nothing specific, I assumed, just a general symptom of vehicular old age. Then came a dull ninety-minute drive on a fairly smooth tarred road which ends – some miles beyond the Lena ferry turn-off – at

Mokhsogollokh, a big industrial settlement dedicated to manufacturing those precast concrete slabs which make possible the rapid construction of multi-storeyed blocks. By Siberian standards this is a densely populated area. A few hamlets of two-storey wooden houses, standing in large paddocks, were dispersed over treeless, slightly hilly land offering minimal grazing to black and white cattle.

From the turn-off we descended steeply – and suddenly the olive-green Lena appeared, seeming to the south like an inland sea. Its low left bank, six miles away, was a scarcely visible line on the horizon. This Bestyakh ferry, a vital link in one of Yakutsk's few supply lines, is approached by a narrow, stony, precipitous track blasted out of a high cliff. It then took Mitya fifteen minutes to back on to the aged mini-barge; already four trucks were aboard, leaving barely enough room for us. I disembarked to watch a ferryman and Sergei, Mitya's mate, placing short planks half-under our wheels which had sunk deep into the sand – golden, but of a muddy consistency. Repeatedly the engine roared and the bus shuddered as it failed to get a grip on the planks; not until spades had been used did it move backwards. Then began my hero-worship of Mitya as he cautiously manoeuvered and I gazed down in awe at wheels mere inches from the edges of the gangplank.

This was my farewell to the Lena. I stood on deck, wearing my *shapka*, as a small almost soundless tug pushed us across the lazy flow. In a coldly blue sky, layers of long slim clouds were poised above the wide horizon – tinted green and copper, pale gold and navy blue, reminding me of a noon sky in midwinter Ireland. When I looked at my watch on the far side, it astonished me that we had spent exactly an hour crossing that six-mile expanse. The Lena is hypnotically soothing. Much has been written about 'the spirit of place', some of it tiresomely fanciful, but truly the Lena spirit does take one over.

Driving off the barge was also quite tricky: more soft sand and planks. Then very slowly the bus climbed a gentle slope towards an extremely rough track and as we jerked on to level ground it collapsed, suffering from dehydration. No one seemed surprised. Sergei hurried down to the Lena with two red plastic buckets and when another two were needed several passengers wandered into the bushes – men to the right, women to the left. As the exigencies of our journey bit harder, this seemly modesty had on occasions to be discarded.

Onwards then, never exceeding 15 m.p.h. on that erosion-ravaged track linking the Lena to the Amur Yakutsk Automobile Highway. The AYaAD, a Stalin era achievement (built 1930–37), runs almost due north for 725 miles from Bolshoi Never on the Trans-Siberian to Yakutsk. In the words of the *BAM Guide*: 'It anticipated the strategy of the BAM – to create a direct path of transportation that cuts across existing lines of communication, regardless of cost or engineering difficulty.' No one will ever know the AYaAD's cost in human lives. It has now been pompously renamed 'the M56' as though it were a motorway instead of a third-class road.

Onwards for only twenty minutes; where the track joined the M56 a new and quite distinctive rattle troubled Mitya. We stopped and were advised to lunch at the truckers' café at the junction while the rattle was being tracked down. The bus had two wheels in front and four behind; seeing the two right back wheels being removed I assumed a puncture – all the tyres were baldly puncture-prone. My blood curdled slightly when I observed the reality: a shattered rim, cracked in two places. Morbidly fascinated, I stood watching Mitya and Sergei doing ingenious things with screws. Exuding determination, they worked as a team, exchanging few words. To my eyes that cracked rim was a non-starter, a component which could not reasonably be expected to take us safely over 400 testing miles where every revolution of the wheels would threaten the men's improvisation. But to Mitya and Sergei this defect was just one more challenge that had to be met. And meet it they did; our future problems were not wheel-related. Their improvisation had obviously been both mentally and physically taxing, yet neither took any nourishment or rest before we went on our way at 1.10 p.m.

For hour after hour we were crossing low forested ridges with little to differentiate them. Here the brief Siberian autumn was almost over, leaving the taiga drab, already frostbitten, the birches and beeches naked and puny, the pines and spruces an unattractive yellowy-green beneath their dust coats. Three months of summer dust had thickly coated everything within range: only in Africa have I seen the like and drivers switched on lights when going through these dense clouds.

Our bus being tightly sealed could not protect us from the unpleasant smell and a sore drying of the nostrils. Mercifully, rain fell within an hour – light rain, yet enough to bring relief.

The approaching traffic was mainly commercial, trucks taking one or two AYaM (Amur–Yakutsk Mainline) freight wagons to Yakutsk from the railway's terminus at Aldan. These Soviet-era vehicles emitted the distinctively foul fumes of adulterated diesel and now, remembering BAM's immensely long freight trains, I could under-stand why some Yakutsk Greens support the AYaM's extension as the lesser of two evils. Most city-dwellers, according to Feodor, were pro-AYaM for pragmatic reasons, blaming air and road transport for their high living costs.

Unlike the Lena and the M56, AYaM will scarcely be affected by weather conditions. It could both speed up urban development and give access, helped by short feeder roads, to natural resources as yet unexploited: which is why the indigenous peoples and the rural Sibiryaki foresee it wrecking their whole way of life. When 480 miles had been built, political/environmental considerations stopped work on the remaining 285 miles plus a six-mile bridge over the Lena. In 1994, not long after Yakutsk inherited the project from Moscow's Ministry of Transport Construction, multi-party elec-tions were held, voters' views became important and the govern-ment gave to rural votes what some saw as 'disproportionate weighting' – hence the stoppage. But inevitably those voters lost out to the developers and in 1999 construction was resumed, though at a snail's pace for funding reasons. The government has confidently asserted that a completed AYaM will pay for itself in seven years by carrying 65 per cent of Yakutsk's freight. Similar predictions were made about BAM and some Greens denounce AYaM as another White Elephant. Only time can tell whether or not it makes eco-nomic sense.

The M56 is so motor-car unfriendly that we met only two convoys, of six and five vehicles, both stationary because one of their number had broken down. Before our own major breakdown we passed eight trucks in trouble, three changing tyres, the others operating on engines having piled pine branches as Danger signs on their side of the road. M56 litter consists mainly of discarded tyres and tubes. Twice I did fifteen-minute reckonings and counted twenty-three and twenty-six tyres on my (right) verge; no doubt an equal number defiled the left verge. Even allowing for AYaM's seventy years of existence – and the durability, as litter, of tyres – this seemed unaccountably bizarre, not to say profligate. In sensibly frugal societies, worn tyres serve as raw material for footwear, floor coverings, draught excluders, children's toys and roof anchors.

The rain had stopped when I registered a new sound, a mysterious, erratic thudding or bumping, as though someone were hitting the rear of the bus with a mallet. Was this another defect being made manifest, or merely the bus's reasonable reaction to a neglected gravel surface? Then our pace slowed, and slowed – to cycling speed – to walking speed – and at 4.20 we stopped in the miserable little settlement of Uluu. Everyone silently disembarked, accepting that this was a major mechanical crisis.

According to a new blue EU-style signpost on Uluu's outskirts, we had covered 162 miles (plus the ferry) in the eight hours since leaving Yakutsk. And Uluu is more than a hundred miles from anywhere else. A road-workers' base, a truckers' café and a logging industry in abeyance explain its existence. Beyond the Uluu river our track could be seen steeply climbing yet another taiga ridge, its slopes a hazy blue-brown beneath a low grey sky. To the north was the ridge we had just crossed, to the east Uluu trailed along a bluff above the road. To the west, below the M56, lay the original road-builders' abandoned (mostly) wooden shacks, their roofs fallen in and walls collapsing. A ramshackle hut opposite the bus, standing a little apart from Uluu's houses beyond a wide ditch, was identified by my companions as our 'rest room'. Out of curiosity I investigated its two gender-specific compartments which were equally horrific – and I'm not fussy. Surely, given an infinity of taiga on all sides, it's unnecessary to have such a concentration of faeces old and new within noseshot of people's homes.

Tools were strewn all over the road as Mitya and Sergei struggled with an engine defect of prodigious complexity. Gabriel, the only English-speaker on board (limited English), regretted he couldn't translate the word for the problem which in any event would have meant nothing to me. Then Sergei and Mitya went in different directions, sifting through Uluu's numerous piles of long-discarded machinery for a length and quality (or thickness) of wire to meet their requirements. The engine occupied the rear of the bus directly behind my seat and I stood gazing at it, wondering if the dissimilar bits of protruding wire attaching *this* to *that* were part of the original design or responses to earlier crises. While several lengths of scrap were being unsuccessfully experimented with, I toured Uluu.

Bleak disorder prevailed – buildings scattered awkwardly over uneven slopes, no discernible main street or central path, broken concrete steps leading from one level to another. On the highest level stood a large school and administration building, both in dire need of repairs.

The difference between a 'relocation' settlement and a village is always sadly apparent. Although in feudal times many villages were artificially contrived, our contemporary villages, at least in the 'undeveloped' world, seem like organic growths on a landscape. But settlements such as Uluu, Stalinist spin-offs, have at their foundations a haunting accumulation of fears, griefs and privations. Usually the privations remain. Uluu's terraced, two-storey concrete block houses appeared to be either unoccupied or inhabited by families so destitute their homes gave the impression of being derelict. That last was the case, I realized, when the generator was switched on at dusk and dim lights appeared behind windows curtained with old newspapers. There were few cultivated gardens and the new roadside kiosk stocked little more than the sort of chemically impregnated fizzy drinks and snacks consumed in lethal quantities by truckers on every continent.

The only visible inhabitant was a small boy dragging an empty plastic beer bottle by a length of string, then standing on tiptoe to peer into the big cardboard cartons used as litter-bins. In one he found a glass beer bottle and, wearing a gleeful expression, was about to smash it when he noticed a babushka watching and hastily replaced it in the carton. Seemingly in Uluu the culture of impunity does not protect junior glass smashers, Then a second inhabitant appeared, a young man carrying buckets to the river to fetch water.

Back at the bus, Gabriel told me that Mitya and Sergei had sought local help but none was forthcoming. Soon we saw them finding yet another sort of wire in the carcass of a lorry that years ago had been pushed off a low cliff above the river. The light was fading fast and a snow-heavy sky formed so tight a lid that nothing marked the west as the sun sank: all around, the horizon was monochrome. To keep warm, I trotted briskly down to the river, now a shrunken channel, filmed with algae near the banks. In midstream stood several dumped cranes, looming out of the dusk like skeletal dinosaurs.

The café was predictable, its low hardboard ceiling smoke-stained, plastic vine leaves hung like bunting from corner to corner, its linoleum worn between the few little tables, its striplighting harsh, its expired TV sharing a corner with two ikons of the Virgin Mary. Food was limited: bus loads don't normally make demands on Uluu. The available bortsch and *pelmeni* had quickly disappeared and now potatoes were being boiled in bulk while the elderly proprietress dexterously chopped cabbage with a hunter's knife.

Outside, three men passengers were strolling up and down the road, their *shapka* ear-flaps pulled down, pausing occasionally by the bus but rarely making any comment as they observed Mitya and Sergei continuing to experiment non-stop with bare hands in a below-zero temperature. They were now working in the dark, literally if not metaphorically. Their own torch was broken. None of the locals, it seemed, had a torch. None of the passengers had a torch; mine is a fixture for a bicycle, recharged by daylight, therefore NBG if confined to a rucksack. When the two began to use their cigarette lighters as candles, deep within the oily engine cavity, I decided (given my run of ill-luck on this journey) to remain outside the bus. Three parked cars were visible and I wondered – why not ask one of the owners to shine his headlamps on the cavity? Gabriel explained: those cars were duds, retained to provide spare parts for motorists in distress. Then a truck approached from Yakutsk, momentarily illuminating the scene of action, and suddenly Sergei gave a 'Eureka!' yelp. He had seen something which enabled the bus's lights to work again, after some complicated fiddling with connections that sparked like fireworks when touched. A brilliant bulb came on above the engine which was then left running. For more than an hour noxious thick black fumes poured into the night, whirling around the men's legs as they stood leaning forward into the cavity, persisting in what seemed a hopeless task.

Most passengers had long since taken themselves off in different directions. Some of the men were drinking vodka and playing cards in the café, others were playing chess in the shop, their board laid on its counter. Little groups of women were huddled by the café stove, doing crossword puzzles; others stayed on the bus, emerging now and then to smoke. No one complained or seemed angry or impatient; the most evident reaction to this delay was half-amused resignation.

By 8 p.m. it was snowing lightly and the afternoon's rain had turned to ice on the road. With luck our problem would not be solved until the morrow. Mitya had by then been on duty for twelve stressful hours, hadn't eaten all day and surely needed sleep and sustenance before driving us hundreds of miles on a dodgy surface, iced and likely to become icier, with three notoriously difficult passes towards the end of our journey. Apart from that consideration – not entirely self-protective, partly prompted by genuine concern for Mitya and Sergei – night travel through mountains is frustrating. The little to be seen from a bus is better than nothing and assuredly I would not be passing this way again ... (That's one of the features of old age; when living in overtime, the possibilities once entertained – 'Some day I may return' – are no longer realistic.)

Again I marched down to the bridge, then up to the signpost, never going more than half a mile from the bus. Apprehension chilled me when Mitya quietly summoned us back to our seats at 9.45. There was none of the cheering that might elsewhere have been deemed appropriate, nor any smiles or slaps on the back for Mitya and Sergei – except from me, who marvelled at their tenacity and inventiveness. These Siberians, so emotional and volatile in so many situations, phlegmatically trooped back to their seats as Mitya, not allowing himself even a cup of tea, settled into his cab looking weary but resolute. I had a clear view of his face reflected in the driver's mirror.

This felt like emergency time and I took a first gulp of vodka while recalling all those news reports which explain, 'It is thought the driver fell asleep at the wheel ...' Who could blame Mitya if, in our well-heated bus, he did fall asleep? Uneasily I watched Sergei nodding off, instead of engaging his mate in stimulating conversation.

For me to feel anticipatory fear is not normal; I'm fatalistic by nature. But certain experiences can warp one's nature and in January 1990, in Rumania, a motor accident left a bit of me warped for ever. In my book about that journey the whole story was not told because so soon after the event I couldn't bear to re-live it, as one does re-live when writing. The edited version went like this:

Twenty-four hours later I was lying [semi-concussed] on my bed in a Satu Mare hotel room ... I could remember the bald-tyred Sebis car sliding slowly off a steep icy road – so slowly that I had time to ask the driver, 'Is there something wrong with the steering?' Then came a moment of incredulity (incredulity, rather than fear) as the car went over the edge. When I came to I was lying on sacks in the back of a State farm grain truck ... I only vaguely recall my fellow-victim being admitted to the hospital where, it later devastated me to learn, he died within a few hours.

In fact that young man died because I had bullied him into taking the front passenger seat. A huge hunk of machinery, wrapped in sacking, occupied most of the back seat and the young man was an unusually large Rumanian, both tall and broad. Therefore I vehemently argued against his squeezing in with the machinery and finally overcame his concern for my comfort. So he died at the age of twenty-four while I, securely wedged between door and machinery, survived – aged fifty-eight. For many months the realization 'He died because I bullied him' was never far from my consciousness. That tragedy induced a guilt nonetheless overwhelming for being intellectually recognized as baseless. And now, because of my warped bit, an icy road in Siberia was making me fearful, stirring vivid recollections of a car slowly sliding off a black-iced road, down a mountainside...

The bus was hellishly overheated, as Siberian homes are in winter, and repeatedly I had to clear the window of our fug. Mitya drove very slowly across ridge after ridge after ridge of taiga, each slope's roadside signs recording its gradient, and gradually the gradients were getting steeper and icier. All the M56's new signs looked as though they had strayed off some European superhighway. Their incongruity, on this ill-kept two-lane gravel track, seemed to match the new Russia's free-market fantasies. Around midnight an almost full moon tried to shine through thinning cloud and a tentative wind began to sway the treetops. Then I fell into a deep sleep – until the sound of the engine cavity being opened just behind my head woke me at 3.15 a.m.

Wiping the window and gazing out, my heart missed a beat. More than a foot of snow had just fallen, the first of the season hereabouts, and each tree, bush, twig, cone and blade of grass carried its luminous burden. The clouds, having delivered their load, had dwindled to wisps of silvery vapour drifting high in a royal blue sky. Few stars could compete with the brilliance of the moon as it shone upon a taiga transformed. The impression of brightness was extraordinary. This seemed neither day nor night but a time apart, a mystery world of softly shining radiance, of still and perfect beauty.

I zipped up my jacket, pulled on my *shapka*, scrambled over high piles of luggage – wincing as The Knee protested – and joined the nicotine addicts already grouped on the verge. They were viewing, still without comment, the re-exposed engine. Gesturing expansively, I exclaimed 'Beautiful!' in Russian – one of my few words. Everyone smiled, nodded, looked gratified; Siberians revel in a foreigner's appreciation of anything Siberian. To them this wonderland was no novelty, but at that moment I could sense their genuine sharing in my exhilaration. A propensity for littering landscapes does not, oddly enough, have to go with an insensitivity to natural beauty.

I had assumed the collapse of the Uluu innovation. But no, here was an entirely new problem, a copious leakage of oil. We could hear it steadily dripping and see a swelling pool of blackness on the whiteness of the verge's carpet. The temperature would have made headlines in Ireland in January: to Siberians it was merely a touch of autumn in the air. I stared, incredulous, as Mitya and Sergei, clad only in jeans and T-shirts, lay flat on the thickly iced road for a full five minutes, their heads under the engine, seeking with ears and fingers the source of the leak. When they thought they had found it, further improvisations began. Meanwhile the smokers had returned to their warm seats and I set off up the road, keeping on the powdery snow of the verge. I needed to be alone amidst this magic and felt selfishly grateful for our new crisis.

Here I again felt the power of Siberia's silence. Silence is something I seek on my journeys, an aid to sanity that has by now been entirely banished from our 'developed' world. But this was an aloof, almost intimidating silence – perhaps an excluding silence? I wondered if I would feel comfortable camping alone in the taiga. Or would I feel unwelcome? Possibly Siberia's spirit of place is hostile to outsiders.

During the next hour and a half three trucks passed, all carrying freight wagons, but the AYaAD highway code does not require anyone to offer assistance, even in the small hours, unless it is directly sought in some extreme emergency. And hereabouts our third breakdown would be rated as no more than an unfortunate minor incident, a routine annoyance, not life-threatening. Quite possibly one of those trucks would have to cope with a comparable set of problems before reaching Yakutsk.

By five o'clock I was so cold, despite ceaseless walking, that prudence dictated a retreat to the bus. As the heating system didn't work when the engine was off its temperature had dropped far below freezing and some sleepers were awakening and rummaging frantically through their luggage for warmer garments. I unrolled my flea-bag, snuggled into it – only my nose left exposed – and within moments was again asleep. I then had a slightly disturbing dream (no doubt immensely symbolic and significant if Jungified) about my three granddaughters, at that date aged six, four and two. They had grown up and become astronauts and were planning to migrate to Venus because they found Mother Earth uncongenial. I have always lamented the squandering of resources, intellectual and economic, on space travel, given our own planet's needs. But when I suggested cancelling the Venus spacecraft and investing in projects to make Mother Earth less uncongenial, I was told it was too late, money couldn't repair the damage. In my semi-nightmare all three girls looked like their mother, though in reality they resemble their father. Rarely do I remember dreams but this one was sharply clear when I awoke at 6.30 to hear the engine roaring triumphantly only inches from my ears.

Now the first glimmer of dawn showed a road made extra-treacherous by frozen snow: and still those three challenging passes lay ahead. Seven or eight miles took us to the small city of Aldan where I hoped Mitya and Sergei would feel the need for sleep-banishing caffeine. But if they did they resisted temptation when we briefly pulled into the bus station. There Mitya firmly rejected five would-be passengers, advising them to wait for a more reliable vehicle. Then we pressed on, our heroes looking grey with exhaustion but maintaining their stoical attitude to life's little setbacks.

In the 1920s prospectors found astounding amounts of gold and mica throughout this area. An indigenous village, Nezhametny, became a miners' settlement called Aldan in 1924 and a recognized 'city' in 1939. For sixty years the paranoid Aldan Gold Company closed the area to all foreigners, evidently not trusting their own staff to refrain from collaborating with gold thieves. Even now, I'm told, strangers are spied on by a population bred to be xenophobic. And in the new Russia Aldan has become notorious for its thriving heroin market and high rate of AIDS-related deaths. Or so they say in Yakutsk.

Soon the sky was cloudless, an intense blue, and the surrounding expanses of deep snow had a diamondesque glitter and sparkle, creating an illusion of *movement* across the landscape. This was another sort of terrain, miles of open tundra, then patches of thin taiga. Very slowly we climbed towards the first pass. The bare larches and birches had become inverted candelabras, whitely incandescent. The tall slender pines were wearing layered skirts – pirouetting models posing for a photographer. In the slanting morning sunlight small shrubs with delicate branches sheathed in frozen snow seemed the creation of some divinely inspired silversmith. Bulky boulders wore cloaks of snow, fringed with icicle needles. Even the old tyres were now acceptable: one could fancy them to be the coruscating coronets of giantesses. And all this I would have missed but for the oil leak.

Our fifth breakdown came at 8.20 a.m., exactly twenty-four hours after leaving Yakutsk; the engine growled erratically, groaned pathetically, then stopped. At once everyone disembarked, looking amazingly cheerful – perhaps because glad of an opportunity to empty bladders. The men promptly unzipped and stood with their backs to the bus making yellow circles in the snow. The women, giggling like schoolgirls, confabulated. For as far as the eye could see, this mountainside made no concessions to modesty; the slopes on both sides were too steep for us to leave the road. So the men were laughingly requested to keep their backs turned while we women bared our bottoms in unison along the verge.

For the heroes' sakes, though not for my own, I was glad this breakdown proved trivial. Within twenty minutes repairs had been effected by the adroit use of a short length of wire, picked off one of the Uluu dumps and providently cherished. Plainly Siberian bus and truck drivers, and their mates, have to know much more than the basics, must be capable of imaginative expedients in response to singular crises not dealt with in a manual. Perhaps Russians have a special flair for this sort of thing; they did, after all, win the space race.

Siberia's mountains being in the junior league, none of the three passes was very impressive. Approaching the highest – Tit-Ebe, below the 4,800 foot Evora peak – the snow glare made me blink and I was relieved to see Mitya wearing dark glasses. On either side long, smooth-topped mountains had the configuration of hills despite their altitude. Then post-Rumanian terror gripped me; here sheet ice covered the road and Mitya had been on duty for more than twenty-four gruelling hours. It helped that I had come to regard him as a superman; his face in the mirror showed no tension, only calm alertness, as he took us up that pass at walking speed. I reflected then that he and Sergei were of the stock who 'opened up the east' (voluntarily or involuntarily) and, unlike the breed who opened up America's west, they have not been softened by generations of affluence.

From the top of the pass we saw ahead two trucks in trouble. Their balding tyres could get no grip on the sheet ice and with huge spades their drivers were digging into the black earth of the verge and laying a carpet on the road. Gabriel explained that this heavy snowfall and sub-zero temperature, arriving some two weeks earlier than usual, had taken everyone by surprise. Normally road gangs would have been on duty to lay that carpet.

For a mile or so, on the road's uncarpeted side, we descended yard by yard, our movement scarcely perceptible. Then Mitya had to contend only with the humdrum hazards of the M56: craterous pot-holes, permafrost molehill-like eruptions, eroded verges and so on. I unclenched my fists and took another, celebratory, swig of vodka. South of Evota's range the snowfall had been much lighter and lay only on the ground; the sparse vegetation and wayside tyres remained unadorned. As bright sunshine streamed into the bus one could see how every jolt was dislodging clouds of fine dust from its crevices.

Towards noon Mitya at last gave in (probably for our sakes) and we stopped to eat at the little settlement of Khatymi where a dozen trucks and vans were parked near two large cafés. Our heroes led us into the largest: bright, clean, crowded, offering soups, stews, salads, *pelmeni*, potato cakes, confectionery, tea, coffee, beer, spirits and wines. I realized that in little Khatymi, between Aldan's goldmines and Neryungri's coalmines, we were back in a 'developed' region.

Smelling good food, we happily formed an orderly queue, our mouths almost visibly watering. Unlike BAM passengers, bus passengers travel ascetically and I had observed no one eating anything since our meagre Uluu suppers.

The service system had a Soviet flavour. Slowly a twenty-person queue shuffled forwards, parallel to the counter. At the till orders were given to one grumpy-looking girl and payments made to another. Then, clutching their receipts, customers moved away to stand between the tables awaiting the loud shout that would, after a long delay, summon them to the other end of the counter where they exchanged their receipts for a small tray. To pass the time, one could watch through an open door three other girls chopping, mixing, frying and grilling at a leisurely pace. Finding a seat was difficult; there were not enough of the round metal tables meant for two but having to accommodate four or five.

The second pass, the Durai, would scarcely count as such in, for instance, the Balkans, And the Chumakan pass is also quite mild. Approaching it, the road can be seen swirling up a highish taiga ridge with the aid of two well-engineered Z-bends. Because of the hardships inflicted on Stalin's prisoners the construction of this stretch in the 1930s, without any of today's colossal machinery, cost very many lives. From the crest of this ridge we were overlooking the vast

Neryungri-Chulman plateau – mostly taiga – and beyond, far to the south-east, rose a long range of chunky mountains loaded with new snow.

As Neryungri's long lines of blocks came into view, on a lower ridge top, I wished I had some appropriate gifts for Mitya and Sergei. At home their achievement would have been acknowledged by the passing around of a hat but here both the bus's unroadworthiness and our heroes' mechanical marathons were completely taken for granted.

A few passengers disembarked at Neryungri's AYaM station, some two miles from the city centre. Then, evidently as a 'thank you' for our cheerful acceptance of multiple misfortunes, Mitya – despite his own exhaustion – took everyone to their widely scattered individual destinations, instead of leaving us all at the bus terminus. I was put down near the PNILZ hotel at 2.20 p.m., exactly thirty hours after leaving Yakutsk. A slow cyclist, doing an average of 8 m.p.h., could cover those 456 miles in only twice that time.

When, back in Tynda, I told my M56 story to Pavel, he opined that it helped to explain the collapse of the Soviet Union. Apart from matters extraterrestrial, the Party set no standards of reasonable efficiency but conditioned its citizens to accept the consequences of inefficiency (as we passengers had done) and make the best of what was available (as our heroes had done).

I then told him another story, having first explained that in Britain and Ireland public transport is outrageously – sometimes criminally – inadequate, inefficient and expensive, goading its victims to complain vociferously seven days a week. For example: in May 2002 I found myself on a Limerick–Dublin train so overcrowded that I and eight others had to travel in the inter-coach space, standing for hours, unable even to sit on our piled luggage, fuelling each other's rage by swapping 'awful journey' yarns. Subsequently I joined that army which regularly writes furious letters to the press and elected representatives. Such protests of course have no discernible effect, though some argue that without them all concerned might sink to even lower levels of incompetence and irresponsibility.

Contrasting such Irish/British ordeals with my M56 experience, I suggested to Pavel that there is much to be said, from the mental health angle, for Siberian laidbackness, generating a communal atmosphere of calm resignation. The seething resentment felt at home by over-charged, inconvenienced passengers achieves little or nothing, is an expense of emotional energy in a waste of anger.

# IO

## Where a Coalmine is 'A Must'

In 1970 fewer than a thousand people lived in the remote little village of Neryungri on the banks of the narrow Chulman river. Then one of the world's largest coal deposits was discovered nearby and within two years a 'priority Komsomol project' had built a settlement for geologists and pioneer miners. Now Neryungri's 70,000 inhabitants make it Sakha's second city, though to me it felt more like an over-grown settlement, lacking a centre but with a certain dishevelled attractiveness. Occupying an airy site on a long high ridge, it completely contradicts the standard image of a dusty, dark, polluted mining town huddled in the shadows of grimy hillocks. The five- or nine-storey blocks (all white with green trimmings) stand far apart and well back from extravagantly wide and delightfully tranquil streets; often it is safe to defy the little red man because nothing is coming from any direction. To the north-east, beyond all those distant open-cast mines, level taiga stretches away to gleaming snowy mountains. Some citizens are said to suffer from chronic nostalgia for their faraway birthplaces yet the atmosphere is cheerful. Neryungri has no unemployment problem and its future looks secure. At the present rate of extraction the Neryungri field itself will be dug out by 2007, but the rest of the South Sakha coal basin holds an estimated forty billion tonnes.

Apart from Severobaikalsk's uniquely congenial Yacht Club hut, Neryungri provided my most agreeable Siberian accommodation. The PNILZ Hotel is near the edge of the city, on one of several short streets of 1972 terraced houses, and no high-risery could be seen from my window. It is really a small hostel, used by the usual complement of Chinese traders and by graduate students working at the Scientific Research Earthquake Laboratory of Yakutsk State

University. To be in an all-wood building, designed on a human scale, where the floors sloped perceptibly, the stairs creaked and earth tremors had realigned the rafters was wonderfully soothing. Here the rooms ($8.30) go in pairs, two sharing a tiny hallway and loo with wash-basin; downstairs is a communal shower-room where on arrival I scalded my scalp, a minor mishap yet quite painful for days. No one had warned me that Siberian pipes sometimes deliver water that is literally boiling. Neryungri's heating had just been turned on and though I left my window wide open, day and night, I always awoke sweating in the small hours. The PNILZ staff and my fellow-guests spoke not a word of English but everyone was welcoming – at first in a slightly hesitant way, being baffled by the solitary wandering babushka. (I like the general use of that term to address any female of my generation, much as 'Father' is – or was – used to address all Catholic priests in Ireland. It makes one feel secure, with an unambiguous and respected role in society.) Neryungri's language barrier was very high; in three days I met only one English-speaker.

By chance my first shopping trip took me into an establishment still adhering to Soviet-era procedures. Originally a miners' concessionary store, now apparently open to everyone, its prices were almost European rather than Eastern Siberian: a litre of milk 16 instead of 22 roubles, two litres of *pivo* 40 instead of 55 roubles and so on. But the time-cost was considerable: fifty minutes to buy a litre of milk and four litres of *pivo*. My fellow-shoppers were sensibly buying in bulk. Surveying the wide range of food industry goods which had been pushed even as far as Neryungri, it struck me that Snickers, given its revoltingly obvious etymon, must hold the world record for brand name vulgarity. No wonder it has been adapted by Russians who resent the consumerist tidal wave; *Snickerizatsiya* (Snickerization) is now a scornful synonym for Westernization.

Stage One of this shop's procedure involved much computer work to produce an invoice (in duplicate) listing the customer's requirements. Behind the computer sat a sullen sallow young woman with infected facial spots and purple hair dragged back into a stringy ponytail. (Had the purple dye caused the spots?) Stage Two involved queuing at another counter, then presenting the invoice to a gloomy elderly man who took it to regions unseen for further arcane processing. Behind his counter was a scene of chaos, a long low store full of half-unpacked crates and cartons. When he re-appeared the procedure was interrupted by a noisy fifteen-minute row between himself, the computer woman and a delivery man who had just parked his van outside and whose documentation was evidently not in order. The victims of this outbreak of hostilities, two elderly couples and myself, stood meekly to one side, clutching copies of our invoices, while the emotional temperature soared. However, I had by then realized that Siberians enjoy histrionics, that what may look like an enmity-for-life confrontation is quite likely to end with the protagonists sharing a *pivo*. In this case the delivery man lost; his sheaf of chits having been decisively rejected by the young woman, he scowlingly reloaded his van and drove away. We could then move on to Stage Three, the handing back of one's invoice with the goods available ticked off. After which one paid the young woman (Stage Four) and re-queued at Gloomy's counter to collect the goods (Stage Five). My roubles were unwelcome and the changing of a 100-rouble note caused extra delay. As the *BAM Guide* explains:

> Many purchasers in stores and cafés use a card. These are not credit cards but Zolotaya Korona smart debit cards. In an isolated one-industry town like Neryungri, these help to solve Russia's perennial cash problem, since most of the wages circulate within the town.

Near the PNILZ I found a tiny store selling bread and caused consternation by picking up a loaf. In such shops it is *verboten* to touch food before paying for it, one must ask for the items required; but on recognizing me as a foreigner the saleswoman laughed forgivingly. When I pointed to myself and said 'Irska' she pointed to herself and said 'Ukraine!' Then impulsively she lent across the counter to shake my hand. I got the message; we were fellow-Europeans in this god-forsaken Asian outpost of Russia's empire.

That evening I presented my hard-won litre of milk to the trio of cleaning-women who, when not at work, sat around in the PNILZ's lower corridor chatting and chuckling and drinking tea. Siberians do even worse things to milk than our own dairy industry and nowhere more so than in Neryungri. That litre had an ominous pinkish-brown tinge, suggestive of mastitis, and tasted proportionately foul.

Sakha retains one pleasing old-fashioned custom: when I boarded a crowded bus to the coalmine a youth at once offered me his seat. In Yakutsk I had noted in my diary:

> Here no elderly (or even middle-aged) woman is expected to stand on a bus. Instantly a child of either sex, or a youth, or a young man if he's the youngest on board, gives up his/her seat. Today one of two primary schoolboys sitting together stood up for my benefit. At the next stop his companion, busy counting small coins to make up his fare, failed to notice another babushka getting on. Immediately she tapped him lightly on the shoulder and he leaped to his feet looking guilty.

The No. 3 took us down six miles to the fast-flowing (even in September) Chulman river, then up to the end of the public road where stands the mine's nine-storey headquarters, incorporating a dozen shops and a canteen for 3,000 employees. Beside it, and dwarfing it, the crushing plants' many stacks were sending columns of white and black steam and smoke into the blue-grey sky. Here the entire visible landscape has been transformed within less than three decades; the long steep black ridges are manmade, likewise the shallow black valleys. The *BAM Guide* has to be on its own when describing a visit to a coalmine as 'a must', but now I could see the point. All extremes are exciting, whether pleasurably so or not, and this mine is truly Siberian in the sheer enormity of everything to do with it. The truck tyres seem millwheel-sized (in fact many are five yards in diameter) and each truck has a centipedal number of wheels. The first I saw advancing towards me was equipped with the equivalent of helicopter blades protruding from its cab; I couldn't begin to imagine what its function might be.

The mine runs a fleet of 2,500 vehicles and beyond the crushing plants are the truck company's headquarters; in a colossal repair workshop many oily men were making delicate adjustments to the innards of 2,300 h.p. monsters (average price $2million). The *BAM Guide* reports:

Maintaining the fleet is demanding as the trucks have to work 24 hours a day, 365 days a year, in temperatures as low as minus 50°C. In summer, the problems are just as bad with coal dust storms choking and even destroying the truck's engines. The drivers work 12-hour shifts with two months of holiday a year. They are only allowed to drive for five months each year as longer exposure to the continuous vibration and constant physical effort in controlling a 200-tonne truck can do them permanent damage. The workers spend the remaining five months a year working in the vehicle repair shops and on other less demanding jobs in the mine.

Opposite the workshop a road barrier was overlooked by a large 'No Entry' sign and an empty sentry box. Lest the sentry might be lurking nearby I rapidly retreated, again conscious of my visaless state. Then the manmade landscape inspired a plan: it should be possible to reach the opencast mines beyond the sentry box by following a truck road along one of the ridges. Some way down the road, past the bus stop, I turned on to a faint footpath and crossed a mile of rough ground, scattered with shreds of taiga, to the base of a ridge where a succession of tipper-trucks were dumping 'overburden', hour by hour enlarging the ridge. ('Overburden' is the dark earth, six to seven hundred feet deep, that covers the seventy-foot-deep coal seam.) Seen from afar, these 200-tonne trucks looked like beetles, ceaselessly crawling to and fro along the ridge's flank. When I came closer, and could watch the dumping 300 feet above me, I held my breath as each massive machine backed closer and closer to the very edge of an unstable precipice, then slowly the driver tipped his load which streamed towards me beneath a plume of dark dust. Before continuing to the far side of that ridge I equipped myself with a pine branch to help me up the steep skiddy slope. Then I was on the truckers' road, specially constructed of reinforced concrete slabs three feet thick. The drivers ignored me as I followed their route to a scene of Dante-esque desolation, a vast expanse of taiga being systematically torn asunder.

Until noon I strolled, unchallenged, around this wounded place where the clank of machinery seemed weirdly to emphasize Siberia's silence. Equally uncanny was the absence of visible people, every worker being hidden within his metal cage. The distress I would normally feel, while witnessing such a violation of natural beauty, was now subsumed by my fascination at the sight of so many mechanical giants doing such extraordinary things, working rhythmically and precisely, smoothly co-ordinating their complicated tasks, one machine taking over from another as a certain stage was completed. I had never thought to find myself being mesmerized for hours by the extraction of coal while not understanding anything I was seeing. Perhaps the mystery of it all added to the fascination.

On my way back to the bus stop I paused to count freight wagons crossing a high railway bridge above the road; trains pulled and pushed by three engines frequently leave the crushing plants. Having counted to eighty I gave up; there were at least another eighty, moving at walking speed towards Tynda like an exaggeration of a train in a small boy's drawing.

Beside me on the bus sat a pale spotty youth with broken teeth, frowning as he read an engineering textbook – in English. By then booklessness was again afflicting me so I said, 'Excuse me, I see you're reading an English book, please can you tell me if there's a bookshop in Neryungri?'

Reading and speaking a language are not identical skills. The lad went tense, darted a startled sideways glance at me, smiled nervously, muttered something incoherent and bent over his page of diagrams. Later I discovered one bookshop, its stock predictably uncontaminated by foreign volumes.

Next morning I looked out on to a still, soft, all-white world, the snow six inches deep. But soon the sun shone warm and the thaw had started as I walked to the Orthodox church for my Sunday choral fix. This rather graceless red-brick edifice, its newly gilded cupola conspicuous from afar, marks the reconciliation that had taken place between Church and State by the 1970s. Much bigger than St Nicholas's in Yakutsk, with a more mellow interior, it was only half-filled by the week's main service. The long-bearded priest, elderly and portly, looked rather bored in contrast to his two deacons, slim and solemn youths who performed their rituals with elegance and dignity. The choir couldn't compete with St Nicholas's but made up in fervour what it lacked in melody.

Young men with oil-ingrained hands – observed as they lit candles before their favourite icons – formed a big minority of the congregation. Oksana had told me that Neryungri is among the towns where Orthodoxy was boosted inadvertently by an evangelical mission called 'Eurovision' which raised funds back home in the United States by describing Siberia as 'a land with No God, No Bible, No Hope'. Such missions proliferated during the early 1990s when their rallies were attended by thousands to whom both Westerners and religious meeting were a novelty. In Siberia, Eurovision's Director once reported, more than 50,000 came forward to receive Christ after fifty-five meetings in sixty-three days. The majority of course 'came forward' merely to be polite to foreign visitors who so obviously yearned for this response and few were genuine converts. However, Oksana made the point that such missions turned many youngsters bred in atheist homes towards the faith of their fathers (or great-grandfathers), giving them a taste for Christianity though they didn't savour the way it was served up by evangelists.

In Irkutsk, on trolley-buses, I had twice seen groups of loudly proselytizing youths with large crosses on their T-shirts and fanatical gleams in their eyes. Possibly they belonged to one of the recently imported quasi-religious cults which from time to time attract police attention. In addition to alienating student victims from their parents by using chillingly efficient psyop techniques, they tend to fundraise by persuading recruits that stealing valuables from their own homes, for Christ's sake, is a shortcut to heaven. This is when the police go after them, usually sending local leaders scuttling to find refuge under the cult founder's wing, more often than not in California. Those Irkutsk preachers were not allowed to ride far and the passengers' hostility to them was quite scary. Given other circumstances, one could imagine the sort of treatment they might receive. On being ejected from the buses they removed their 'uniforms', revealing unprovocative shirts beneath.

Observing Neryungri's congregation – repeatedly crossing themselves, bowing, praying half-aloud, moving around to kiss their most revered icons or light another candle – I wondered how much they knew or cared about the chronic divisions that plague Orthodoxy. The Soviet-moulded ecclesiastical Establishment at present in control occupies Camp I. The Orthodox Church Abroad, intent on restoring Holy Russia as was and steadily gaining support within Russia, occupies Camp II. The intelligentsia wing, uncompromisingly opposed to any reunion of Church and State, occupies Camp III. Each camp distrusts and detests the other two and at intervals verbal hostilities break out. In brief, it's all very Christian.

I emerged into a bright wet city, slushy underfoot with the drip of fast-melting snow loud in every direction and the sky cloudless. In the noon sun one sweated, in the shade one shivered. Walking down to the AYaM station to book my ticket for Tynda, I saw the roads, pavements and rough paths between blocks becoming rapidly flooded. Those who built Neryungri in record time, and who are commemorated by several dire monuments throughout the city, concentrated all their skills on permafrost and earthquake problems – admittedly more important than drainage.

In 2002 Neryungri was the AYaM passenger service terminus, but if all goes according to plan Sakha's second city will be relegated to a branch line while the mainline goes through the nearby town (also mine-centred) of Berkakit. Therefore Neryungri's station seems large and grand out of all proportion to its present or future significance. Here are marble walls, twelve-foot-high potted plants, vaguely Gothic windows of garish stained glass, ecclesiastical-looking chandeliers, bouquets of plastic flowers hanging above the ticket office guichet.

Only five stood ahead of me in the queue. However, each one had some major problem which required the friendly, patient young woman clerk to consult many files and make many telephone calls involving prolonged struggles to get connections. I had been queuing for one hour and fifty minutes, according to the Moscow-time station clock, when I stepped forward to the guichet – just as it closed, for the clerk's well-earned lunch break. By then six women and five men stood behind me and we all moved to sit on the front row of plastic chairs, maintaining our queue order. (Hundreds of chairs furnished this waiting-room.) During the next hour several others arrived, including a thin-lipped woman in a sealskin coat, carrying a miniature poodle who wore a plaid jacket and a twee pink ribbon on his topknot. As the clerk returned we all stood up and Mrs Sealskin moved swiftly forward to place the poodle on the guichet shelf. Pointedly I thrust my passport and roubles past his sharp little nose and in firm tones requested my *platskartny* ticket to Tynda – conscious of my fellow-queuers' support. Mrs Sealskin, enraged, said something sneering about '*platskartny*' which prompted the man next in the queue to make a taunting remark about the poodle. My ticket purchase took only moments; annoyingly, the one daily train departed at 6 p.m.

Pain compelled me to seek a bus back to Neryungri; my coalmine trek, and the walk to the station, and then that queue, had overtaxed The Knee. As I stood by the roadside, the man who had denigrated the poodle reappeared with a friend and they thumbed a passing car, then beckoned me to join them. Evidently this was Neryungri's informal taxi system, hitching a ride for a few roubles; but of course the foreign babushka was not allowed to contribute her mite.

By now the city was seriously flooded as torrents raced down slopes. Yet many Sunday afternoon strollers were enjoying the sunshine, though crossing roads meant fording ponds and streams six feet wide and six inches deep.

In the PNILZ a young man awaited me; he had seen the foreigner in church and it wasn't too difficult to trace Neryungri's only tourist to her lodgings. Pyotr was a Muscovite, a junior accountant at the coalmine, condemned by his firm to two years' exile in Neryungri which he hoped would be rewarded by rapid promotion. He hated Neryungri. 'It is uncivilized, the people are stupid, there is no one speaking English and I need to practise English. When I am promoted in Moscow I must speak good English with our American clients.' The mine employed a few foreign English-speakers, he explained as we went upstairs, but they were senior men who wouldn't mix with a junior accountant. Pyotr looked shocked when I took a two-litre bottle of *pivo* from the bedside cupboard and offered him a glass. 'I am not drinking alcohol, I am a very good Orthodox Christian.' Historically, teetotalism and Orthodoxy don't go together – rather the reverse – but I nodded respectfully, concealing my surprise.

We talked for more than an hour without finding any common ground though Pyotr didn't seem to notice that failure. He displayed equal prejudice against Jews, Roman Catholics and Muslims. People talked a lot about the mafia but it was really Jewish financiers behind the scenes who were wrecking the new Russia's economy. The Pope was a religious imperialist trying to bribe the Russians to leave their Holy Mother Church and become a Vatican colony. The Chechnyans were 'all primitive fundamentalists, Islamic fanatics and terrorists. In the eighteenth century they asked for the czar's protection and you can't break agreements when it suits you!' My deploring the Russian army's extreme brutality in Grozny provoked him to rudeness. 'You're blind!' he exclaimed. 'You will believe any bad thing said about Russia!' Here were no shaded areas; Pyotr could tolerate nothing even indirectly suggesting a Russian imperfection. Yeltsin's alcoholism was 'a typical example of Western propaganda'. It was not true that the Kremlin tried to hide the Chernobyl disaster, that when the *Kursk* sank Putin turned down offers of Western help or that contaminated meat from the Chernobyl area was being illegally sold in Moscow. All anti-Russian propaganda! Foreigners complained about the Siberian tribes being Sovietized but 'uncivilized people must suffer, they can't keep up with us. That's why they die out anyway all over the world. It's the survival of the fittest, we can't go against Nature.'

When Pyotr looked at his watch and invited me to a film I made polite but negative noises. He then went to the loo and found it waterless, which set him off on another exile's lament. In fact Neryungri's water supply was less erratic than Yakutsk's – more often on than off – and in the PNILZ (unlike the Kolos) our bathroom was always provided with two full buckets.

As we said goodbye the western sky was all bronze and purple and the temperature way below freezing. 'Tomorrow winter will start here,' Pyotr gloomily foretold. 'The colour of the clouds is their winter colour. In Moscow now it's still autumn, a good season. I don't understand why you came to this place.'

At sunrise the fineness and lightness of the falling snow were deceptive; by ten o'clock a smooth blanket covered Neryungri and when I looked down from its ridge visibility was nil. Ancient little snowploughs worked away on all the main streets but not much gravel was being strewn; this early fall had surprised the municipality. Interior heating quickly melted some of the snow on roofs and around windows but now no water was dripping: the icicles lengthened even as one watched. By noon the cleared streets were sheets of ice; heavy trucks couldn't cope with mild inclines and had to be abandoned. Everywhere icicles were forming, including between the wheels of vehicles. Cars and buses moved very cautiously. Schoolboys going home at lunchtime enjoyed snowball fights, happily shouting. Dogs, equally happy, rolled in the snow. Most people were wearing black leather ankle-length coats or knee-length jackets and high boots, everything fur-lined. From now on the climate, rather than fashion, would determine outdoor wear.

At 2 p.m. it was hard to believe that only twenty-four hours earlier the sun had felt *hot*. The temperature was still dropping and I had left my *very* cold weather garments at Severobaikalsk, not expecting to need them so soon. It was time to move to the safe warmth of the station waiting room. Back at the PNILZ I said my goodbyes and set off on foot, my post-Rumania phobia again operative. It seemed less phobic when, on that downhill walk, I passed two cars that had slid off the road – one landing on its wheels, the other on its side. Luckily the drop was no more than twenty feet. On the slight slope up to the station a truck loaded with two freight wagons was hopelessly stuck. Presumably such crises are avoided when Neryungri gets its winter act together.

Many of my fellow-passengers had already assembled, perhaps also taking refuge from winter's abrupt arrival. Most were reading, or busy with crosswords, or had their chess sets out. In one corner five men still wearing their *shapkas* were hunkered around a mammoth picnic. The large restaurant beside the waiting room remained unused, apart from a mother breastfeeding her baby. A generational conflict provided the only diversion: over-protective mother versus bossy babushka as a baby practised walking and laughed each time it fell. Babushka regarded falling as a natural part of the process, mother disagreed and eventually burst into tears which made one suspect this issue was merely the tip of a rather large iceberg. For the next two hours I reread *Lord Jim*, thrice going outside to observe developments; by five o'clock the temperature was minus 21 °C and the several vehicles parked in the forecourt had been left with their engines running.

At 5.50 the train doors were opened and the steps let down. In a quarter-full *platskartny* my only companion was an Aldan woman who oozed friendly curiosity and enjoyed the mini-dictionary game. That morning she had had a nerve-wracking journey through the blizzard across those three passes. She ran a pharmacy in Aldan and was going to Tynda to buy antibiotics made in China.

Our *provodnitsa*, tall and thirtyish, wore carmine lipstick, blonde ringlets in a ponytail and a big smile. Unlike most of her kind, she was chatty and bright-eyed. She should have been off work this week but her boyfriend had just proposed marriage by e-mail from Khabarovsk so she had exchanged rotas with a colleague and was hastening to his arms. Recently the railway workers' free travel concession had been withdrawn and they had to pay half-fare which she couldn't possibly afford all the way to Khabarovsk. Then her mother came around, selling golden-brown potato cakes, filled with minced meat or vegetables and kept hot in a hay-basket with a metal base beneath which charcoal glowed.

Through the dusk I gazed at a snow-smeared, axe-mutilated taiga where the ponds were already iced over and the streams had begun to freeze along their edges. As the landscape became more interesting the light faded. No bedding was provided for this short six-hour journey but I slept soundly on the leatherette bunk until my companion shook me awake. We shared a taxi to the Yunis where I was given a 'welcome back' hug by Masha, the stout body with tousled ginger hair who always slept on her divan bed below the Reception counter.

Pavel knew nothing of my second accident and on the telephone sounded at first puzzled – then flatteringly pleased by my unexpected return. After we had arranged to meet at 11.30 I set off for the market's Chinese canteen. Tynda remained snow-free but its avenues of leafless birches looked wintry.

Entering the market from the rear, I chanced upon the butchers' corner, an open-air abattoir, and noticed something suspicious. Siberia's family-reared pigs are said to be uncontaminated by growth hormones, antibiotics and chemically treated feed; yet here were two

throats being cut and the noiselessness of the procedure (pigs are pro-
verbially noisy at this stage) suggested the use of an anaesthetic. I
paused to watch buckets of blood being carefully collected before the
heads were sawn off and placed on a long counter – returning me to
the Ireland of my youth, to the days before EU regulations, hypocrit-
ical squeamishness and excessive affluence took pigs' heads off the
market. The carcasses were then heaved on to a three-foot-high
block – with difficulty, these were giant boars – and disembowelled
and carved up by two husband and wife teams, the men wielding their
cleavers, saws and hunting knives not very skilfully while the women
held the carcasses steady. Customers began to arrive as quivering
hunks were slapped on to the counter – still warm, steaming in the
cold air. This fresh meat was less than half the price of Yakutsk's deep-
frozen pork.

After breakfast I did what I couldn't do on my previous visit and
walked to the crest of the taiga ridge above Tynda. On its lower slopes
the BAM builders erected scores of temporary dwellings, at least half
of which became permanent when block construction fell short of
The Plan's specifications. Outwardly these shacks look wretched
enough but some have newish extensions, the majority have electricity and my glimpses of several interiors showed neat and cosy homes.
Many large railway containers, converted to dwellings thirty years ago,
have been stripped of all fittings and left sprawling at odd angles
between trees and shacks. I wondered how they had got to this steep,
roadless slope so far above the railway – perhaps by helicopter? Here
too are dumps of rotting and rusting matériel not needed for BAM's
completion. Further up the ridge and deeper into the trees, some of
these have been used to build authentic shanty-town huts, lacking all
amenities. The occupants are ragged, dirty, hungry-looking Sibiryaki
families who stared at the passing stranger with a mixture of nervousness and hostility. One never sees such people in BAM town centres.
Pavel described them as 'alcohol drop-outs' who somehow survive by
trapping, fishing and if possible stealing.

Beyond all this, a soft path led gradually upwards through pines and
larches to an abandoned radio mast on the ridgetop. The view was
curtailed by the lie of the land and the thickness of the taiga, but an
encounter on the way down provided ample compensation. Near the

edge of the town a small slender shining creature darted across the road – my first glimpse of Siberian wildlife. I stood still, trying to trace its movement, then saw it swiftly ascending the trunk of a tall spruce. For the next fifteen minutes I followed its progress as it flowed from tree to tree apparently effortlessly, sailing across distances prodigious in relation to its size. Thrice it descended and paused to nibble at pine cones and once I was almost within touching distance and held my breath, now able fully to appreciate its cream-coloured belly, sleek chestnut flanks, ebony back and tail – the fluffy tail seeming bulkier than the body. It had tufted ears, a pointed nose, quick bright eyes, deft and delicate forepaws with which it extracted the seeds from the cones. Then, registering my presence, it was gone into the high branches – beauty incarnate, perfect in shape, colour, texture, movement. The trite phrase 'it made my day' can be a statement of fact.

I found Pavel in rather low spirits; a few recent incidents involving his university friends in various cities were troubling him, incidents to do with 'destructive bribery in the groves of academe'. Plaintively he continued, 'Soviet corruption was widespread, but rare in the academic world. Russians had intellectual integrity and were proud of it and respected for it internationally.' The cynical and ruthless precision of the bribery pay-scale struck me as peculiarly morally repulsive: 200 roubles for a 'satisfactory' mark, 300 for a 'good' mark, 500 for 'excellent'. A lecturer/professor with scores of students does very nicely, thank you. Some degrees can be bought for $50, paid in dollar bills.

Pavel went on, 'Some say it's all about cutbacks, the Soviet ethos of free and *valued* education is fading. Academic staff on low pay are tempted to demand bribes to survive. Poor parents can't pay for schoolbooks and know they couldn't anyway afford university bribes so they've no incentive to keep children's noses to books. Many pupils don't want to learn, or not until it's too late to catch up. It doesn't help that all corporal punishment is illegal, teachers daren't lay a finger on a pupil. Some deal with persistent troublemakers by punishing their whole class, setting everyone tasks like picking up litter before they're allowed home. So it's left to the classmates to punish him or her – usually him! This is an offshoot of the communal way of thinking and some classmates don't hesitate to lay sticks or fists on an offender. In the worst cases pupils go before the Principal, parents are called to a conference and if no improvement follows there's expulsion. We have special schools in big cities for hard cases, I believe like US boot-camps. Real education is neglected, a tough routine leaves no energy over for being disruptive. But then what? Too often prison! People say, "They're born criminals, that's their fate." I don't agree, I hate this system, I'd let teachers frighten junior pupils with a small stick. Then they might not grow into seniors ending up where staff are allowed big sticks. Most hard cases come from families that give them no love or discipline, no discipline because no love. Then they have children of their own and don't know how to love them – and how to break this chain reaction?'

I said, 'Listening to you, I might be back in Ireland, discussing our own inner-city problems. And I've never heard of anyone, anywhere, with the answer to your question.'

We were on our way, during this conversation, to one of Tynda's ten municipal schools; Pavel had hastily arranged a visit after my tele-phone call. Access to the only fee-paying school, recently established, was not possible at such short notice. To compare the two would have been interesting. Later, someone obliquely suggested that the private school's founder preferred to avoid such comparisons.

In a long, outwardly shabby five-storey building a staff of fifty (all women apart from the sports master) teach 700 seven- to eighteen-year-olds. Two years previously the interior had been redecorated and it seemed everywhere was dusted, scrubbed and polished every day. At noon the high, wide corridors were full of laughing, scampering juniors and more sedate but no less animated seniors. Uniforms are out but sartorial competitiveness is discouraged and everyone was neatly and suitably dressed, the seven-year-old girls still wearing their 'First Day' white hair-ribbons. The excited reaction to my presence, though politely – even charmingly – expressed, made me feel extra-terrestrial.

One of the English teachers – Polina, Pavel's friend – joined us for our tour of large bright classrooms, a much-used well-stocked library including a comfortable reading annex, a theatre with a full-sized stage, elaborate props, heavy royal blue curtains and seating for 800, a huge gym-cum-sports hall equipped for basketball, indoor football and much else, a science laboratory of (to my untutored eye) stunning sophistication.

I asked Pavel, 'Is this a showpiece school?'

He laughed. 'You have a suspicious nature! For Tynda it's average – but here is a lucky town.'

We lunched in the canteen, furnished with tables for four, of grey-white flecked formica. The placement was informal, staff and pupils together eating simple wholesome food freshly cooked in the many-stoved kitchen by a staff of eight. I noticed easy teacher/pupil relationships, all mingling in the queue at the counter separating canteen from kitchen. Most of the teaching staff, Polina said, were in mid-career with a few trainees and a few near retirement age. When she introduced the unexpected Irishwoman to various colleagues, the older generation were noticeably less at ease with me. Pavel remarked that nowadays most trainees are either very unusual, with a genuine enthusiasm for teaching, or not very bright and grateful to have found any job. Out of their monthly salary of $100 (3,000 roubles), they must pay an average of $33 rent and, if without dependants, 13 per cent income tax.

Afterwards, in Polina's senior classroom (décor: dove grey and powder blue), twenty shyly smiling pupils rose to their feet as I entered and chorused 'Welcome to Tynda! Welcome to our school!' They sat two to a desk, the sexes segregated, and though none had ever before met a Western foreigner several were brave (or fluent) enough to ask questions. The rest whispered to Polina, pleading with her to translate for them.

The first question, 'What do you think about Harry Potter?', came from a goodlooking girl with ash-blonde hair and high cheekbones. Ripples of laughter greeted my reply: 'I don't think about him, tell me what you think.' The ash-blonde promptly replied, 'It's a bit like Tolkien but easier to read.' A distinguished-looking youth in the front row of the boys' aisle added, 'Russians like magic mixed in with ordinary life. We like to believe in some impossible things.'

Many questions followed about my domestic circumstances. As always, my living in a village caused bewilderment – surely people who write books must live in *cities*? Only farmworkers or loggers or fishermen live in villages! 'How many rooms in your dacha?' Then gasps of astonishment and squeals of incredulity – *seven* rooms for *one* person! 'Are you very, very rich?' To correct that misapprehension I listed what I don't possess: car, TV set, central heating, washing machine, microwave oven, computer. But this merely compounded their confusion. Then came name-signing; as I had discovered elsewhere, the Siberian young are avid autograph hunters and a Western autograph is much coveted. I did my duty by Polina's class and thought that was that. Not so – as we left the school an hour later scores of anxious-looking children were waiting around the steps, albums open, pens at the ready. Cheers broke out when I began to sign; it's satisfying to be able to give so much pleasure so easily.

Polina accompanied us back to the Yunis and expressed a fear that soon overall standards might fall, compulsory schooling having been reduced from eleven to eight years. Now pupils are allowed to do the final two years only if they pass a tough examination.

Pavel nodded. 'We're crazy, throwing out the educational baby with the Party bathwater. It was a very healthy baby that might have become the country's saviour.'

The following morning was cold and dull, a pewter sky pressing down on Tynda. Yet by 11.30, when Pavel and I passed the town hall, its digital temperature 'clock' read 9°C. In midwinter Tynda's average noon temperature is minus 27°C and Yakutsk's minus 40°C.

We were on our way to the municipal library where I sniffed the air appreciatively; all libraries smell the same. The high galleried atrium was a luxuriant jungle of potted trees, shrubs, vines, all looked after by devoted volunteers since Tynda could no longer afford indoor gardeners. Every leaf shone with health, every delicate fern had its special needs catered for, every cactus bristled vigorously. When I commented on the wealth of plant life in schools and offices, and in all Siberian homes, Pavel said, 'You don't know about eight months of whiteness, for you snow and ice and frost look beautiful and romantic. For us it can seem sterile and threatening. We must have greenery, growth visibly happening, to refresh our souls. We enjoy winter, playing sports in snow and on ice – we have to enjoy it, people couldn't keep sane if they didn't enjoy their environment for two-thirds of the year. But we're not natives, Sibiryaki are not genetically programmed to accept the eight-month ordeal.'

On our way up the wide staircase, its banisters handsomely carved, we admired (or not, as the case might be) the gallery's permanent art exhibition, showing the works of local painters and promising school-children. In the library's long airy rooms trees flourished in every corner and vines had been trained to drape themselves gracefully between History and Fiction, Economics and Science, Biography and Reference Works. Few books had been acquired since 1992 and in some sections volumes were displayed front-wise to fill depleted shelves.

'It's not just because of cutbacks,' said Pavel. 'This library was always too big, all BAM towns were designed by unrealists. They had to believe the railway would bring industry, trade, more people. Instead, populations are going down.'

The juvenile section, catering for pre-reading toddlers through to teenage science fiction addicts, remained well stocked and had its own reading room equipped with rows of small desks and comfortable benches around the walls. The other two reading rooms were for students and adults. I used to wonder how the Siberians, confined within such tiny flats, got through the winter evenings without freaking out. Here was part of the answer: a high percentage of the population troops off to reading rooms.

Pavel said, 'This was part of the Communist way. Homes were for eating and sleeping in. Other activities – intellectual, artistic, athletic – were communal, free of expense, so keeping everyone conformist and dependent on the State. But also giving them opportunities like their forefathers never had.'

Nearby was the Palace of Culture, often incorrectly translated, said Pavel, as 'House of Culture'. Every city has one (or several) and Pavel explained, 'The Soviets thought back to the czars' palaces and said the proletariat should also have special places but for everyone, sharing culture to enrich ordinary lives. Not grand baroque structures to be looked at but palaces *in spirit*.'

Tynda's palace felt sadly underused and urgently needed redecorat-ing. Here were a cinema, theatre, concert hall, soundproof recording studios and multi-purpose rooms where adults were taught arts and crafts before the roubles ran out. In recent years the concert hall was mainly used by Tynda's choir, 'famous throughout Siberia,' boasted Pavel. The cinema showed three films a week to diminishing audiences. 'It's the same all over the country,' Pavel mourned. 'Russians were regular filmgoers before '91 and proud of our industry, which was more than an industry. It was an art we were famous for, ever since Sergey Eisenstein's *Battleship Potemkin* in 1925. In the history of world cinema he's like a Shakespeare figure. And even today we do have outstanding filmmakers – but frustrated. Ticket prices are so high since the mid-Nineties people with satellite TV give up the cinema. Our production is only a tenth of what it was but still the quality is fine.'

We next visited the Music College, founded in the mid-1990s by a celebrated Tynda musician now living in Moscow, whose name I forgot to write down. His foundation flourishes in a large building previously used by the Communist Party; their logo remains above the entrance. Offices have been converted to attractive music rooms and children from the age of seven up pay 200 roubles ($7.50) each term for an hour's one-to-one tuition five days a week. With the Director's permission we intruded briefly on a few of the lessons and to my embarrassment a nine-year-old clarinettist and a ten-year-old pianist (both boys) were asked by their teacher to perform for the guest – which they readily did, looking rather pleased with themselves, so I stopped feeling embarrassed. One eight-year-old violinist with a Botticelli angel's hairstyle to match her features was excitingly talented and regarded as a future 'star', though everyone was careful not to tell her so. As we drank tea with the Director we saw this beautiful lass going home, wearing her violin case satchelwise. Pupils are expected to practise seriously and families unable to afford an instrument can apply to the foundation for an interest-free loan.

This was the acceptable face of new Russian capitalism – or do I mean old Russian philanthropy? The college's conversion and furnishing had involved as many local artists and craftsmen as possible. Pavel indicated the strips of red carpet running the length of corridors that had been refloored with intricately patterned cedarwood parquet. 'All this is Tynda work, a very big change from everything coming from factories far away!' On the corridor walls hung several large bas-relief wood panels depicting Siberian birds, fish, animals, carved in marvellous detail. 'Commissioned from a local genius,' explained Pavel, 'to help the revival of one of our most ancient indigenous traditions.'

As we left the college the rain came: cold, heavy, straight down. I suggested waiting for a bus to the railway station but Pavel obviously thought public transport unsuitable for a Distinguished Visitor and insisted on walking through the downpour to fetch a taxi.

This journey to Severobaikalsk was made for ever memorable by Vali from Dushanbe, now resident in Tynda. He occupied the lower bunk opposite mine and was travelling with his slim, gold-toothed wife and her hard-faced, silent mother. Aged thirtyish, tall and obese, he had short greasy hair, a forehead so low his eyebrows almost hid it, a big loose mouth and three chins. He wore tracksuit trousers and a too small T-shirt and often made porcine noises, clearing his nose by snorting into his throat. Less often, but to noisome effect, he farted. He ate more than seemed possible: a meal every few hours (noodles, potato salad, salami, Bush's legs, cheese, hard-boiled eggs, two sorts of bread) and in between apples, chocolate, grapes, toffees, biscuits. This may have had something to do with his unfortunate and repellent skin condition: infected pimples, and the purple scars of earlier eruptions, covered his whole visible body. When not eating he removed his shirt and obsessively squeezed yellow pus from the spots on his torso, considering each trophy with morbid satisfaction before transferring it to the BAM blanket. He sat up only to use a hand-mirror while squeezing facial pimples. Otherwise, even when eating, he preferred the reclining posture and his belly, when he turned sideways, looked like something extraneous and unpleasant placed near him on the bunk. He also suffered from a permanent erection (the medical term escapes me) to which he frequently drew his wife's attention, inviting her with eloquent gestures to sit astride him – invitations which she declined, while glancing at me and giggling and providing him with yet another snack to take his mind off his penis. Inevitably, Vali aroused guilt. One should feel sorry for someone afflicted by multiple disorders: dietary, dermatological, sexual. But rapidly I came to loathe him, with a peculiar intensity. Making the snobbish assumption that people who travel coupé don't behave like Vali, I wondered about the journey back to Moscow ... Could anyone survive five days with a Vali as their *platskartny* companion?

Towards sunset I moved to the window at the end of our coach and sat on the litter-bin. This was my third journey on BAM's Tynda–Severobaikalsk line yet the landscape looked unfamiliar, transformed by the advent of winter. As we gained altitude the frozen streams, so frisky and sparkling in August, lay inert like dead pale grey serpents. The nearby jagged rock peaks seemed all the more ferocious above their slopes' snowy softness. Then, to the west, a fan-shaped rosy effusion reached halfway up the sky, flanked by grey-blue blizzard clouds. As dusk fell, the first flakes appeared.

During the night, after one of Vali's problems had been dealt with, he needed sustenance and his wife hastened to the samovar, returned with a dish of noodles, was thrown off-balance by a BAM jerk and spilled very hot water over my head. As I picked bits of noodle out of my hair Vali shouted angrily at his wife and the man in the bunk above me shouted angrily at Vali. Then Vali's mother-in-law woke up and shouted angrily at everybody, which brought upon us all the wrath of our *provodnitsa*. She whispered, making the point that this was the middle of the night when passengers were entitled to silence. But her whispers were menacing and cowed all concerned. Vali resigned himself to a cold repast, belching loudly between courses, and I, having been provided with a clean pillow, slept on.

The Evenk weather god, the deity in charge of this region, was kind to me next morning. Sitting with my mug of tea on the litter-bin, I could see the last stars fading in a clear sky. A scattering of conifers on a wide valley floor turned from black to green – and suddenly the distant white summits of the Chara range were pink, then radiantly gold. At which point our *provodnitsa* (who had the shape and demeanour of a bulldog) arrived to reprimand me for sitting on the litter-bin at an hour when passengers needed to deposit their nocturnal garbage. (Mainly beer cans, I observed, while standing by the window.)

BAM runs close to the southern shore of the fourteen-mile-long Big Leprindo Lake and on its opposite shore 8,000-foot mountains rise sheer from the water. The sun had now gained strength and above the lake mist was writhing, concealing and revealing the jade surface, dispersing and reforming around the gaunt peaks, draping silver scarves over the range's shoulders. But this early calm was deceptive and as we approached the Severomuisk Pass a blizzard was blowing, fine snow being driven horizontally. We crept up that dicey marvel of Soviet engineering with visibility down to fifty yards – not enough to veil the hazards of the track. On the long descent the snow thickened until we were wrapped in whiteness – an eerie feeling, our train seeming an alien, self-contained entity, defying both the terrain and the elements.

This, however, was autumn in Siberia. Down at Lake Baikal's level, no snow had yet fallen and the trees were still aglow. Near Severobaikalsk, a freakishly beautiful phenomenon appeared. In the long valley behind the lakeside mountains, layered banks of cloud – way below the dark blue bulk of the summits, not far above the ground – had taken on sunset colours and were streaked orange, yellow and fiery red, as though the sky had fallen to earth.

At 8.40 p.m., as promised on my ticket, we halted in Severobaikalsk. By courtesy of Pavel I had sent an e-mail to Rashit, saying how much I was looking forward to seeing the Yahins again on 4 October. Deliberately I had left vague the time of my arrival on 3 October; I planned to spend that night in the Severney Baikal Hotel in the Old Town, not far from the Yahins. But Siberian hospitality is not so easily dodged. By some mysterious means Rashit had ascertained not only which train I was on but which coach I was in and I stepped out of my *platskartny* into the welcoming arms of Mrs Yahin. When I had with difficulty dissuaded her from carrying my rucksack we walked through the town centre, then in pitch darkness on rough paths through the wide belt of taiga separating the New Town from the Old. I thought, 'Lucky Siberia! Is there any town now, in Europe, where two elderly women would feel completely safe walking through unlit woodland at night?' Only the path's roughness bothered me; a disability like The Knee makes one twitchy about stumbling and falling.

Rashit condemned my plan to spend the next twelve days in the Severny Baikal hotel. I must stay in the Yahins' luxury (by my standards) flat in the New Town, at a ludicrously low rent – a flat hallowed by the presence of Colin Thubron, during his Siberian journey.

# 11

# Reunions

In the New Town I was conveniently close to most of those who had earlier befriended me and living in a flat created the illusion of being part of Severobaikalsk, rather than merely observing the town from a hotel. Not that block life is convivial; I made no new friends among my immediate neighbours. There is something isolating about blocks of flats, be they state flats in Siberia or luxury flats in London. Packing hundreds of human beings into one purpose-built edifice is a bad idea, not how we were meant to live. In the Old Town, the Yahins and Yulia had normal relationships with their micro-communities; there was casual toing and froing between homes, friendly chatting and not so friendly arguing. The neighbours mattered, contributed to daily life in lots of little ways. The New Town's block-dwellers seemed much more centred on family and close friends.

I was alone on the shore for my sunrise reunion with Lake Baikal. Rounded banks of deep pink cloud were touching the sharp crags, now snow-blunted, of its guardian mountains. Waves pulsed loudly on the gravel and sand, curling whitely before a strong wind. As I walked the wind dropped, the clouds faded to shades of grey – were broken – and through them streamed rays from the hidden sun, tinting the distant summits until they matched the autumn taiga on the cliffs above me. Then Lake Baikal, responding gloriously to the subdued light, became a trembling expanse of bronze.

Perhaps the lake's emanations have influenced Severobaikalsk. I can't complain of unfriendliness anywhere in Siberia but this town's relaxed amiability and spontaneity seem exceptional. People generally have time to spare for a foreigner who can't speak Russian and the numbers of townsfolk who welcomed me back – taxi-drivers, street cleaners, market stallholders – created a homecoming atmosphere.

One local friend suggested that all this may have something to do with the area's protected status which has left people aware of their particular relationship with the Hallowed Sea. The very existence of a BAM town of course violates Baikal's integrity but I understood what Grigori meant; Severobaikalsk now intrudes as little as possible. Moreover, these 'Children of BAM', unlike many peoples privileged to live amidst great beauty, do appreciate their good fortune and wax poetical about the changing colours of lake, mountains and taiga, about the wild flowers in summer, the ice sculptures in winter, the various seasonal scents of the forest. As in Tynda, I noticed a strong local loyalty and an aversion to what Moscow represents. Although many young from both towns find work in their Siberian university city, the urge to migrate further west seems weaker than one would expect.

On my way back from the lake I visited Yulia in her draper's shop near the station market. The hugging was vigorous, the tea and toffees instant, the family news good – though business could be better. Elvira had won a prize for her anti-globalization essay and, much more important, Feodor had joined the army. In August Yulia had been fretting about his keeping bad company, drinking too much *pivo*, wanting to go to some faraway college or institute where he would surely drink even more *pivo*, maybe take drugs, meet bad girls who might have AIDS. He had never been away from home, with the maternal brake off anything could happen, at his age a boy needs paternal control, his behaviour might be a reaction to his father's death just as he left school. So on his eighteenth birthday she wanted him to join the army where he would, she believed, be strictly disciplined – and last week he had joined!

Yulia's vision of the army as a moral safe haven puzzled me, as did her ignoring of the Chechnya threat. Elsewhere I had met three mothers who, on realizing that their sons were at risk as expendable junior recruits, had borrowed unspecified sums of money, flown to the relevant military bases and ensured that those boys were not sent south.

The Gladkovas' spacious three-roomed ground-floor flat, bright and comfortably furnished, was not far from the station; their sitting-room window gave a good view of BAM movements. After Accident II, this family had been prominent among my corps of carers. Mila, a teacher, spoke fluent English; her husband Roman, an assistant train-driver soon to 'graduate', was a man of few words, none of them English. Their daughter Katya, by now aged one minus a week, was a remarkably outgoing and enterprising infant who, when we first met in August, impressed me by being already out of nappies. ('Disposables' were not yet on sale in the BAM Zone where mothers had too much sense or too little cash to make them profitable.) Mila and Roman had married after a three-year courtship, then had to live with the older generation for another three years until this flat, bought with parental assistance, became available. Now the rapidly rising costs of electricity and heating had begun to worry them. Shortly before Katya's birth Mila took a year's paid maternity leave; on her return to work the babushkas, both living only ten minutes' walk away in different directions, undertook to share babycare. She confided that she would like to start a second baby soon but for economic reasons it seemed sensible to wait until Katya was seven, then she could guide her through her first year at school while at home with the infant.

When Mila started work during the 1998–99 economic crisis, neither she nor her teacher mother was paid anything from September to March. 'It's lucky my father is a professional fisherman! We lived on fish and dacha produce, though our dacha is very small.'

Even as an assistant driver, Roman earned more than double Mila's salary. She said, 'A woman is very secure with a BAM driver husband. He is under daily observation for any sign of alcoholism. Every three years he has a detailed general health check and special sight and hearing tests for his reactions to crises simulated on computers. He drives for twelve hours maximum, then must take sixteen hours' rest in one of the hostels you see in most stations. After twelve years' service he can move to other jobs but have free train travel for life. Not many move. Most BAM workers, whatever their job – track crews, ticket sellers, freight superintendents, laundry workers, *provodniki*, drivers – belong to BAM builder families, committed to the line even if Moscow jeers at it!'

I like the Siberians' tendency to congregate in their kitchens, invariably small but very much the centre of the home. Mila apologized for the meagreness of my 'welcome back' lunch; she had been teaching until 2 p.m. So we were on Siberian short commons: omul smoked and salted, potato salad, beetroot, a mature hard cheese made near Irkutsk, excellent black bread and homemade butter and a bottle of Caucasian white wine. Katya lunched with us, devouring an astonishing number of green grapes after her long breastfeed.

Then to the living-room to view the recent christening; in August I had heard this event being planned by Mila and her friend Tanya, the godmother-to-be, also a teacher and another of my devoted carers.

'Christ parents,' explained Mila, 'are very important for us and always Tanya and Alexei will be Katya's soul-relatives with a duty to advise.'

Orthodox christenings are group ceremonies and the video showed forty candidates: four one-year-olds, a few children aged about ten, the rest adults including a fifty-two-year-old man. Mila left halfway through the three-hour ceremony, ostensibly to do something urgent about the imminent feast, in reality because she couldn't bear to watch 'my precious beloved' being thrust deep under the water three times in rapid succession. I don't blame her. Watching this immersion in an enormous square tank, I was appalled. As were the traumatized infants: this is surely enough to give them aquaphobia. When the priest handed Katya back to Tanya the new Christian's mouth was wide open and her eyes screwed up but shock had rendered her soundless. However, recovery was rapid; the last shot showed a beaming Katya toddling between the feasters' legs, dismembering a slice of christening cake as she went.

Another teacher friend, Vera, told me next day 'Getting baptized has become "fashionable" in some circles, it's not always a sign of personal religious fervour. Or it can be a way of showing how *Russian* you are, nationalism replacing the Soviet *Union* of many different faiths and races.'

Vera's grandmother had just died, aged eighty-five, in her home town near Moscow where her mother now was, organizing the funeral. Vera had longed to go too but they couldn't afford both fares.

We had already discussed mortality, during long Yacht Club sessions, and Vera had looked shocked on hearing that I don't believe in an afterlife. Her own belief system flummoxed me. When TV showed President Putin attending a Christmas service in St Basil's cathedral in

Moscow she switched off, enraged, seeing the Orthodox establishment and the new 'democratic' leader as hypocrites, reviving an old
collaboration to exploit ignorant people's superstitious fears. Yet, to
secular ears, many of her own convictions sounded like superstitions.
She had been more emphatic, less self-conscious than Yakutsk Feodor
about post-mortem communications, some occurring in dreams that
were more than dreams, others when the spirit returned to its home
– not as a scary ghost but in a companionable way, blessedly soothing
for the bereaved. So influential are the dead that when a bad person
dies his/her grave is a danger, therefore cemeteries should be far from
towns – despite their being, traditionally, places of pilgrimage where
family members (mostly women) go on 'ancestors' Saturdays' to pray
and converse with the dead. Vera's paternal babushka, still very much
alive and coincidentally occupying the flat next to mine, could
remember the 1930s when churches were being closed or destroyed
and believers instead brought their bread, eggs and flower offerings to
the cemetery. No wonder the Soviets' attempts to introduce crema-
tion failed – sometimes spectacularly, as in Kiev in the 1960s where a
crematorium costing three million roubles and seven years' work was
decisively boycotted and quickly fell into ruin.

Vera (sounding like someone trying to reassure herself) argued that
anyone happy to die without any prospect of an afterlife must have a
closed mind. I opened mine enough to concede that an explanation
is certainly needed for animals' reactions to phenomena unseen. A
century (or a decade) hence, scientists may have discovered that our
brains' electronic impulses, projected into the atmosphere, go on functioning long after our bodies have rotted. Anything seems possible,
nowadays.

Aged twenty-eight and unmarried, Vera was by Siberian standards
only inches from the shelf. Eighteen months previously Vasili had
abruptly deserted her, for no apparent reason. Then news came from
the university city where they had lived together for two years as post-
graduate students; Vasili had married a young woman who owned her
own flat, recently inherited from parents killed in a blizzard-induced
Aeroflot crash near Magadan. 'But I didn't give up hope,' said Vera.
'We were so happy, we'd plans to marry and have a baby when we got
jobs. How could she tie him down for ever with a free flat?' This hope

was boosted by 'my magic woman', an elderly widow, living in the fishing village of Baikalskoe, with whom Vera could discuss all her emotional problems and from whom she received 'spiritual advice and herbal medicines for the soul'.

Then, in the middle of September, hope was further boosted by rumours that Vasili's marriage was in danger because he very much wanted a child and *she* didn't. 'Everyone knows she's paranoid about pollution and monster babies,' said Vera, her tone not conveying sympathy. Now the magic woman was predicting that Vasili would divorce before Christmas and return to Vera if the situation could be adroitly managed: Vera was given a bottle of 'special' water from a secret source in the mountains, a little to be drunk daily for a month to hasten the reunion process.

Is it natural for people to regress to magic potions in response to major socio-political turmoils and tensions? But that doesn't explain the millions of Roman Catholic pilgrims from stable 'advanced' countries who throng to places like Lourdes, Fatima, Medjugorje, showing a similar faith in miracles and 'holy water'.

Even casual visitors to Siberia must notice the disparity between male and female lifespans; in my age group there are conspicuously more women than men. Mrs Sikorski, Tanya's mother (Olga to me: the range of Russian given names is oddly limited), was yet another whose husband had died suddenly in his early fifties, while Tanya was still at her teacher training institute in Nizhny Tagil. And now she had to worry about Tanya's health and about her own beloved brother who was dying.

Tanya admitted her mistake: she should never have nagged at her parents until they agreed to Nizhny Tagil instead of Irkutsk. This distant industrial city of 400,000 in the Urals, ninety miles north of Yekaterinburg, seemed glamorous to the nineteen-year-old Tanya because it was so far west. By the time its sinister dreadfulness had become apparent it was too late for her to turn around the bureaucratic tanker and she was condemned to four years in one of the former Soviet Union's ten most polluted cities, a place out-polluting even Bratsk. According to official figures it tops the chart for cancer, asthma and various lung and heart diseases. The Federal Government has designated it an 'environmental emergency zone', which entitles it to special financial assistance from Moscow. And for five years the US provided 'technical assistance' – environmental education training courses for the local population.

'But it's not the local population need education,' said Tanya acerbically. 'It's the people running the iron and steel plants, the chemicals and plastics plants, the coking plant and many small plants. The Federal Environment Ministry says every year two tons of toxic substances per head of population are pumped into the air – that's *800,000* tons!'

Tanya set out for Nizhny Tagil as a healthy, sturdy child of BAM; she finished her course prone to occasional asthmatic attacks, with permanently cracked finger and toe nails and a heart condition needing regular monitoring. Her doctor, quoting Nizhny Tagil's rate of foetal abnormalities, advised her not to risk having children for at least three years.

When first we met in August, Tanya had been reluctant to join me for a *pivo* at Irina's bar on Leningradski Prospekt. She suggested moving to another source of draught *pivo*, behind the outdoor market, where the tables were screened by wickerwork 'walls'. Awkwardly she explained that she likes a cigarette with her *pivo* and on Leningradski Prospekt someone might see her smoking and report back to her mother and then she'd be in very big trouble. (Severobaikalsk, despite its population, has certain village characteristics.) To me this indicated an over-authoritarian mother – I hadn't yet met Mrs Sikorski – but on hearing Tanya's medical history I could understand such protectiveness. (By the time my daughter was twenty-three I had abandoned the anti-nicotine struggle, in which I'd been handicapped from the start by my own addiction to mini-cigars. Eventually, in Rachel's case, motherhood conquered nicotine; in certain important respects the younger generation are more responsible than some of their parents were.)

Mrs Sikorski's biologist brother, Nikita, was sent to the Chernobyl area soon after the catastrophe – then aged thirty-three, with a baby daughter. He spent most of the next three years helping to measure the environmental damage, observing, amongst other things, grossly enlarged fungi, fruits and vegetables in all the surrounding forests and dachas. On his return to Moscow his wife became pregnant but a scan revealed what they feared. The next pregnancy, four years later, showed even more hideous deformities.

'Uncle is forty-nine now,' said Tanya, 'and not expected to be fifty. When he first went to Ukraine his wife couldn't be told where he was going or why – he wasn't told himself until he arrived. The rest of the world knew what had happened a month before we did – you look like you don't believe that but it's *true*! Even though the radio-active fallout was ninety times what came from Hiroshima. We'll never hear how many thousands of families' lives were ruined, I mean families from outside the area, when a member was sent in to be exposed for years. How many centuries will the Chernobyl curse last? People have moved back to live in the danger zone because the Moscow and Kiev governments broke their promises to give other accommodation. Farmers are selling contaminated meat very cheaply in Moscow markets with no government health checks and in other markets where they can bribe inspectors. Uncle says mushrooms and berries absorb contamination most and are still a big threat but the local people don't listen. Poor people can't afford to avoid free food. You'd expect leaders to learn from Chernobyl that you can't make secrets of catastrophes, but the *Kursk* submarine showed our new Russia isn't so new! Why didn't Putin beg for outside help in the first two days when experts say rescue was possible? One of my best Nizhny Tagil friends lost her fiancé, can you imagine what those families suffered? For us all it was like a nightmare. But maybe the new Russia is a little bit new, there was more angry talk in public about the *Kursk* than Chernobyl. Or is that because radioactivity is so hard to understand? Everyone can feel pain about young men trapped in a box at the bottom of the sea!'

Once a day someone had to visit the Gladkovas' so-called dacha in the Old Town, to feed and water Lev the guard dog and clear away his deposits. As Mila and I walked there on a brilliantly sunny Saturday afternoon, with Katya in her buggy, Mila explained, 'This dacha is where Roman and his sister grew up while their parents were BAM building. Now it's only a store for what's grown in the little garden.'

Inside the padlocked gate a huge handsome red-brown mongrel snarled frenziedly and Mila warned, 'Take care, Lev's good at his job!'

There wasn't enough space for me to give him a wide berth; I could just keep out of reach as he lunged at me frantically, standing on his hind legs at the end of a long chain. His small insulated kennel had brick stilts. 'It's small,' explained Mila, 'so his own body heat warms it in winter.' Although deprived of exercise and human company, Lev's relationship with Mila was loving. And he did have one companion, the Gladkovas' ancient black and white tom – the only scruffy-looking cat I saw in Siberia – who had found block life intolerable when the family moved and repeatedly returned to his birthplace.

The two-roomed dwelling, without hallway or kitchen, was no bigger than the plastic hothouse. 'My brother and I grew up at the end of this lane in the same sort of place,' said Mila. 'We had Third World childhoods, no electricity, sanitation or tap water. But we knew about nothing else and were happy. For our parents it was harder, they deserved all the privileges they got.'

On our way back I asked Mila, 'Why do you need a guard dog?'

She laughed 'I could see you were bothering about him! We need him because now this town has criminals as jobs get less and pay lower and more and more come from Central Asia and other Muslim places. You and Mrs Yahin were crazy to walk home that evening in the dark. We've had two schoolgirls raped and murdered this past three months. Ten days ago in my own block a forty-five-year-old handicapped woman disappeared from her flat – not any small trace of her since. She worked in the market, a taxi collected her every morning, the market managers paid for it. She was to go on holidays and was talking about having saved roubles. People believe she was murdered so the flat could be well searched by the taxi-drivers' friends, Muslims from Azerbaijan. She was a nice quiet person, I knew her a little. She seemed lonely, no relatives, and now no one is making a fuss with the police so they're not looking very hard to see what happened.'

Perhaps my usually reliable antennae were malfunctioning in Severobaikalsk where they never registered the level of risk credited by Mila.

We found an agitated group of neighbours gathered outside the entrance to the Gladkovas' stairway, gazing down at a litter victim, a large black-and-tan sheepdog who had jumped on to a broken bottle and, apparently, cut a tendon. He refused to walk, explained his blood-stained owner, a slim youth on the verge of tears. When he had been bandaged a taxi must take him to the vet. At once Mila offered the Gladkovas' car: Roman was at home, would be happy to oblige. The youth's mother (over the verge of tears) rushed upstairs for a bandage and ten minutes later the patient was en route to the vet who lived far away in Severobaikalsk's 'Hampstead'. (In Tynda, Pavel had remarked that glass-wounded dogs were the vets' main source of income.)

'Sometimes cars are useful,' conceded Mila, as we carried the buggy up the steps. She had tried to overcome Roman's car-lust ('our only quarrel!'), arguing that a car would be a pointless extravagance, given Severobaikalsk's motoring limitations. 'But mostly Russian men win' and now Roman's eleven-year-old vehicle gave him great joy, not least when it broke down, challenging his mechanical ingenuity. An old Russian car, he informed me, was much superior to those posh Japanese four-wheel-drives that present themselves as tough all-terrain champions but in fact can't cope with Siberian tracks as well as a humble Russian saloon.

Severobaikalsk's traffic is dangerous because so sparse. On wide straight boulevards the few vehicles drive at motorway speeds and as you amble across a street a car may suddenly loom into view only yards away. It's up to you to take action, the driver has no time. But at least you can be reasonably sure that he's sober; throughout the BAM Zone drunken driving is severely punished. Arguments, excuses – even bribes – are futile. Breathalyzing is rigorous and after the first offence (more than half a litre of *pivo*) licences are cancelled for a year, then cancelled for ever after the second offence.

Speeding by sober drivers is treated more leniently. 'My' block overlooked a long wide street only recently tarred but not provided with pavements. Post-tarring, several pedestrians had been killed or injured, prompting the erection of 40km speed limit signs – soon removed during the night – replaced – removed again. Then the municipality implicitly admitted defeat and set about laying pavements instead, a work in progress during my tenure.

'A carefully conducted inquiry found that 67 per cent of boys and 46 per cent of girls regularly drank alcohol.' This sounds like a quote from a contemporary survey of the recreational habits of Irish juveniles. In fact it comes from a 1901 survey of the recreational habits of rural schoolchildren, aged seven to thirteen, in Moscow province. That survey had been prompted by an increase in heavy drinking among women. One small boy, when asked 'Are you not ashamed to drink?', cheerfully replied, 'Why should I be ashamed? Aunty, mamma, uncle and little sister drink, why should I not drink?'

Alcoholism has afflicted Russians to an alarming extent since at least the Middle Ages when observers noticed that drunkenness was among the few vices thought to need a sermon to itself – most vices being dealt with in bulk. Famously eloquent preachers against excessive drinking included St Theodosius Pecherskii (died 1074) and the early twelfth-century Abbot Daniel of Chernigov. Presumably the nature of the alcohol, vodka, is at the root of the problem; in those days English peasants safely drank small beer with every meal including breakfast.

Ivan III's attempts to limit fifteenth-century vodka sales had no appreciable effect. Ivan the Terrible unsuccessfully tried to restrict drinking to his friends and followers and in 1552 set up the first taverns for this purpose. In the seventeenth century the remarkable Patriarch Nikon, who wielded a certain amount of secular as well as spiritual power, banned the sale of vodka on holy days and formed a council to regulate the tavern-licensing process. Towards the end of that century Peter the Great's imbibing became an international scandal; he required his court and distinguished foreign visitors to compete with him in marathon binges such as soccer fans enjoy. Even more shocking – *much* more shocking – his Drunken Synod of Fools and Jesters staged soft-porn 'entertainments' parodying Orthodox religious ceremonies.

The teetotal Catherine the Great squeezed as much state revenue as possible from her sodden subjects by auctioning tavern licences. The consequent proliferation of vodka outlets was soon raising 25 per cent of the total state revenue. When St Tikhon of Voronezh, outraged by this development, preached rousing anti-vodka sermons to attentive congregations (he was widely revered and loved), the vodka-sellers and their government supporters forced him to retire early from his bishopric.

In the 1860s Alexander II scrapped Catherine's tax-farming system on the grounds that licence-holders, impatient to recoup their high fees, had become too ingenious, not to say unscrupulous, in their marketing methods. But his alternative ploy, taxing both the distillers' output and the shops' sales, backfired badly. Unlicensed shops and taverns mushroomed, competition lowered prices and vodka consumption went off the scale. In 1886 a desperate State, striving to stop workplace drinking, made it a serious crime for employers to part-pay in vodka.

Alexander III (1845–94) came up with yet another ploy, the state control of vodka sales which in theory would provide responsible supervision of both quality and quantity. In 1894 the Minister of Finance instituted the State Vodka Monopoly, earnestly assuring everybody that it was not designed to increase government revenues. Nobody believed him. Five years later a survey revealed both increased vodka sales and a thriving new bootlegger subculture.

Since the early 1880s numerous temperance societies had been in action, with much support at all levels of society; peasant women, and Russia's many women doctors, were especially active. Alcoholism was now recognized as a disease rather than a vice, with no shame attached to seeking help. Some doctors considered heredity a key factor, therefore the children of alcoholics must be warned never to touch the stuff because they would be incapable of moderate drinking. The Society for Fighting Against Alcohol in the Public Schools was presided over by Professor A.A. Kornilov of Moscow University.

One drying-out clinic reported on a four-year survey: their average male patient had been spending 48 per cent of his wages on drinking 1.40 bottles of 80-proof vodka every twenty-four hours. 'Korsakov's disease' – alcoholic paralysis and alcoholic paraplegia – is so called because Dr S.S. Korsakov, having an abundance of cases within reach, identified it in the 1890s. An international medical congress in Moscow recognized his achievement which by 1914 had generated more than 400 works, in numerous languages, discussing his research.

Heated controversy surrounded hypnosis as an effective cure. Psychoanalysis was just coming into fashion and in 1911 Dr Pevnitskii, once a vociferous hypnosis proponent, read a paper before Moscow's Commission on the Question of Alcoholism fervently promoting the

Freudian way forward. But he conceded that however effective psychoanalysis might be, the convalescent alcoholic needed longterm support from a temperance society or brotherhood. At that time many leading Russian specialists advocated techniques later adopted by Alcoholics Anonymous.

A more traditionally Russian solution was favoured by a St Petersburg psychiatrist, V.E. Ol'derogge, who paid the governor-general of Finland 2,500 roubles for an uninhabited island in the Gulf of Finland on which he planted colonies of alcoholics who could not possibly escape to Vodkaland. In some medical circles, including the Society for the Preservation of Public Health, it was judged appropriate to confine a patient to a clinic for up to two years if he seemed 'a danger to himself, to those around him, and to society'.

Most of the temperance activists had a hidden agenda. Given the undeniable and undenied fact that Russia was suffering increasingly from alcoholim, *why* had so many succumbed to this disease? Answering that question (the answers were varied and contentious) gave closet reformers an opportunity indirectly to criticize the status quo and suggest social, economic, even political improvements, speaking not as disloyal subjects of the czar but as public-spirited citizens deeply troubled by a debilitating national handicap. Anti-alcohol days were organized and enthusiastically supported by large crowds, to the government's disquiet. Impassioned anti-Monopoly speeches could have powerful and complex political undertones. Police spies attended those rallies and in December 1909, at the First All-Russian Congress on the Struggle Against Drunkenness, twenty worker delegates were arrested.

A disproportionate number of activists belonged to the medical professions and in 1904 a group of brave physicians argued openly that until people had civil rights nothing of significance could be achieved by the temperance societies. They and many other angry doctors joined in the 1905 Revolution, after which the campaigners demanded, for citizens both male and female, the right to veto the opening of new vodka outlets in their home districts. In 1911, in St Petersburg, the Russian Medical Society of Doctors Promoting Temperance was founded.

A year later Ernest Gordon, an American writer on Europe's anti-alcohol movements, calculated that when the Monopoly brought in 750,000,000 roubles, 17,000,000 went to distillers as premiums and 2,000,000 funded the Guardianship of Public Sobriety. This bureaucracy-bound government body (the Czar's very own temperance society) preached 'moderation' while halfheartedly trying to lure people away from taverns by providing free public entertainments. Count Leo Tolstoy, who ran his own uncompromisingly teetotal temperance education movement, condemned the Guardianship's hypocrisy and was backed by a spokesman for the Kazan Temperance Society who complained that many Guardianship leaders themselves drank excessively and were either lazy or cynical about fostering 'moderation'. Shortly before his death in 1910 Tolstoy pointed out that the Monopoly had helped to fill the State's coffers astonishingly quickly after the disastrous Russo-Japanese War (1904–5) and that one-third of Russia's revenue was now vodka-derived.

By 1913 the authorities were fearfully aware of 'anti-alcoholism' as a major political issue. Mounting public fury, ostensibly focused on the State Vodka Monopoly-cum-Guardianship of Public Sobriety charade, finally got to Nicholas II – a good guy in his feeble way and a connoisseur of fine wines who would never have exposed his sensitive taste buds to the numbing ravages of vodka. He decided to see for himself what all the agitation was about and it seems his conscience then came out of hibernation. He wrote:

> The journey through several provinces of Great Russia, which I undertook with God's aid, afforded me an opportunity to study directly the vital needs of my people...With profoundest grief, I saw sorrowful pictures of the people's helplessness, of family poverty, of broken-up households and all those inevitable consequences of insobriety. We cannot make our fiscal prosperity dependent upon the destruction of the spiritual and economic powers of many of my subjects, and therefore it is necessary to direct our financial policy towards seeking government revenues from the unexhausted sources of the country's wealth and from the creative toil of the people.

Once the Czar had spoken, even those Duma members who happened to own distilleries were silenced. Reluctantly, on 14 February 1914, the State Council approved a bill to limit vodka consumption by allowing local authorities to ban sales, given a two-thirds majority vote of an area's residents. More than 800 petitions for closures had been granted by 1 July. Then urban and provincial authorities were given 'prohibition powers' and most major cities promptly voted to become 'dry'. A month later, on the outbreak of the First World War, Nicholas decreed that during mobilization only first-class clubs and restaurants could sell vodka, despite Tolstoy's much-quoted observation that nobles drank even harder than peasants. Soon after, the Czar banned all vodka sales for the duration of the war. This left the temperance campaigners gratified but not wholly satisfied, still demanding permanent and total prohibition. Then the Monopoly was abolished, there being nothing legal left to monopolize.

Prohibition, though welcomed by so many with relief and rejoicing, had predictable consequences: a higher death-rate from experiments with alcohol substitutes, the home distillation of millions of gallons of vodka and therefore a shortage of grain for bakeries – which contributed significantly to those bread riots credited with sparking off the 1917 February Revolution in St Petersburg.

By this stage one group of socialists, who for decades had been using the Monopoly as their most effective political weapon, were protesting that prohibition was a tyrannical law, interfering with the people's freedom. However, the teetotal Lenin banned the production of all alcohol, including wine, and in 1918 assembled a Commission to Combat Drunkenness and Pogroms, its first task to track down home-distillers. Many medical professionals had backed the Bolsheviks in the vain hope that socialism could conquer alcoholism but Communist Russia failed to find a replacement for all those vodka roubles. As Patricia Herlihy puts it: 'Lenin reluctantly ended prohibition and created a new state vodka monopoly that went into effect in 1925, the year after his death.' (Professor Herlihy's *The Alcoholic Empire* is a gem of a book, witty, harrowing and compassionate.)

As if to make up for lost time, Russian men, women and children at once plunged into an ocean of vodka and within two years the new monopoly was providing 19 per cent of the Soviet State's revenues. In 1929 15,000 Irkutsk schoolchildren turned out to demonstrate against this relapse, as did very many others all over the country. But in 1930 Stalin ordered an increase in vodka production; alcoholism was no longer to be acknowledged as a problem. In 1994 three Russian contributors to the *International Journal of the Addictions* reported that between 1940 and 1985 vodka consumption increased 7.4 times.

Mikhail Gorbachev became General Secretary of the Communist Party in March 1985 and his first policy move (900 years after St Theodosius's eloquent anti-alcohol sermons) was signing into law a resolution 'On measures to Overcome Drunkenness and Alcoholism'. This initiative horrified the Minister of Finance, the Minister of Trade and the State Planning Commission, all to a great extent dependent on vodka taxes. Soon the Gorbachev-inspired All-Union Voluntary Temperance Promotion Society had fourteen million members energetically preaching total abstinence – with their tails up. Gorbachev is as adamant a teetotaller as Tolstoy and Lenin. Vodka production was quickly halved, liquor licences issued to restaurants were more than halved, the legal drinking age went from eighteen to twenty-one and vodka stores remained closed until 2 p.m. But very soon sugar vanished from the shops and had to be rationed. Buckets also vanished: the home distillers were at it again. By 1988 *samogon* ('moonshine') production had become the Soviet Union's main growth industry and Gorbachev was forced to abandon his dream of leading the Russians into pastures dry. By 1991 blackmarket vodka cost five times the official price. Gorbachev then admitted, from his retirement dacha, that his anti-alcohol policies had cost the State 49 billion roubles, equivalent to the costs of the Armenian earthquake and Chernobyl.

After half a century of simply ignoring the problem, the pre-1917 acceptance of alcoholism as a disease has for some reason been replaced by a more condemnatory attitude, possibly partly owing to Gorbachev's campaign: he openly despised drunkenness as a moral defect. According to some concerned Russian observers, this change is deterring many alcoholics and their families from seeking medical advice, though between 1990 and 1995 the numbers receiving treatment increased fivefold.

Inevitably, the post-Soviet chaos has exacerbated the situation. When the state monopoly was again abolished in 1992, consumption increased as cheap, untaxed foreign vodka poured over the borders. A year later Boris Yeltsin set up yet another state monopoly, echoing the 1894 excuse: the government's public health worries. But this time monopolizing didn't work, collapsed in the general shambles.

International criminal gangs regularly smuggle into Russia from the US millions of gallons of 192-proof grain spirits. By 1997 raw ethanol was being despatched from Georgia, at the rate of 800 truckloads a month, to be transformed into *samogon* – a cruel liquid undeserving of the poetic sobriquet 'moonshine'. The Government vodka tax was raised by 40 per cent during the first five months of 2000; uncoincidentally, those months saw the registering of 15,823 deaths from alcohol poisoning, 45 per cent more than during the same period in 1999.

Sadly, it is not a sobering fact that today's Russian adolescents are less likely to celebrate their sixtieth birthdays than the 1900 generation. In 2000, it was officially estimated that Russia's alcoholics number eighty (80!) million. But in that survey, how was 'alcoholism' being measured? Would I have been included because I drink many more 'weekly units' than women are supposed to absorb? In any event, I should draw no conclusions from my own limited observations in an underpopulated territory. Severobaikalsk's strict enforcement of the drink-driving law may be a wholesome local idiosyncrasy. I can only say that in many places along my route I sensed either strong anti-alcohol undercurrents or a grim disapproval of vodka, as distinct from *pivo*.


Ossip dominated the Sikorski household, ruling as an absolute monarch whose humans must obey his every whim. The curtains on the living-room window had been chosen to match his enormous gorse-yellow eyes and his record-breaking silver and chestnut coat. Never before had I met a cat with a coat so long and a tail so bushy. When I took out my camera he jumped on to a small table by the window and (this was almost unnerving) *posed* for me, sitting upright against that matching background, beside a shapely Chinese vase, his unbelievable tail hanging down from the table's edge while he looked back at me, over his shoulder, with those unbelievable eyes. As I marvelled at this, cats being notoriously hard to photograph, Tanya smiled and said, 'He's used to cameras, everyone wants a picture of Ossip, they say he has to be seen to be believed.'

I had been invited to supper, a banquet prepared by both mother and daughter, who each specialized; Olga was famous for her creamed turkey and fried cabbage, Tanya for her salmon and mushroom casserole, and caramel and gooseberry ice-cake smothered in real cream. We were joined by Mila, and later by Tanya's boyfriend Yan, a Buriat and mildly epileptic, very shy and charming. Olga gave no hint that she disapproved of him, not because he was a Buriat but because of his epilepsy; in future Tanya would have enough health problems of her own to cope with and Yan's prospects, in the new hard-nosed Russia, were not good.

Irkutsk-born Olga had always worked in the BAM bureaucracy, as had her husband, and now she held a senior post but felt apprehensive about the future. Privatization was looming for all Russia's railways. At least 35 per cent of employees were to be sacked – probably more in the BAM Zone – and while the State planned to retain ownership of the tracks, competing private companies would take over various aspects of management. (I didn't like the whiff of that dog's dinner produced by the mincing of British Rail.) Ticket prices, which seemed so reasonable to me, had gone up by more than 50 per cent in the past year, causing much hardship, especially in Siberia. As the workforce and capital investment were reduced, the BAM in particular and rail services in general would have to lower their standards and again raise their prices. All this was typical, said Olga, of the Putin régime. Recently the Duma had approved the first moves necessary for the privatization of the telephone system, the State only to retain ownership of the cables. This 'reform' would certainly bring higher charges and possibly abolish the free calls now enjoyed within cities and towns. (And they are very much enjoyed; even in summer Siberian telephonic verbosity is noticeable and I'm told people chat to their neighbours for hours during winter.)

As for the regional electricity boards, also overshadowed by privatization – Olga gestured despairingly. Often scores of blocks were left without heat and light when power was cut off to force local authorities to pay their bills, a ploy unthinkable in Soviet times, at least within Olga's lifetime. 'It's the sort of thing you associate with Stalin,' she said, 'but now it's inspired by capitalism. The wheel of Fate turns in strange ways in our country. And nobody asks, "If the poor can't pay the authorities, how can the authorities pay the electricity boards?" We need a real political opposition in the Duma and there isn't one, only the fake opposition of the Communist Party and it isn't allowed the freedom to make honest criticisms. Democracy is no nearer than it ever was, in Russia.'

Polya dropped in at the coffee and homemade vodka stage – whiskey-coloured vodka, matured with cedar seeds. Polya was Mila's cousin, a vivacious young half-Buriat radiologist whose work left her little free time. For weeks she had been struggling to buy a flat from the municipality and we all listened sympathetically to the latest instalment. At a certain point she had to pay for four date-stamped forms, valid for only three days after purchase, to be filled in and witnessed and presented to four different offices. But the queues are so long that she could register only two forms within three days and had had to buy two more. Is this a sort of collective madness? Or a clinging to the old ways for fear of something worse, like more job losses? Were these bizarrely convoluted and irrational procedures designed in the first place to create jobs?

Yan, his shyness eased by two vodkas, was able to cap Polya's contribution. One of his university friends wanted to move from Irkutsk, his birthplace and family base, to Novosibirsk where, as an economics graduate, he had been offered a job – lowly but with prospects – by a US corporation. While a student he had resided legitimately at Novosibirsk though registered as a resident of Irkutsk. But now, as a twenty-five-year-old graduate, he could not register as a resident of Novosibirsk because he had no family living there.

In Olga's view, the retention of internal passports and residence permit regulations was not the result of inertia or ignorance about other systems. 'It shows Putin wants to keep democracy *out*! Under Yeltsin, even under Gorbachev, we relaxed and felt more free to criticize openly. Since 1 January 2000 that's been changing, at first slowly, now faster and faster. Putin cuts back on support for most state institutions but gives extra power and funding to law-enforcement agencies. The police beat up opposition political meetings. The Kremlin again controls most of the media, taken over from the big-business gangs who'd got control by the end of Yeltsin's time. Putin loves the Americans' "War Against Terrorism", all groups he doesn't like can be called "terrorists", given no media chance to make their arguments, imprisoned without trial for ever. When the US is doing that to groups they don't like, the West can't criticize Putin for doing the same!'

Everyone listened in silence, no one commented. Most of my friends among Siberia's younger generation seemed cynically indifferent to everything connected with politics, not unlike their contemporaries throughout the superficially 'democratic' West.

Severobaikalsk's Ecology Centre stands on the edge of the Old Town, an attractive wooden building, long and two-storeyed with lots of space at present being wasted for lack of money. Its staff of four highly trained young women (paid $50 monthly by the government) test soil and water in an inadequately equipped laboratory, the only one in the North Baikal area. Its Director denounced in anguished tones those who control special grants for the preservation of Lake Baikal. His complaints were standard: money squandered on conferences in luxury hotels, lavish monthly dinners, pretentious workshops, fat fees for fat consultants – those last made his eyes dilate with rage. Much talk and theory, long reports on expensive paper circulated worldwide – but little action and nothing left over (not one dollar!) for Severobaikalsk's Ecology Centre where valuable work could be done, given a fraction of those squandered funds. To us such institutionalized corruption, bred in the Rich World and reaching its apogee at UN conferences, is familiar. To the Director it seemed astonishing, bewildering, profoundly shocking – such behaviour by people posing as concerned ecologists, saviours of Baikal! He quoted a Siberian Duma representative who had recently accused Putin of deliberately neglecting Siberia as part of a campaign again to concentrate power in the Kremlin. 'Siberia is too big to be worth the effort, but it's taken Moscow four centuries to realize that. It's five million square miles, more thinly populated than almost anywhere else, not really suitable for settlement and development.'

The Director spoke no English (Tanya interpreted) but he gave me an introduction to Grigori from Nizhneangarsk, an agrobiologist and ecologist who did.

At six-foot-three, erect and broad-shouldered, Grigori looked especially conspicuous in Siberia. Aged fiftyish, he had lupin-blue eyes, short grey hair and the mahogany tan of someone who spends most of his day outdoors. Appearances aside, he was not an average BAM Zone citizen. For more than 180 years his family had lived in the Baikal region, since the exiling of his politically incorrect (in czarist eyes) ancestors, both paternal and maternal. In the new Russia he found himself maintaining that radical tradition; with a chuckle he described himself as 'almost still a Communist'. Fiercely committed to the Baikal Basin, he continued bitterly to resent BAM. When the destruction of the lake shore began he was aged twenty and I didn't need to be shown the 'before' photographs, taken by himself and his father, to empathize with his resentment. (For me, something comparable – not as drastic but more widespread – has happened with the degradation of so much of rural Ireland to accommodate holiday bungalows and motor vehicles.) He had always scorned the BAM dream (new industries supporting thriving communities) and too soon his scorn was justified. Mila had observed, 'Some of my parents' age group are bitter because BAM is called a "mistake", but all the same they're proud of what they did. BAM happened, they made it happen, it's still happening and they cling to that.' Grigori didn't have even an illusory sense of achievement to sustain him.

Lake Baikal, Grigori foretold, is doomed. Even if industrial pollution could somehow be curbed, the 'leisure industry' entrepreneurs, wearing their 'eco-tourism' fig-leaves, could not. Yet he saw a faint glimmer of hope for Siberia as a whole, emanating from the trend that makes most Siberians despair. 'In the eighteenth century the scientist Mikhail Lomonosov, the man who founded Moscow University, told Catherine the Great Siberia would make Russia rich. In the twenty-first century German Gref, the Kremlin's economic development minister, is telling Putin Siberia will make Russia poor. Earlier this year a new government strategy for our development was announced, planned by Leonid Drachevsky, Siberia's Putin-appointed boss. He reminded us Russian history has been dominated by Siberia. Generations of Russians felt fascinated and awed and ambitious when they thought about it. Giant efforts went into trying to populate it by force or subsidies. But now Drachevsky has admitted this new plan will probably be "successfully forgotten" – his phrase. I hope he's right, I think he is – Siberia's decolonizing itself. The Chukotka region population has gone down 65 per cent, Magadan more than 50 per cent – millions are moving west and there's room for them there. Our main expert on population says Russians of working age will decrease annually by a million from 2005.'

Grigori belonged to the minuscule Labour Party of Russia whose solitary Duma deputy organized a campaign that compelled the government to modify some of its more vicious proposals for municipal 'reforms'. The party's campaign against the new labour laws had been less successful. The IMF, as destructive in Russia as elsewhere, was directly responsible for those laws which severely reduced the rights of trade unions and women, lengthened the working week and increased employers' powers in a variety of regressive ways. Simultaneously, their profit tax rate dropped from 35 per cent to 24 per cent. And in 2000 their social contributions had been reduced from 38.5 to 35 per cent. 'Meanwhile,' concluded Grigori, 'official figures give 27 per cent of Russians living below the poverty line, something not to be imagined in Soviet times. I was teasing you when I said I'm still a Communist, but I'll always be a socialist.'

Few could boast of Grigori's 180-year-deep roots in Siberia but most of my friends liked to talk about their mixum-gatherum ancestries. Vera, for instance, knew that one of her maternal great-great-grandfathers was a prosperous *kulak* from the Moscow region exiled to Siberia with his Caucasian noblewoman wife. Vera's father was the descendant of courageous serfs who fled east to escape serfdom. By the time her parents married class-consciousness had been so obliterated (Vera claimed) that their forebears' contrasting nineteenth-century backgrounds were of no consequence. Yet in twenty-first-century Russia Vera seemed quite proud of that noblewoman's input, while emphasizing the healthiness of its being 'irrelevant'.

Vera's paternal grandfather puzzled me. A devout Orthodox Christian, with many icons in his living-room, he spoke no English but invited Vera and me to visit him one evening because he wanted to explain to the foreigner how things *really* were, in the Soviet Union, for Orthodox believers of his generation. Vera confided, 'He's a bit strange about this, it's not that he's so old and getting muddled, it's that he hates Cold War propaganda about religion.' A heavy evening followed, as much for Vera, who takes her interpreting duties seriously, as for me.

Mr Narizhny, a sprightly octogenarian, had a thick mane of snowy hair hanging to one side of his small, narrow head, creating an almost busby-like effect. Recently widowed, he now lived alone and his flat, unlike the average Siberian home, was slightly grubby and more than slightly untidy. When Vera had made tea my 'corrective' session began. Proof existed that the Soviet Union had never been an atheist state. The Party from the beginning protected freedom of conscience, its 1919 Eighth Congress affirmed the religious freedom of all citizens, the 1977 Constitution reaffirmed that – and so on. During the Civil War most clergy supported the White Army. Afterwards, the Russian Orthodox Church Outside of Russia, based in the US, consisted only of émigré right-wing Russians and collaborated with Western propagandists. (Vera, sensing my impatience as she translated, looked apologetic.)

Then Mr Nariznhy challenged me, leaning forward over the kitchen table, looking me straight in the eye from behind his thick spectacles. Did I believe all the propaganda about the Party's repression of Christians? I admitted that I did, had never seen any reason to doubt it given the documentary and visual evidence.

Mr Nariznhy nodded and sat back and continued at length with a few confusing digressions about the advanced state of civilization among the Rus *before* the coming of Christianity from Byzantium in 988 – and the divisive role played by the Uniate Church in the Ukraine – and the short-lived Renovator movement inspired by the Revolution amongst those clergy who had not fled abroad. He admitted that Russians saw the Church as part of the czarist regime and raged against it for years. During that period the 'freedom of religion' guarantee was ignored by Party leaders, national and local; they either passively condoned or actively encouraged the killing and imprisoning of priests, monks and nuns, the looting of monastery treasuries and the destruction of churches or their use for sacrilegious purposes. All that was part of the Revolution, regrettable but understandable. And why not insist on the separation of Church and State, and Church and schools, and forbid the teaching of religion in schools? That didn't happen only in Russia, A big shift came in 1941 when Orthodoxy's moral and practical support for Mother Russia's war against Nazism proved that in times of crisis the Party needed the Church as much as the czars ever did. The next shift came after Stalin's death when the Party adopted a Special Resolution admitting the mistakes made in conducting 'scientific atheistic propaganda' among the population. Over the next generation a minor religious revival took place and Mr Nariznhy's clerical friends, who co-operated with the State's new Council for Religious Affairs, were accused by the émigré Church of having become Party puppets.

Here Mr Nariznhy paused, laughed and wondered why the émigrés weren't pleased that Church and State had found a way to live together. Christianity, after all, was supposed to promote forgiveness and reconciliation. The Orthodox Church *in* Russia had, he asserted, learned from the Party about how to put some of Christ's teachings into practice. That was why it protested publicly against the Vatican's condemnation of Liberation Theology in the 1980s, those Roman Catholic thinkers having arrived at many of the same conclusions as their Orthodox clerical contemporaries.

Suddenly Mr Nariznhy looked very tired. When I thanked him for informing me and he had thanked me for listening, Vera said, 'All those years of anti-Communist propaganda worry him. He says it means our experiment will never be understood by the rest of the world. It was complicated but outsiders only want to think it was all bad – it failed, and that's good, and now it can be forgotten about. I tell him all sorts of scholars will be studying it in the future but he doesn't believe me.'

When Vera had made a pot of soup for her grandfather we walked back to my flat and she said, 'Many of our local Party leaders were only pretend atheists. Some were very frightened to see churches looted and abused and icons treated disrespectfully – used like bits of scrap wood for making a box or patching a barn door. Some gave orders to loot and destroy only because they were even more frightened of the real atheists at the top, the ones who got rich from all the stolen gold and jewels. My great-grandfather gave such orders in Irkutsk but he whispered to his family it would bring bad luck to Russia. He was right – see Russia now!'

I said, 'I hope at his age I'll be as mentally vigorous as your grandfather.'

Vera chuckled. 'You won't be, with all that *pivo* rotting your brain cells. He's always hated alcohol.'

When Tanya and I walked to the shashlik bar, overlooking the Yacht Club, Lake Baikal's blueness was at its most improbable, both dark and brilliant under a cloudless sky. I exclaimed, 'This is a new colour!' and Tanya said lovingly, 'Baikal has many moods, quickly changing, always changing, like there's some artist undecided which way he wants his painting but every way it's beautiful.'

We sat outside, on the long verandah, keeping our *shapkas'* ear-flaps down. The bar's Alsatian bitch (a family member, not a guard) lay near us in the sun suckling five fat fluffy pups. When we parted in August Tanya had been on the eve of her teaching career and now she told me how much she enjoyed the ten-to-fourteen-year-old classes. But she was having quite a hard time with some of the restless seniors who saw her as virtually their contemporary and sensed her novice's nervousness. There were other tensions, too; one class of eighteen comprised eight nationalities: Armenian, Azeri, Belorus, Buriat, Georgian, Tatar, Ukrainian, Russian. Given Severobaikalsk's stressful economic circumstances, their all being the Grandchildren of BAM did not automatically forge bonds strong enough to counter racism.

The BAM towns have a much higher birthrate than the Russian average of one or two: families of five or six are common. 'The poorest have most,' complained Tanya, 'and usually they're Muslim. Why have so many when you can't afford to feed and clothe them? Some come to school too hungry to concentrate – what's their future? We're all afraid that soon Muslims will be in a majority in BAM towns.'

Certain Siberian conversations made me feel I hadn't left home; here were loud echoes from arguments about the Mirpuri, Jamaican and other communities urged to settle in Britain after the Second World War to help reconstruct 'the Motherland'. Tanya did not appreciate my pointing out that Muslims who were forced or encouraged to become BAM builders a generation ago can't now be rejected because their culture promotes a higher birthrate than the Russians'. Indignantly she quoted the case of Mila's uncle who lives in Kazakhstan (now a Pentagon satellite state) where his ten- and twelve-year-old sons are compelled to learn the local language and must often deal with unnerving passport-related problems.

I already knew about the serious intimidation of Russian residents throughout the new Central Asian republics, families who can't afford (or don't wish) to leave regions where they may have been rooted for generations. Yet in Siberia, as Tanya now forcefully reminded me, peoples from all those republics are still accepted as citizens and never officially discriminated against, whatever personal prejudices may be shown. 'If in Central Asia they can shout "Tajikistan for the Tajiks!" and "Uzbekistan for the Uzbeks!" and so on why can't we shout "Siberia for the Russians!" and send them back to their independent republics?' I was tempted to remind Tanya that Siberia is a Russian colony; but in the BAM towns, founded several years after my daughter was born, such historical retrospection seems irrelevant.

As we chewed our way through below-standard shashlik Tanya diagnosed 'A very old pig' and went on to speculate about the Islamic taboo on pork. At the Nizhny Tagil institute she had chosen to do a 'World Religions' course and been told by her lecturer (one she respected: she didn't respect them all) that Islam had some good laws, like avoiding alcohol and usury, and some bad laws allowing multiple wives and downgrading women. She looked not merely sceptical but disbelieving when I remarked that not so long ago, in some cultures and in some respects, Muslim women enjoyed more legal rights than European Christian women.

I had been uneasily watching the pups frolicking in the middle of the road and as we were leaving the almost inevitable happened – because a driver, who could see them clearly, wouldn't slow down. The four siblings were much puzzled by the still corpse, apparently uninjured but for a little blood oozing from nose and mouth. The distraught bitch repeatedly pawed at the victim, turning him over and over, sniffing and licking and whining. Tanya was looking quite queasy (perhaps I was, too) and she hurried back to the bar to advise the family to confine the survivors.

Our Islamic exchange had a sequel on the following evening when Tanya (equipped with a seemly scarf to replace my male *shapka*) invited me to view Severobaikalsk's surrogate Orthodox church. This

long, low, wooden building in the Old Town, previously a municipal office, would have to serve until enough money had been collected to complete the real church; soon after its foundations had
been enthusiastically laid, the money ran out. Numerous blue collection boxes, discreetly marked with a little cross, stood at strategic
points in the railway station, post office, bank, market, palace of
culture: but contributions were few and small. Some 60 per cent of
the town's population are 'believers', Tanya reckoned, though not
regular church goers. Unfortunately their faith doesn't enhance their
earning capacity.

When Tanya reminded me that in Orthodox churches women are
not allowed to go beyond a certain point I asked, feigning gormless-
ness, 'Why not?'

Promptly Tanya replied, 'Because we know a woman was the first
sinner, Eve made Adam sin.'

'Hmm!' said I. 'So what do you suppose it does for Orthodox or
Roman Catholic women to be taught they're inferior to men, can't
become priests or enter the holy of holies?'

Tanya laughed. 'I suppose you think we're no better than Muslims!'

My teacher friend Vera had, she told me, been named after the
heroine of Tchernychevski's novel *What Are We To Do?*, written in
the prison fortress of Peter and Paul before he was condemned, in
1864, to fourteen years' hard labour in a Siberian mine. His Vera was
the New Woman, a suitable partner for the New Man then evolving
within the Nihilistic wing of the intelligentsia. She was resolved to
study science, earn her own living when married, wear short hair and
spectacles and cultivate the deportment of a (New) young man. Victor
Tissot, a French journalist and travel writer who toured Russia in the
1870s, detested the New Woman but conceded:

> Women have given to Nihilism and the revolutionary associations a
> very strong contingent. When courage, passion and self-abnegation
> have been requisite, they have often surpassed their brethren! It was
> looked on as a disgrace to take any pleasure in art or needlework,
> because in the old schools the study of French and music, and lessons
> in dancing and embroidery, had taken the place of more serious
> occupations.

These old schools – Institutes for Young Ladies of Gentle Birth, Russia's first girls' schools – had been founded at the end of the eighteenth century by Catherine the Great. Madame N. Jarintzoff, writing just before the First World War, recounted some of her grandmother's memories:

> The teaching of the visiting masters was not bad, but deportment and fanatical loyalty [to the czar] were the prevailing notes...Every girl worshipped one of her chums and many of the silly little creatures pined miserably away if their admiration was not accepted. It was a usual thing to eat chalk and drink ink for the purpose of attaining "pale and fragile beauty". A great deal of young strength perished within those thick walls.

Knuckles were rapped hard for breaches of etiquette and pupils who failed to share their hampers with the staff were made to stand in a corner of the dormitory all night. The daily diet was only slightly more appetizing than chalk and ink and occasional rebellions proved that not all the pupils were thoroughly cowed. At the Institute of St Catherine, one summer Sunday, a mass protest was efficiently organized. Reacting to inedible soup, 400 young ladies, at a signal from their leader, simultaneously flung their soup plates into the sunny garden through open dining-hall windows. The staid, elderly headmistress, sitting on her raised dais the better to supervise table-manners, was so discombobulated that the mutiny went unpunished – and the cooking improved.

Ten-year-old girls were despatched to St Petersburg from distant estates and spent all of the next seven years 'within those thick walls' – unless their parents were very rich or exceptionally loving, in which case horse-sledges might be sent, two or three times during those years, to fetch daughters home for Christmas. Such journeys often lasted a week or more and required three huge sledges: one for the young lady and her chaperone, one for the numerous servants, one a well-stocked kitchen.

In general, the nobility were not prone to pampering their young. Small boys going home on holidays from the Military Cadet Corps college often had to arrange their own transport, wandering through the market area, looking for some kindly peasant who would give them a lift in his goods wagon for hundreds of miles. Boys were brought to this college at the age of six by their military (usually) fathers and handed over to nanny-figures in whose arms they could cry themselves to sleep. Floggings were administered on Saturdays – but only for indiscipline, not for academic inadequacies. No great demands were made on these lads' intellects, a fact that too often became apparent when they took to the battlefield. But physical endurance tests were routine and sometimes unpleasant in strange ways. The evening before a General's inspection, cadets from the age of ten upwards had to go to bed in tight wet white breeches, to ensure that on the morrow these would be even tighter and crease-free.

The militaristic Nicholas I (1796–1855), who never quite recovered from the Decembrist Uprising that marred his coronation, longed to replace all Russia's seven universities (breeding grounds for every sort of czar-threatening notion) with more Cadet Corps colleges where young gentlemen could learn how to kill rather than how to think. When advised by his Minister of Education, Count S.S. Uvarov, that such closures might boomerang he compromised by greatly reducing student numbers, completely excluding the lower orders and banning discussion groups. However, these restrictions were less hampering than they might seem. Russia's universities were quite new, by Arab or Western European standards, and very disorganized and largely dependent on German and French professors and lecturers – more French than German after Bismarck's alarming achievement.

The Crimean War gave St Petersburg a very nasty shock and then came the reforms (but nothing *too* drastic!) of Alexander II (1818–81). In 1858 a decree ordered the founding of gymnasiums (approximately equivalent to grammar schools) for the academic education of girls. A year later one determined young woman (the niece of a professor) marched alone into a lecture hall of the University of St Petersburg asserting her right to a university education. As nobody argued with her she came regularly to lectures and worked hard for a degree. Remarkably, the numbers of men and women students were almost equal by 1861, when rebellions broke out in both Moscow and St Petersburg universities causing lectures to be suspended for months. In 1863 the Council of St Petersburg University conferred about these unsettling developments and wondered, 'What rights should women students be allowed?' After less acrimony than one might expect, it was agreed that they should be allowed honours degrees but no professorships until women's colleges had been established. At this many took umbrage and migrated to Switzerland, joining the Nihilist colonies then enjoying political asylum status. In 1868 a Russian girl won the highest degree at Zurich's Medical School where scores of Russian girls were studying by 1873. Many more scores, who could not afford to live abroad, thronged into St Petersburg's medical faculty to qualify as midwives while awaiting permission to practise as doctors. This soon came; the Ministry of the Interior authorized a Medical Institute for Women from which hundreds of doctors graduated within the following decades. Europe's first technical school for women was founded in Russia. In the 1890s the world's first woman civil engineer, a Russian, graduated – and, at Kiev University, two women were appointed to the Professorships of History and Mathematics. Tchernychevski's generation of Veras – with their bobbed hair and mannish demeanour – had not been play-acting, had meant business.

Madame Jarintzoff's long-forgotten but vividly informative *Russia: The Country of Extremes* deserves reprinting. Writing in 1914, she thus concludes her chapter on 'The Educational Revolution':

> The most marked feature of the last decade has been the influx of the lower classes into educational centres of all kinds; so great has this been that an alteration has been effected in the character of the Intelligentzia, particularly in Moscow ... The original body of highly strung intellectual refinement and self-sacrifice has come to recognize a new strain in its organism, a constituent more sturdy, more 'sporting', and somewhat less idealistic ... There may be many forces latent in the Country of Extremes.

By the late nineteenth century the disadvantages of a largely illiterate population, in a state keen to modernize its trade and industries, had been perceived to outweigh the advantages of keeping the lower classes in political quarantine, isolated from infectious subversive printed matter. The rural literacy rate rose from less than 10 per cent in the early 1880s to about 25 per cent in 1913. Meanwhile the urban authorities were adopting literature as a good cause. Between 1880 and 1895 St Petersburg's Literacy Committee published some two million copies of 'the Great Russians' and other cities had similar committees. *Niva*, a weekly mass-market illustrated magazine, brought out cheap editions of Dostoyevsky, Chekhov and Gorky. Schoolteachers, though as ill-paid then as now, quite often bought these editions for their poorer pupils' benefit.

By February 1917, despite acute wartime economic difficulties, newspapers, pamphlets and leaflets were cascading from the presses all over a dying empire. There were soldiers' papers, peasants' papers, national papers. The four Bolshevik dailies each had print runs close to 100,000. The Mensheviks' one daily wavered between 25,000 and 96,000. The pamphlets' print runs were in tens of millions. Nobody has ever counted the leaflets.

Romances, thrillers, adventure stories had become popular even before 1917 and when the 'latent forces' took over, and put universal literacy near the top of their agenda, they found themselves with an expanding mass of insatiable readers whose printed diet had to be rigorously controlled. The Union of Soviet Writers held its first Congress in 1934. (Maxim Gorky, cajoled back by Stalin from his years of self-imposed exile in Italy, had helped to found it.) 'Socialist realism' was born then, presented as the guiding principle 'to unite all writers supporting the platform of Soviet power and aspiring to participate in the building of socialism'. Interestingly, it did not demand total subservience to Russia's 'cultural revolution' but was defined as the apogee of Europe's finest literary traditions, foreign as well as Russian. Dickens, Tolstoy, Zola, Balzac and Stendhal could lawfully be mentioned in the same breath as Chernyshevski, Gorky himself and such post-Revolutionary novelists as Fadeyev, Furmanov and Gladkov. When the Union handed out official posts, stodgy proletarian writers devoid of talent, who during the 1920s had manufactured dreary works based on 'the dialectical materialist creative method', were almost ignored. It seems the Party, while relentlessly censoring Union members' output, did dimly understand that without some scope for genuine creativity writers (and scientists) would simply cease to function.

Conforming writers (the majority) enjoyed 'perks' such as their non-Union colleagues could only dream of: villas in tranquil rural surroundings likely to encourage one's muse, urban mansion flats, holiday homes on the Black Sea coast, sanatoria at bracing altitudes, well-equipped hospitals. Publishers' advances and 'material-gathering' trips were arranged by the Union, secretaries were laid on to type the final version. In 1936 fourteen writers were earning more than 1,000 roubles monthly in royalties, about forty-five times the average wage. Even in the 1960s and 1970s, when pay scales had in general become much more equal, successful writers were unmistakably rich. Yet state subsidies kept book prices low, hence the packed shelves in every home I visited.

According to Sofya, my poet friend in Tynda, most senior editors at the state publishing houses were men of limited education and distinctly plebeian tastes, often themselves failed writers. These had a markedly dumbing-down effect on the Soviet empire's visible literary output, but despite their influence a fairly wide middle-brow stream also flowed. And then came a conspicuous gap. The 'Greats' – writers of flawless professional integrity, like Mandelstam, Babel, Pilnyak, Akhmatova, Pasternak – were silenced. Some had attempted to conform but found their muse paralysed by the Union of Soviet Writers ambience. Some emigrated, some translated and/or wrote children's books in which they occasionally inserted messages too subtle for editorial eyes to see. Some wrote on, defiantly, and died in labour camps.

Most of my friends being teachers, I had within a week involuntarily acquired the status of Severobaikalsk's 'Writer in Residence'. To both pupils and staff, all foreigners were intriguing, as were all writers, and a *foreign writer* was a most wondrous thing. Timetables were disrupted for my (and I hope the pupils') benefit and the more I saw of this town's schools in action the more impressed I was.

The buildings varied from long, solid, two-storeyed wooden structures in the Old Town (800 pupils, sixty-five teachers), skilfully built in 1975, to drab concrete edifices in the New Town not so skilfully built ten years later. However, all the interiors were equally well maintained and overheated and furnished with healthy potted plants – shelves of them – and in some corridors and hallways stood groves of palm trees. The Old Town pupils envied the New Town's modern schools with their gyms on the premises, not in a nearby Nissen hut, and couldn't understand my preference for the handsome wooden buildings. This thought pattern (or emotion pattern) was familiar, a mirror image of the rural Irish determination to build brash bungalows instead of traditional farmhouses.

My overall impression was of children and adolescents relatively unharmed by the consumer society's aggressive exploitation of youth but several older teachers sought to correct that impression, railing against the West's pernicious influences. Although consumerism can't take much of a hold on a town as poor as Severobaikalsk, to the extent that it can it sometimes does, as when hard-earned money provided by parents for schoolbooks is diverted to pirated pop group tapes. But the West could scarcely be blamed (or could it?) for the weakening of community bonds. Previously parents and neighbours co-operated in their surveillance of a district's youth but not any more ... Teenage pregnancies are increasing as virginity is lost (or sold) ASAP. In one school a fourteen-year-old had recently had a baby whose sale for 15,000 roubles to a rich childless couple was arranged by the hospital. This not uncommon deal, generally regarded as the best outcome for the baby, is a questionable deterrent; 15,000 roubles seems a huge sum to many families. Fast-spreading STDs, for which free treatment is no longer available, are not taken very seriously by the younger generation. When I tentatively mentioned 'AIDS?' there was denial. Yet given the numbers of students who go to Irkutsk (and other) heroin-haunted universities, can Severobaikalsk be AIDS-free?

After sessions in the classrooms came sessions in the staff common rooms where I inwardly saluted what can only be described in a stodgy phrase – those teachers' devotion to duty, despite low pay and long hours. The two shifts made necessary by space and staff shortages require most teachers to work long hours five days a week, starting at 8 a.m. Most walk to work, which can mean leaving home an hour or so earlier and not getting back to the family before 7 p.m. In Severobaikalsk a high percentage of children come from what we would coyly categorize as 'disadvantaged' backgrounds, yet there was a sense of collaboration in the education process; it wasn't something being imposed by an alien authority. If a pupil with a problem knocked at the staffroom door during the lunch hour, s/he would be admitted and the problem given due consideration. Most surprising of all, to me, was the custom of teachers visiting all their pupils' homes once a year, to enable them to adjust their teaching to each child's family circumstances.

In one of the Old Town schools, at the end of a classroom session, an ebullient sixteen-year-old girl asked, 'Babushka, may I kiss you?' When I replied, 'Of course, and hug me if you wish,' all ten girls rushed to kiss and hug the first Westerner any of them had ever met – another counter to the myth that Siberians are xenophobic.

Because of those school visits, word spread that I was a writer from Ireland and on my walks through the various districts parents occasionally invited me in to their flats or dachas, fed me omul or bliny (or both) and asked many questions. Ireland's length being less than Lake Baikal's made them doubt our status as an independent nation. Several asked, 'What academic qualifications does an author need?' and were bewildered to hear that I left school at fourteen. But one shrewd mother, a school cleaning-woman whose fifteen-year-old daughter was interpreting, observed, 'Maybe universities don't teach how to write books and people wanting to write them can.'

Day by day it was getting colder and on 13 October I needed long johns and an extra-heavy sweater for my sunset walk to Severobaikalsk's 'Hampstead'. This small privileged suburb stands on high ground above a long lagoon separated from Lake Baikal by marshland and a hamlet of fishermen's dachas. Here the narrow tarred roads are pothole-free and have street lamps, the one- or two-storey homes are newish and spacious with fine fretwork around windows and doors, the small gardens are devoted to flowers rather than vegetables, the large well-polished cars are unblemished, the gates sport post boxes which receive deliveries whenever a plane brings mail to Nizhneangarsk. (Between Siberian towns surface mail can take four to eight weeks, therefore the art of letter-writing was never much cultivated. Now e-mail is popular when and where telephones work but my message to Rashit from Yakutsk, by courtesy Feodor, never arrived.)

All day the temperature had stayed some way below zero and the lagoon was beginning to ice over. (Lake Baikal doesn't freeze until early December.) As I gazed down at the sunset shadows of the dachas on the intricate ice patterns, a huge hound came bounding towards me, barking aggressively. He looked half-Rottweiler and half-Doberman, an unattractive cross though doubtless useful. Standing on the edge of a steep cliff, I had no alternative but to address him in amiable tones. He stopped barking and seemed perplexed – at which point his owner appeared, sternly summoning him. I recognized the young man; he had been behind me in the bread queue at the market and was visually memorable: tall, thin and pale, with red-gold hair *en brosse* and a hooked nose, wearing a tweed jacket and gabardine trousers that assuredly had not been bought from a Chinese trader in Severobaikalsk. And he recognized me – equally visually memorable, in my way.

Yuri spoke fluent English and invited me in for a whiskey or gin and tonic. He was recuperating after glandular fever in the family's nearby holiday home. The family lived in Irkutsk where his father was now a businessman and his mother ran a private maternity clinic. Their holiday home was furnished and decorated with a disconcerting mix of kitsch and elegance, the former inevitably cancelling out the latter. There was a resident maidservant, an elderly Buriat woman whose subservience to Yuri held undertones of resentment. When I expressed a preference for *pivo* she was despatched to a lean-to store in the next road.

Seemingly Yuri's father had held high office in the Party; a large yawn-making album commemorated the family's round-the-world tour in 1982 when Yuri was aged eight. Parents and children (his sister had since been killed in an Aeroflot crash) stood or sat beside the Taj Mahal, Sphinx, Statue of Liberty, St Mark's Square, Big Ben, etc, etc. Already, then, his father was 'getting into business for his hobby'. Yuri felt sanguine about the new Russia; there had been disasters and crises and there would probably be more of the same but with the right connections people could always get by ... In 1994 his family had moved from Vladivostok, where he was born, because 'elements from Japan, South Korea and China were moving in, making business a bit messy and dangerous'. His mother was Irkutsk-born so they had strong connections there; her father, too, had been a Party person of consequence.

Pouring himself a third whiskey, and me a third *pivo*, Yuri embarked on a sad story – 'If we were younger we would be same as Romeo and Juliet!' His Juliet was very beautiful – photographs were drawn from the inner pocket of his tweed jacket. And they loved each other very much, had been in love for five years, should by now be married with two children. But she had links with a foreign environmental protection agency and disapproved of his working in the family business (by implication, environmentally unsound). His parents distrusted her, said she only wanted to marry him to spy on the business, getting information to pass on to her foreign friends who would, allegedly, pay her well for it. Yuri also loved his parents and if he married her they would feel betrayed and reject him. There had been big family rows and now her parents were urging her to find a less contentious mate; she had many admirers and was aged twenty-six and they were impatient for grandchildren and she loved them and it was all getting too stressful … Being anti-abortion was part of her environmental mindset so her parents might one day have an unwelcome grandchild. Here Yuri paused and sniggered before explaining that Indian condoms (imported by Siberia in bulk) are much too small for Russian men, the relevant Indian dimensions being far inferior. Although I have no built-in objection to discussing penile dimensions in a clinical way with acquaintances, this comment made me feel uncomfortable – even slightly affronted. It was a self-conscious display of 'sophistication', meant to convey that Yuri was no longer bound by those conventions which would have made it unthinkable for him to share such a 'joke' with a Russian babushka. (The joke's racist tinge is another issue.) Yuri continued, 'They burst though they cost so much, then people won't waste money on them and this makes even more abortions. My mother's clinic has to get rid of so many babies my father says it should be called an "anti-maternity" clinic!'

When I declined his half-hearted offer to escort me home Yuri looked relieved. A very cold wind had been blowing since sunset and as I crossed the pedestrian bridge over the BAM line the stars were being quenched by snow clouds.

Severobaikalsk has two libraries, municipal and BAM, the latter providing an exceptionally well stocked and pleasantly furnished children's section, much used throughout the year. 'Here are hatched many bookworms,' said Mila proudly.

The municipal library shares the Palace of Culture with music, art and dancing schools, and with the Winter Garden, an unusual amenity cared for by my friend Marina who doted on every leaf and tendril. Palm and fig trees, infertile banana plants, jungle vines and flowering cacti happily coexist in a domed, galleried space needing some repairs; the moist warm atmosphere essential for their wellbeing doesn't suit Siberian construction methods.

On my first visit to the Palace I paused, unseen, to admire a class of eight- to ten-year-olds practising a complicated folk dance. Then their teacher noticed me and a special performance was put on for my benefit – the boys leaping and stamping in their knee-high black boots, the girls wearing spangled satin slippers, all their movements dainty and precise. 'Gender stereotype!' muttered Vera, my guide.

The Palace's many long corridors double as an art gallery, exhibiting the best of the work produced locally over quarter of a century – some of it outstanding, none mawkish like the mass-produced paintings sold in the markets. Vera grumbled because art students must now pay a small monthly fee so I gave private enterprise a push by suggesting the sale of paintings in, for instance, the post office, an outlet used by the more talented of my home town's artists. But this struck Vera, and my other friends, as a very odd idea. To them painting is something you do for fun, allowing the whole community to enjoy your work for free. As we sauntered along the corridors we could hear junior musicians diligently practising on pianos, violins, a clarinet, a cello. 'They will give us concerts in the winter,' said Vera.

The eve of my departure coincided with Katya's first birthday party at which I was the only non-family guest. On discovering that Katya's great-grandmother was six years my junior I felt like someone's great-great-grandmother. All guests arrived food-laden and the menu was long: omul in five forms, red caviar pie with flaky pastry, pungently herby meatballs roasted in butter, two whole roast chickens, pork casseroled with lemon and mushroom, creamed potatoes, roast potatoes, grated fresh raw cabbage, pickled cucumbers and tomatoes, salami in three varieties, chilli purée, cheese and bread. And there were homemade forest berry juices, Moldovan red wine, *pivo* in three-litre bottles, home-distilled vodka 'purified' with cedar seeds. And invisible in the kitchen, awaiting its psychological moment, was The Cake.

By now I understood a Siberian domestic eccentricity which at first had puzzled me: the use of tea plates instead of dinner plates, despite the amount of food on offer. It is *because* of the ample spread, which leaves no room for large plates on small tables.

During present-opening time Roman videoed Katya's every move and smile. Then, instead of becoming over-excited and fractious, the birthday girl obligingly fell fast asleep when put in her cot in the bedroom and fourteen of us sat down to eat around a table made for six.

This was my third banquet in less than thirty-six hours; after a few months in Siberia my waistband needed drastic readjustment. Earlier, one of the Old Town schools had laid on a memorable farewell lunch in the staff common room. And the day before, Yulia had outwitted me. Her mother was visiting from Perm and she wanted us to meet – when could I call? At three next afternoon, I said, a time chosen to avoid a meal. But of course Yulia postponed lunch to include me.

Siberian parties are slow-paced and not until 10.15 did The Cake with its one candle appear. To my horror, Katya was roused and expected to blow out the candle to provide the grand finale to Roman's First Birthday Party video. Naturally she didn't co-operate, howled in distress, only wanted to continue sleeping. Great-grandma and I, sitting together, exchanged glances and didn't need a common language to share our disapproval of the video cult smothering parental good sense.

Great-grandma – small and muscular, shrewd and vigorously out-spoken – had told me (Tanya our interpreter) that she knew the BAM Zone would 'fail' when the authorities admitted, in 1985, that it could never feed itself, must always import 80 per cent of its cereal and dairy needs from Western Siberia. She recalled the Zone's diet before that date: meat rarely available, fresh milk reserved for children and in-valids, potatoes, cabbages and carrots the only vegetables.

The Research Council on Agricultural Development in the BAM Zone, established in 1976, was soon joined by the Scientific Council on the Problems of the BAM. Two years later Brezhnev asserted: 'The newly developed economic regions should be provided with their own agricultural base and should be in a position to supply themselves with their own animal products and vegetables.' He had forgotten why most of Siberia remained unpopulated at the end of the second millennium. The whole BAM Zone then depended on twenty-seven farms which contributed less than a quarter of the minimum food needs of five of the seven administrative districts, leaving the others with nothing. Aiming for the impossible, Moscow ordered the creation of 33,000 hectares of grazing land and 96,600 hectares of meadowland, to be achieved through deforestation and the destruction of river eco-systems on a tragic scale. In 1985, when the Agricultural Academy of the Siberian Division of the Soviet Academy of Agricultural Sciences formally abandoned BAM Zone self-sufficiency, it emphasized that technically enough food could be locally produced – but at too high a cost.

Grigori supplied me with all that information, then added, as I closed my notebook, 'Like in all advanced countries but more so, our rulers imagined science and technology could overcome every natural obstacle. *Experts* could do it! All those *councils* had thousands of scientists and engineers being tossed around like clothes in a washing machine not able to stop to think anything through. Or in many cases *afraid* to make honest judgements against grandiose projects. In 1976 we'd experts on the ground – my father was one – who *knew* the BAM Zone couldn't be forced to produce enough food. We didn't need nine years of environmental vandalism to prove it!'

Grigori's mood was sombre that evening. A project involving more environmental vandalism, on a grand scale, had been revealed with a flourish in Moscow. A recently discovered oilfield on Evenk territory promised to be as productive as Kuwait's and the Russian oil company, Yukos, had decided to build a 1,550-mile pipeline to China at a cost to them of more than $2 billion. The Chinese would pay $500 million to take it another 500 miles from the border to Daqing. Starting in 2005, a daily flow of 600,000 barrels would greatly assist the Kremlin's coffers and China's industrial expansion while making Yukos Russia's largest oil company.

'We're being shown the deal as a big victory for the Putin administration though even an efficient pipeline would be a crime. Who cares that we've a history of inefficient leaking pipes that poison thousands

of kilometres? With Evenkia's seismic shifts, and temperatures dropping to minus 60°C, could anyone build this line efficiently? One of
Yukos's advisers sort of admits it's a gamble, mentions the oilfield being
"difficult to exploit" but "the economics make it viable and minimize
the risks". Another fantasy about what *experts* can do!'

Evenkia – west of Sakha, in the geographical centre of the
Federation – is one and a half times the size of France with no roads
(transport is by canoe and small motorboats) and a population of about
18,000 of whom 3,000 or so are Evenk. These reindeer herders, like
Siberia's other 'little peoples', were threatened once the Russians
arrived. In the 1650s imported smallpox wiped out, it is said, 80 per
cent of the northern Evenk and several other tribes. (But in seventeenth-century Siberia who was around accurately to estimate these
losses?) As the centuries passed, populations were further depleted by
syphilis, influenza and vodka. Yet the Evenk maintained their traditional way of life until the Soviets 'disappeared' their tribal chiefs and
religious leaders and compelled them to become collective reindeer
farmers instead of nomadic herders.

In the early 1990s such farms were privatized or simply abandoned.
Then the pioneer oil prospectors arrived, hungry for fresh meat, and
some 95 per cent of the domesticated reindeer were exchanged for
crates of vodka, to which many Evenk had become lethally addicted
when Sovietization induced despair – the sort that also sends suicide
rates rocketing. They had bred their own unique sub-species of broad-
backed riding reindeer, now almost extinct; only wild reindeer survive
in the untouched taiga.

Grigori's sociologist son Georgi, newly graduated, had considered
working with this branch of the Evenk and hitched a lift to the area
in an oil company helicopter (much to his father's disapproval). He
returned lamenting 'a lost cause' – there was, he reckoned, no battle
to be fought. In the village of Kuyumba (population recently reduced
to about 150 adults and fifty children) he had found that a third were
alcoholics. Within the previous three years twenty-four people had
been murdered (ten of them women), six people had killed themselves
and Soviet era statistics indicated that the average life expectancy was
forty for men and forty-five for women. In the six years from January
1996, ten adults had died of stomach cancer, a disease hitherto

unknown locally. The manager of the Evenk Drilling Enterprise admitted to Georgi that the river had been contaminated but argued that it will recover, that a price always has to be paid for 'development', that oil wealth will bring roads, bridges, schools, clinics. Already this man had made a brutally unambiguous public statement: 'The Evenk will have to accept assimilation or be exterminated'. He denied that his Russian staff had shot from helicopters so many bears, elk and wild reindeer that the Evenk were short of food and winter clothing.

Before this Evenkia excursion, Georgi had placed some hope in Raipon (Russian Association of Indigenous Peoples of the North), which represents twenty-four tiny tribes almost unknown outside Russia and not very well known inside Russia. Raipon is backed by a Norwegian NGO (Grid) and the UN Environment Programme. Its leader, Pavel Sulyandziga, regards the Evenkia controversy as the greatest test of his organization. Federal law gives the Evenk exclusive land rights in Evenkia, which theoretically should shield them from the depredations of Yukos. But early in 2002 the region's newly elected governor, formerly a senior Yukos employee, granted the oil company all the drilling rights they asked for. And Evenkia's Moscow office is part of Yukos's luxurious headquarters where plans are being made to investigate Evenkia's considerable gold and diamond deposits.

After his chopper tour Georgi felt (and his father agreed with him) that opposition to Yukos's China project should focus not on the legal rights of the bullied and already doomed 3,000 Evenk but on the incalculable environmental damage certain to result from a 1,550-mile wound across territory of exceptional ecological sensitivity.

That evening I wrote in my diary:

It's probably true that these degenerate Evenk (a harsh word but merely factual, not meant unkindly) – have by now lost the skills needed to resume their ancient way of life. As a distinctive, separate people they're about to become extinct; one of their own proverbs says 'No reindeer no Evenk'. Our 'developed' world literally leaves no space for human beings unable to adapt to it, whose survival depends on *not* developing, *not* changing. In the twenty-first century *little* tribes are expendable, few in number, their skills irrelevant. Why should anyone mourn their extinction? In the Evenk's case, it seems Sovietization had already

pushed them beyond recovery point. Whatever superficial concessions
Yukos may make, to placate international opinion, can't rescue them.
But surely only sentimental cranks could feel a sense of loss on hearing
of their fate. What's the loss? The Evenk and their like have nothing
to contribute to the world as we want it to be. It's a pity they've suffered
so much but that's the inevitable consequence of being so primitive, so
unadaptable, so vulnerable to our diseases, including alcoholism. The
rest of the world is moving on and needs oil to keep moving. Tribes
who can't move on are destined to extinction. That's how Nature
works. As Pyotr put it in Neryungri, 'uncivilized people must suffer,
they can't keep up with us'. Changing conditions saw off the dinosaurs
*et al.*, the mammoths and various other unadaptables ... But there's a
flaw in that argument. Man, not Nature, has created the conditions
with which the Evenk can't cope. Talk of oil wealth bringing them
roads, bridges, schools and so on is tendentious. Those benefits are of
no value to the Evenk, are unrelated to their needs *as Evenk*. And
they're only one of many peoples being wiped out on three continents
because we with the power have decided they don't matter, can't be
allowed to impede *our* exploitation of *their* regions' resources.

I marked the eve of my departure by going on a favourite walk, up a
loggers' little-used tractor track that soon became a faint footpath
winding for miles through the taiga. From the crest of this high ridge,
on a clear day, one can see Lake Baikal's guardian mountain ranges
stretching away to east and west – scores of dazzling summits – and far
below a crescent of water is visible, its blueness silvered by distance.
On that track I never met anyone but saw several of those most beautiful little creatures first encountered in Tynda and here quite unafraid.
One could edge up close and photograph them as they fed on cedar-
cone seeds.

That last walk was magical. The night had brought Severobaikalsk's
first heavy snowfall, the bright noon sun lacked thawing heat and all
around me lay a silent sparkling world of trees and bushes, gracefully
bending under their burdens of snow.

As the Yahins were being so hospitable to Pushkin I had decided to
leave him and my camping gear in Severobaikalsk, to return in 2004
and go on from there. Local knowledge is important ('local' being here
used loosely – and widely) and in Yakutsk and Irkutsk friends had
warned me that the Russian Far East is being rapidly globalized. On

11 September 2001, as I excitedly studied my 1973 atlas, Ussuriland had looked blissfully remote, on the isolated edge of Russia, separated from Europe by the immensity of Siberia. Had I looked at the atlas with a more discerning eye, I would have realized that very little separates the Russian Far East from its enterprising Asian neighbours. It was isolated throughout most of the twentieth century only by political/military decree. Geographically, it is vulnerable to whomever decides to build luxury hotels, create theme parks and construct tourist-friendly motorways. Therefore my enthusiasm for that region had waned as my affection for Siberia waxed. Because of this new plan, leaving Severobaikalsk was not the mournful occasion it might have been.

# 12

# Racing the Sun

As we pulled out of Severobaikalsk at 6.05 p.m. local time I realized
that I had become a BAM junkie. Florence Farmborough put it well
in March 1918, while escaping to Vladivostok on the Trans-Siberian.
Her journal records: 'The soothing saunter of our lazy locomotive and
the slowly passing days and nights spent in the wide open spaces, far
from human habitations, have reacted upon me as a wholesome,
bracing stimulus.' (Miss Farmborough, a young English nurse of
uncommon bravery, stamina and literary talent, served with the
Russian army throughout the First World War.)

Some BAM trains have their own 'home towns' and my farewell
support group were very proud of this newish Severobaikalsk-based
model. Evidently it was trying to compete with the Trans-Siberian,
in amenities if not in speed. Our bedding came in sealed cellophane
packs, the pillow-slips and terry-towelling new, the double blankets
of pure wool. Big windows with slatted wooden shutters (an improvement on tiresome lace curtains) were clean both ways but alas!
couldn't be opened. Next door to my coach a buffet car had seating
for ten and a freestanding central bar counter dissociated from the
source of beer in one corner. That corner was also the kitchenette,
where precooked food could be microwaved for those rash enough to
order a meal. Siberians worship microwaves and my friends were
unimpressed when I warned of the two-edged hazard of radiation and
nutriment-destruction. But of course no one argued; it is polite to
make allowances for the babushka generation, those quaint leftovers
from the mid-twentieth century.

At night two deaf and dumb youths, hawking sacks of books and
travelling free as handicapped Children of BAM, were allowed to sleep
in the buffet car – sitting at a table, heads pillowed on arms.

Animatedly they communicated with one another in sign language – much chuckling, many smiles – and their large sacks were almost empty by journey's end.

For all this keeping up with the Trans-Siberian a predictable price had to be paid – intolerably loud piped music, Russian imitations of the most debased ear-searing Western pop. In desperation I traced the control knob to the buffet and lowered the volume, whereupon a young barmaid scowled and turned it up even louder. BAM employees feel proprietorial about everything to do with their railway.

At first I was alone in my four-person coupé, as snow silvered the dusk: not fat, floating flakes but very fine particles like frozen mist, speeding past the window before a strong gale. At a little mountain settlement, some forty miles from Baikal, the snow was a foot deep yet so dry and powdery that the few who embarked left no footprints – merely ruffled it. Here an elderly man joined me, a retired army officer (Viktor) who spoke quite fluent English and promptly sorted out our decibel problem. Using a tone of military authority he ordered the buffet staff to play *real* Russian music, folk or classical, and drastically to reduce the decibels. Sulkily the barmaid and her young male colleague obeyed both orders.

Viktor's face, hands and forearms were dreadfully disfigured; he had led one of the army teams sent to cope with Chernobyl in 1987. Pointing to his radiation burns he said, 'I'm only one, thousands went, many now are dead – and some of the dead didn't look as bad as me. Medical people study to see why some died and others lived after the same or worse exposure. About radiation we have an imagination we know all but we are fools!'

The microwave hazard is in fact triple-edged. Vera had invited me to a Departure Day lunch at which she produced a very special omul pie cooked the evening before. This she insisted on reheating in her microwave despite my protestations that I prefer fish pie cold, don't like it hot. 'So I'll only warm it,' compromised Vera, causing an alarm bell to tinkle faintly. Was I being neurotic? Anyway, I couldn't not eat this dish so lovingly prepared, with elaborately sculpted pastry. It tasted delicious and I enjoyed two large helpings. But I wasn't being neurotic. Five hours later Vera failed to join my support group on the platform – sent a message about an upset stomach.

By bedtime I was feeling rather queasy and by midnight I had a major problem: poisoned gas burps, severe stomach cramps, then an overwhelming nausea. I knew that any change of posture would cause me to vomit copiously; that urge could only be controlled by lying still and biting my tongue. While my body was ordering me to get rid of something undesirable (warmed omul) my mind shrank from the prospect of throwing up in that pristine coach, and possibly victimizing Viktor as he snored gently on the lower bunk opposite my top bunk. I bit my tongue so hard that it bled and for what seemed a long time this mind over matter combat continued. Then the nausea passed and the gut pains worsened – became like sabre stabbings in the belly.

Next morning Viktor exclaimed, 'You look not healthy!' Having heard my story he hastened away to our *provodnitsa*'s lair and soon returned with a steaming mug of some murky-looking and foul-tasting herbal laxative. At noon I had to dash to the loo and after a few more dashes all was well. Triumphantly Viktor clapped his hands and said, 'Now again you look healthy! In Russia we have many, many good medicines from the taiga!'

During a long stop at Ulcan I watched mechanized loggers at work. Each of their gigantic mobile cranes was seizing three 150-foot-long cedar trunks at a go, then following an extension of the railway line to a siding where countless flat wagons had already been loaded. I remarked to Viktor that had BAM not happened, the world would have survived without plundering these magnificent cedar forests. But he couldn't understand why so much needless logging distressed me.

Soon after, we observed a truly extraordinary phenomenon with a fairytale flavour. Across wide, exposed plains of thin taiga, all the tall trees lie down in winter, then rise again when spring comes. Some were already prone, others were gracefully drooping sideways at various distances from the ground.

Beyond Taishet we met several very long freight trains, most of the oil tankers conspicuously new in contrast to the dilapidated Soviet-era rolling stock. As yet the rows of icicles decorating the wagon roofs were only about a foot long; soon they would be a yard long.

Approaching Novosibirsk at dawn, the hoar-frosted pines and larches on distant slopes seemed insubstantial, the glimmering ghosts of trees. Novosibirsk is both the biggest (population 1.3 million) and the youngest of Siberia's major cities; it was founded in 1893, during the construction of the Trans-Siberian's bridge across the Ob' river. Such a palatial railway station must then have seemed incongruous as it rose amidst the wilderness; most of Novosibirsk dates from the 1920s.

Here many passengers wrapped up and hurried out to buy hot potato and meat cakes, crisp brown bliny, long salami sausages, smoked trout. I noticed people reacting differently to the black-iced platform, some striding along confidently, others mincing cautiously. One over-confident young man had a bad fall, cracking his head on the sharp corner of a metal kiosk and lying stunned for a moment.

West of Novosibirsk patchy snow lay on square miles of dark new-ploughed earth, scattered with dreary groups of concrete collective farm buildings (now co-operatives or privatized). Then the railway climbed again and soon was skirting a hidden lake, new snow covering its ice-lid – a flawless expanse of smooth soft whiteness. All that day the sky hung low and the horizons were near. Through diaphanous cloud a pale orb shed its subdued light over the frozen stillness of limitless spaces where everything, from tufted reeds to towering trees, was silver-plated.

Twelve hours and 500 miles west of Novosibirsk we halted at Omsk where I diverted Viktor by recalling that I once owned four cats named Omsk, Tomsk, Minsk and Smolensk. This prompted my companion to reminisce about his year as a young captain stationed in Tomsk, some 170 miles north-east of Novosibirsk and one of Siberia's oldest cities, founded in 1604. For three centuries it was an important commercial and administrative centre on the Great Siberian Trakt, but then came the Trans-Siberian and abruptly it lost status. In Soviet times it acquired another sort of unsavoury status and was closed to foreigners, being one of a cluster of top-secret weapons research and production establishments. Now, said Viktor, tourists are advised to avoid this whole region because its water supply has been contaminated by the underground disposal of radioactive wastes. Lucky tourists, who can choose to avoid it! By Siberian standards the region is heavily populated.

Viktor and I had by then got to know one another quite well and

I admitted to being baffled by his acceptance of what to me seemed outrageous – the deployment to Chernobyl of clean-up teams lacking the best possible protective equipment (there could be no protection in the hottest spots) and Moscow's subsequent indifference to those teams' sufferings.

'But it was our duty,' said Viktor. 'We were needed. When orders come, soldiers go. If they die, that's what happens. Chernobyl was another sort of battlefield. Only death when it came was more slow.'

Viktor's photograph album was substantial; his son and daughter had each provided him with two grandsons. During our half-hour stop at Tyumen a hawker of glass ornaments came aboard and because Viktor bought a swan for my grand-daughters I bought a tiger for his grand-sons. Remembering the brisk trading done through the open windows of Indian trains and African buses I pitied those platform hawkers who, during our shorter stops, could trade only through open doors.

Since sunset a blizzard had been blowing; we were now in the Urals and as the land rose the snow deepened. Even during the darkest hours, occasional huge bonfires blazed by the tracks for the benefit of maintenance crews. A crew is always on duty, twenty-four hours a day, 365 days a year, deservedly earning more than double the average wage.

For me the next day started at 5.10 my time. (It was fun having a personal time, neither local nor Moscow.) Descending from my bunk I washed, made tea, then asked our amiable young night *provodnitsa* to switch on the buffet-car light. Before she did so, I could see snow-flakes pirouetting through blackness. No one else was astir and I reck-oned daylight wouldn't happen before nine or ten my time. Two hours later, approaching Ekaterinburg, the *provodnitsa* – on her way to lock the loo – warned me that for some reason best known to BAM the light must be switched off during our halt. This is another imposing station, surrounded by hectares of freight yards, and its clock said 3.10 Moscow time. Everything was silent and snow-mantled; few got off or on. Peering up and down the long empty platform I wondered where, exactly, Czar Nicholas II and family had disembarked at the end of their last railway journey; they were murdered nearby.

Soon a faint greyness smudged the eastern horizon as King Sol struggled to rise – but he struggled in vain. That was a memorable interlude: BAM racing the sun, keeping us in a pre-dawn twilight for hour after hour as I sat gazing over an endlessly crepuscular landscape of snow-burdened larches, beeches and birches. In this elastic dawn, time as we normally measure it seemed meaningless. Jet planes, rushing us from continent to continent miles above the earth, provide nothing comparable.

Not until noon my time did the sun win this race. BAM was then following the contours of a pine-forested ridge above a narrow curving river, half iced-over, and the light reminded me of a cloudy midwinter Irish morning. For several miles villages straggled along the far bank, below a twin ridge, their colourfully restored churches emphasizing the dwellings' drabness. Further on, where the railway ran parallel to a snow-bound track, men were transporting potatoes on horse-sledges.

The first passengers to appear were three English-speaking men at whom I stared as though they were two-headed. Since leaving Irkutsk six weeks previously I had met no native English-speaker and to Ted Robinson I remarked what a relief it was to be able to converse at a normal speed, using short-cut syntax. He was the leader of a seven-person Australian television team and I couldn't have encountered a more congenial group of fellow-travellers. Politically kindred spirits recognize one another after a few sentences have been exchanged – in this case, sentences about Iraq.

The team had just spent three weeks making a documentary on one of their member's Siberian relatives. When this young man's great-grandfather migrated to Australia in 1912 one of his three children, a toddler son, was left behind with a babushka. Post-Revolution, communications ceased. Now, after much arduous detective work, the toddler's grand-nephew had found his cousins – living in poverty in a hamlet near the ruins of a little church their ancestors had built in the mid-nineteenth century.

West of the Urals we suddenly entered a rainy zone where light snow was thawing on wide fields, exposing short green grass – vividly green, almost homelike. Here the embankment shrubs and birches had not yet shed their leaves; the Urals, puny as they seem, do make a difference.

An hour short of Moscow my respect for our pristine coach was negated by a large jar of red caviar, a farewell gift which I had been assured would survive the journey. When I began to pack and moved it, it literally blew its top, spurting a singularly sticky substance all over the lower bunks. (Happily Viktor had already packed and moved to the buffet car.) There was nothing I could do to repair the damage; a major operation, involving some anti-fermented-caviar detergent, was called for. Guiltily I slunk down the corridor to our *provodnitsa's* office and confessed, using vigorous sign-language. I hadn't seen this buxom blonde smiling once in four and a half days but now she laughed aloud.

We pulled into Kazan station at 6.55 precisely, too early on a Sunday morning for me to ring Clem or Anna. (From Severobaikalsk Rashit had e-mailed Clem on my behalf but, unsurprisingly, his message got lost in cyberspace; many Siberian telephones have not yet come to terms with that novel element.) Ted therefore invited me to wait in his team's suite on the ninth floor of the thousand-bed Stalgothic Hotel Ukraine where I spent a few hours reading the first English-language newspaper I had seen in three months. *The Moscow Times* headlines proclaimed: MAGADAN GOVERNOR GUNNED DOWN: VALENTIN TSVETKOV DIED ON THE SPOT — POWERFUL CAR BOMB INJURES 8 AT MOSCOW MCDONALD'S — ROCKET CRASH DELAYS OCT. 28 LIFTOFF — ARMY SAYS REBELS TARGETED CHOPPER — MEXICAN VILLAGE MOURNS ILLEGAL WORKERS' DEATHS — AFGHAN FOOD SHORTAGE CRITICAL — JAKARTA ARRESTS ISLAMIC CLERIC — PAKISTAN SUSPECTED OF NUCLEAR AID TO N. KOREA — GOLDMAN SACHS BUYING UP JAPANESE GOLF COURSES — and so on and on...

Having returned to the complexities of the twenty-first century, I already felt impatient to be back in relatively tension-free Eastern Siberia. OAPs are entitled to go for the escapist option.

*Dervla Murphy*